HANDFULS ON PURPOSE

SERIES III

BY

Pastor JAMES SMITH

Author of "A Survey of the Wondrous Cross,"
"Spiritual Patterns" etc.

WM. B. EERDMANS PUBLISHING COMPANY

Grand Rapids   1955   Michigan

American Edition

———

Published in 1947, by

WM. B. EERDMANS PUBLISHING CO.
by
Special Arrangement with

PICKERING & INGLIS, LTD.
14 Paternoster Row, London, E.C.4
229 Bothwell St., Glasgow, C.2
Manchester—Newcastle—Liverpool—Edinburgh

Guide to Series 1 to 12

OLD TESTAMENT

NEW TESTAMENT

SERIES 1 to 10 .. By Pastor JAMES SMITH
SERIES 11 and 12, .. By ROBERT LEE
SERIES 13, COMPLETE INDEX TO SERIES

PREFACE.

"Behold, how great a matter a little fire kindleth" (James 3. 5).

LITTLE did we think when, with fear and trembling, we launched the first small monthly part, that it would so soon grow into so many volumes. For this special token of the Master's favour we are sincerely thankful. It is an unspeakable delight for us to know that very many weary gleaners have found therein "Handfuls on Purpose." All who choose to glean here, are as much at liberty to take home for their own use what they find as Ruth was, when she gleaned among the sheaves in the fields of Boaz.

We esteem it a great privilege to have the opportunity of ministering in any small degree, to the encouragement and usefulness of the lowliest of Christ's servants, believing that "inasmuch as ye did it unto one of the least of these My brethren, ye have done it unto Me" (Matt. 25. 40). In this volume, which we trust will also be found helpful in "the quiet hour," we have once more humbly attempted to fulfil the Apostle's injunction, "Let him that is taught in the word *communicate* unto him that teacheth in all good things" (Gal. 6. 8). What we have prayerfully received, we herewith prayerfully give.

JAMES SMITH.

INDEX OF SUBJECTS.

INDEX OF TEXTS.

Handfuls on Purpose

(THIRD SERIES)

———◀┼┼▶———

Expository Outlines. Old Testament

———◀┼▶———

THE FIVE OFFERINGS

---

1. THE BURNT-OFFERING

THE DEVOTEDNESS OF CHRIST
Leviticus 1. 1-9.

A STUDY of these offerings cannot but deepen our reverence for the Word of God, and magnify our Lord and Saviour whom they represent. We should never overlook the fact that all the particulars given concerning these five offerings, which reveal so many different aspects of Christ's life and work, were given to Moses by Jehovah Himself, who knew the character of Christ and His sufferings beforehand. This burnt-offering is "an *approach-offering*," indicating the way to God.

1. The Character of the Offering. Much depends upon its character and the manner in which it was offered.

1. IT MUST BE WITHOUT BLEMISH (v. 3). Not only in the sight of man, but in the sight of God. Christ, as God's beloved Lamb, was without blemish and without spot (1 Peter 1. 19). One sin in thought or feeling would have made Him a blemished sacrifice.

2. IT MUST BE BROUGHT TO THE DOOR (v. 3). The *door* of access to God has been blocked by sin. It can only be opened through suffering and sacrifice. Jesus Christ came for this purpose. Now He says, Behold I set before you an open door.

3. IT MUST BE KILLED BEFORE THE LORD (v. 5). A blameless life is not enough to atone for sin and remove the barrier from the door. Christ must die, and He must die *before the Lord*. His death was Jehovah's doing, and not man's. It pleased the Lord to bruise Him, *He* hath put Him to grief. Atonement has to do with God.

4. IT MUST BE LAID IN ORDER UPON THE ALTAR (v. 8). Everything here must be *in order*, as everything is typical of Him who came to do the Father's will. The nailing of Christ, our Sacrifice, upon the Cross may be here in figure.

5. ITS BLOOD MUST BE SPRINKLED (v. 5). The blameless one becomes the lifeless one. The blood, which signifies life, must be applied both to the altar and to the heart. The *sprinkled* blood saved the first-born in Egypt (Exod. 12). The blood of sprinkling still speaks (Heb. 12. 24).

6. ITS INWARDS MUST BE WASHED (v. 9). The *inwards* may suggest the thoughts and feelings, the intents of the heart, that must be clean before God. All was perfect in the Son of the Highest as our Passover Lamb. He could say, Thy law is within My heart, I delight to do Thy will.

7. IT MUST ALL BE LAID UPON THE ALTAR (v. 9). All was given to God, He offered *Himself* wholly and acceptable. A sweet savour unto the Lord (Eph. 5. 2).

2. **Some things about the Offerer.** We learn from this that—

1. AN APPROACH-OFFERING WAS NEEDED. Because of sin man has forfeited all right and *fitness* to approach God. Jesus is the Way.

2. THIS OFFERING WAS TO BE VOLUNTARY (v. 3). Our "own voluntary will" is responsible for our accepting or rejecting God's great offering for our sins. "Ye *will not* come to Me that ye might have life."

3. THERE MUST BE PERSONAL IDENTIFICATION (v. 4). "He shall put his hand upon the head of the burnt-offering." This is the *touch* of appropriation, it is the touch of faith, the *leaning* of a believing heart.

4. THE OFFERER WAS ACCEPTED IN THE OFFERING. "And it shall be accepted *for* him, to make *atonement for* him." He hath made us accepted in the Beloved (Eph. 1. 6). Glorious Gospel, that by our acceptance of His offering we are made acceptable unto God. Justified freely from all things.

5. THIS PRIVILEGE IS OFFERED TO ALL. "If any man" (v. 2). This is a wide door opened by the infinite mercy of God. Salvation, by the offering of Christ, is brought within the reach of every man who has heard the tidings. He is the *propitiation* for the whole world.

---

2. THE MEAT-OFFERING.

THE PERSONAL CHARACTER OF CHRIST.

Leviticus 2. 1-16.

THERE was no blood-shedding in this offering, signifying that the thought of *suffering* is not connected with it. We have here in type the character and real moral worth of Jesus as the Son of God. In looking at this offering we observe that it was—

1. OF FINE FLOUR (v. 1). Flour is a product of earth, and may refer to the kinship of Christ with man. It was *fine* flour. Though He was truly human He was entirely free from the bran of carnal-mindedness. There was no defect, no coarseness of passion or feeling, all was perfectly even and sincere.

2. MINGLED WITH OIL (v. 4). Oil is an emblem of the Holy Spirit. As the flour was *mingled* with oil, so the presence and power of the Holy Ghost permeated every act and thought of the Saviour. The process of *mingling* the human and the divine is a great mystery. Great is the mystery of Godliness.

3. ANOINTED WITH OIL. " He shall pour oil *upon* it" (v. 1). Oil *in* it and oil *on* it suggest the twofold truth of the *indwelling* and the *anointing*. The Holy Spirit *in* us for guidance and teaching, *on* us for power and service. The Holy Spirit was in Christ from His birth, it was on Him after His baptism at Jordan. So He is in us from our new birth, and on us from the day of our entire consecration to the service of God.

4. COVERED WITH FRANKINCENSE (vs. 2-16). The frankincense was " a sweet savour unto the Lord," and speaks of the satisfaction God finds in a Spirit-possessed and Spirit-anointed life. The life of Jesus was lived in and by the power of the Holy Ghost, and so it was well pleasing in His sight.

5. BAKEN IN THE OVEN. The green ears of corn were dried by the fire and beaten out (v. 14). The *fire* and the *beating* are most suggestive emblems of the *sufferings* of Him who was the Holy One, yet the "Man of Sorrows and acquainted with grief." He passed through the oven of fiery heat in the garden of Gethsemane. The Shepherd was sorely smitten, He was made a perfect meat-offering through suffering. "Ours were the pangs He bore."

6. TO HAVE NO LEAVEN OR HONEY (v. 11). Leaven as a type of sin represents the *secret* workings of deceit and corruption. Honey may symbolise the flattery and applause of men. Jesus Christ was unmoved either by the one or the other. There was no guile in His mouth, He could say, " I am the Truth."

7. SEASONED WITH SALT (v. 13). Salt has a pungent, preserving influence, something opposed to corruption. Such is the effect of the truth as revealed in Jesus upon those who come into contact with it. The everlasting *covenant* and the unfailing faithfulness of Christ to the will of God the Father is doubtless taught by the salt. He abideth faithful. Have salt in yourselves.

8. OFFERED UNTO THE LORD (v. 2). Flour, oil, frankincense, these three, body, soul, and spirit, all presented to the Lord, and accepted by Him. This is the "approach-offering." Through Jesus Christ we have access by one Spirit unto the Father. Present yourselves (Rom. 12.1,2).

9. FOOD FOR THE OFFERER (v. 10). A portion of this offering was given to Aaron and his sons. "It was *most holy*." It was the Bread of God and also of man. It takes the most holy to satisfy the heart of God and the soul of man. It became the food of the offerer only after he had offered it to God. Christ can only satisfy our souls as we present Him to God as our Substitute, and plead the merit of His precious Name. God will not have us to feast our souls on less than that which has brought infinite satisfaction to His own heart.

-----

3. THE PEACE-OFFERING.

FELLOWSHIP THROUGH CHRIST.

Leviticus 3.

IN the peace-offering we may see Jesus as the *Way*; in the meat-offering Jesus as the *Truth*; in the burnt-offering Jesus as the *Life*. In this chapter the peace-offering is brought before us in three aspects.

1. The Ox (v. 1).

2. The Lamb (v. 7).

3. The Goat (v. 12).

As the ox, Christ was strong and patient; as the lamb,

meek and gentle; as the goat, despised and rejected. Or these three offerings may represent three different degrees of appreciation of the offerings of Christ by His believing people. In looking into this offering we notice that—

1. IT COULD BE MALE OR FEMALE (v. 1). In our fellowship with God there is neither male nor female—all one in Christ. Children of the living God.

2. IT MUST BE WITHOUT BLEMISH BEFORE THE LORD (v. 1). Whatever man may say or do concerning His Son, God must see no blemish within or without. Even a demon had to confess "Thou are the Holy One of God."

3. THERE MUST BE IDENTIFICATION. "He shall lay His hand upon the head of the offering" (v. 2). A peace-maker must be worthy of the trust of both parties. The atoning Blood of Christ, shed for all, justifies only those who by faith identify themselves with it (Rom. 5. 1).

4. THERE MUST BE DEATH. "Kill it at the door" (v. 2). If we are saved by His *life*, it is His life from the dead. The life of Christ before the Cross could not save, it was the evidence of His fitness to be the sinner's Substitute before God. Without shedding of blood there is no remission.

5. THE BLOOD MUST BE SPRINKLED ON THE ALTAR (v. 2). The altar signifies the just claims of God. To Him atonement must be made. The propitiation or *covering* from sin made by the death and resurrection of Christ is wide enough for all. The blood on the altar speaks of God's acceptance of the offering.

6. THIS OFFERING WAS MADE BY FIRE (v. 3). The fire of God's judgment has to fall upon it ere peace can come to the erring soul. He suffered for us, the Just for the unjust, that He might bring us to God. In verses 3 to 5 we see that all the choice parts of the offering were laid upon the

altar. The affections and energies of Christ were all toward His Father's glory.

7. IT WAS A SWEET SAVOUR UNTO THE LORD (v. 5). This does not mean a bare satisfaction, as if only a debt had been paid, but a *sweet delight*, as one receiving a great gift. God the Father will be glorified through all eternity because of His Son's obedience unto death (Isa. 42. 1).

8. THE OFFERER HAD A PORTION OF THE OFFERING (see chap. 7. 34). The *breast* and the *shoulder* were taken by the Lord and given back to the offerer. This is most significant. The breast tells us of *affection*, the shoulder of *strength*; both are given to us through Jesus Christ our Lord and Saviour. Love and power come to us by His Cross.

9. IT COULD BE EATEN ON THE SAME DAY AS IT WAS OFFERED (chap. 19. 5, 6). Peace and soul satisfaction come at once when Christ the peace-offering is truly trusted. Instant faith brings immediate salvation.

10. IT WAS TO BE EATEN TILL THE THIRD DAY (chap. 19. 6). The *third* day points on to resurrection. We feed on the love and rest in the strength of our glorified Redeemer till the resurrection morn. The breast and the shoulder will suffice us till the.day dawns and the shadows flee away, when we shall see Him as He is, and be for ever with Him. Meanwhile be thankful and adore.

---

4. THE SIN-OFFERING.

CHRIST OUR SUBSTITUTE.
Leviticus 4. 1-12.

SIN, the sinner, and the sin-offering are all vividly before us in this chapter. Ruin and remedy might be written over it. " If a priest that is anointed do sin." Yes, it is possible even for an *anointed* one to sin, but, blessed be God, provision is made for such (1 John 2. 1). But when religious *teachers* sin, it is like the going wrong of the town clock. Others are apt to be led astray by their example. As Trapp says, "The sins of teachers are teachers of sin." The way of life is a revelation from God. A ladder *let down* from Heaven. So this sin-offering may be mentioned here, because it is the lowest step of the ladder, and the *first* with which we as sinners have to do. Like every other sacrifice—

1. It must be blameless (v. 3). The smallest physical deformity unfitted the ox or the lamb for the altar. The Lord Jesus was perfectly blameless in the eyes of the heart-searching God. In all His close and continuous contact with men and earthly things He remained untainted by the corruptions of lust and of the world. He could touch the unclean and yet be untouched with uncleanness. He was holy, harmless, separate from sinners.

2. There had to be imputation and identification (v. 4). The offerer laid his hand on the head of the offering, identifying himself with the sins imputed to the sacrifice, and also with the sacrifice itself. The laying of our sins on Jesus is not our act, but Jehovah's. "He laid on Him the iniquity of us all. It pleased Jehovah to bruise Him." We *confess* our sins on Him, and by faith lay our hand of appropriation upon Him. He gave Himself for us.

3. The life must be taken. "Kill the bullock before the Lord" (v. 4). The death of the offering had to do with Jehovah. The death of Christ was not an accident, neither was it only an example to us of patience in suffering. *It was a death* demanded by God. So His life was offered to God as a substitute for others. He died before the Lord. He offered Himself without spot *unto* God.

4. The fat was burnt on the altar (vs. 8-10). This fat was a sweet savour unto the Lord (v. 31). The fat is frequently referred to, and occupies a prominent place in connection with the sin-offering. It may represent the riches and preciousness of Christ as God sees it all yielded up as an offering to Him on the altar of the Cross, well pleasing.

5. The body was carried outside. The whole bullock shall he carry forth without the camp and burn him (v. 12). Human reason of itself would never have suggested a change of procedure like this. Why should this offering be burnt outside the camp, and not on the altar like the others? Because it is typical of Him who was made a *curse* for us, and who suffered *without* the gate (Heb. 13. 11, 12), and from whom the Father's face for a season had to be turned away (Matt. 27. 46). God cannot look upon sin, but He looks with compassion on the sinner.

6. The blood must be sprinkled. "The priest shall sprinkle of the blood seven times before the Lord" (v. 6). *The order* in which the blood was sprinkled is sublimely beautiful, and perfectly consistent with the way of salvation as taught in the New Testament. It was sprinkled—(1) Before the Lord. (2) Before the vail. (3) On the altar of incense. (4) Then all that was left was *poured out* at the bottom of the altar of burnt-offering. The priest sprinkled the blood on his way *out*, not as he was going in on this instance, teaching us that the way has been made *from God* out to sinful men. Salvation is of the Lord. But on our approach to God we meet *the poured out* blood, first of all at the altar, which maketh atonement for the soul. Typical of Him who poured out His soul unto death on the Cross of Calvary—

1. AT THE ALTAR OF SACRIFICE we have atonement.

2. AT THE ALTAR OF INCENSE we have intercession.

3. THE BLOOD BEFORE THE VAIL speaks of *access*.

4. THE BLOOD SPRINKLED SEVEN TIMES *before the Lord*

indicates a perfect standing in His presence. Thus we have boldness to enter into the Holiest by *the Blood of Jesus*. Let us draw near (Heb. 10. 19-22).

7. The blessed results. The acceptance by God of the blood of the sin-offering brings within the reach of every believer—

1. THE FORGIVENESS OF SIN. As concerning his sin, it shall be forgiven him (v. 26). Blessed is the man to whom the Lord will not impute sin (Rom. 4. 7, 8). It is a blood-bought pardon.

2. THE ASSURANCE OF THIS FORGIVENESS. "It *shall*." This is the promise of Him who knows the full value of the Blood of His own beloved Son. We are *saved* by His Blood, and *assured* by His Word. In the blood-shedding and blood-sprinkling of God's own Son there is provision made for the sins of *ignorance* (v. 2), as well as for the sins that come to our knowledge (v. 28). "Behold the Lamb of God which taketh away the sin of the world."

---

5. THE TRESPASS-OFFERING.

THE ADAPTATION OF CHRIST'S WORK TO THE SINNER'S NEED.
Leviticus 5; 6. 1-7.

THE voice of the trespass-offering to man is: "He hath *certainly* trespassed against the Lord " (v. 19). In connection with this offering individual sins rather than persons are prominently dealt with. Let us look at—

1. The need. " All we like sheep have gone astray." So a *trespass*-offering is needed. The sins mentioned here are cardinal ones, and prove that all have sinned.

1. THE SIN OF SILENCE when we ought to speak (v. 1). Every privilege of *witnessing* for the truth that is neglected brings guilt. Silence may be sometimes golden, but it may also be criminal. Silence gives consent. How

often do we Christians indulge in this guilty silence for Christ because of the fear of man? "I say unto you, Fear God."

2. THE SIN OF DEFILEMENT through unclean associations. "If a *soul* touch any unclean thing," &c. (vs. 2, 3). The hands and the feet may touch things unclean without incurring *moral* pollution, but not so with the *soul*. It is our *fellowship* with the unclean that corrupts the life. Even the *touch* of sympathy and desire will bring defilement and condemnation.

3. THE SIN OF IGNORANCE, in breaking the commands of the Lord. "If a soul commit any of these things which are forbidden, though he *wist it not*, yet is he guilty" (v. 17). Neither our reason nor our conscience determine what is sin, but the Word of God. Inadvertence or negligence on our part to the *revealed* will of God is in itself sinful. Although Paul says he was forgiven because he did it *ignorantly* (1 Tim. 1. 13), yet *forgiveness* was needed all the same. To say I am not conscious of sin does not imply that I am free from guilt (Psa. 19. 12).

4. THE SIN OF DEFRAUDING our fellowmen (chap. 6. 1, 2). All sin is against God. He holds the man guilty who deceives in any way his neighbour. The apostle realised this when he said, "I am debtor both to the Jew and to the Greek," &c. Defraud no man. How much owest thou?

2. The provision. The variety of the offerings allowed, according to the poverty of the guilty offerers, reveals the adaptability and all-sufficiency of the sacrifice to the need of all. The expense of the offering was reduced to the "tenth part of an ephah of fine flour" (vs. 7-11). A handful of flour was within the reach of the poorest. The *grace* of God which bringeth salvation to all men hath appeared. No matter how poor the offerers may be, the full value and power of the sacrifice was imputed to

them. Our faith may be weak, poor indeed, but it lays hold on a strong Redeemer, the mighty to save. We may have but a poor estimate of the worth of Christ as our trespass-offering, and yet be as perfectly forgiven as those who are rich in faith, giving glory to God. There are no *degrees* in our justification before Him. All these various offerings represent the *one sacrifice* for the trespasses of the people.

Associated with it we have these thoughts—

1. SUBSTITUTION. In every case the offering was *for* the offerer. "Christ loved us, and gave Himself *for* us" (Eph. 5. 2). He died for our sins.

2. RESTORATION (chap. 6. 1, 2). Our Lord Jesus Christ, by the offering of Himself, has restored that which sin and unbelief had taken away. Surely if we are dependent upon the trespass-offering for our restoration unto God we shall willingly restore to our fellowmen what we have fraudulently taken away from them. Freely ye have received, freely give.

3. COMPENSATION. "He shall make amends, and *add* the fifth part" (v. 16). We are to give compensation to our brother man for loss through our acts, because there is in this offering as a type of Christ, not only the payment of a debt, but in a deep, unfathomable sense, the full compensating of God for loss sustained through the ruin of man by sin. Hallelujah, what a Saviour! The death of Christ has made *amends* unto God for our guilt, and *added* the "fifth part" of a glorious Church to the eternal praise of His holy Name.

3. The condition. The provision made by the trespass-offering availed nothing where there was no—

1. CONFESSION. "He shall confess that he hath sinned in *that thing*" (v. 5). *That thing* implies that the confession must come down to *particular* things. The trespass-offering deals with these, and may have special

reference to the sins of the backslider, which must be confessed in detail before restoration can come. Then there must be—

2. ACCEPTANCE. He must be willing to accept God's only way of deliverance from guilt, and be obedient to His Word.

4. **The promise.** "And it shall be forgiven him" (v. 10). This verse contains a double promise, giving a double assurance.

1. ATONEMENT MADE FOR HIM. The priest *shall* make an atonement *for* him. This work is outside of the offerer. This Christ has done for us (Rom. 5. 11).

2. FORGIVENESS EXTENDED TO HIM. Justified freely by His grace. "Through this Man (Christ) is offered unto you the forgiveness of sins" (Acts 13. 38).

AARON AND HIS SONS.
Leviticus 8.

AARON and his sons very fitly represent Christ and His servants.

1. They were CALLED with him: "Take Aaron and his sons *with him*."

2. They were related BY BIRTH, "sons." So we have been *called* in Christ, and *born* from above.

3. They were IDENTICAL IN DRESS (v. 13). The righteousness of God which clothed our great High Priest is upon all that believe.

4. They were ASSOCIATED IN SERVICE (v. 27). We are co-workers together with Him.

5. They RECEIVED THE SAME ANOINTING (v. 30). Baptised with the same spirit. Aaron's sons were all servants.

Let us see in this chapter how they were made meet for their holy work. They were—

1. Washed. "Moses washed them with water" (v. 6). They did not even wash themselves. Wash *Thou* me, and I shall be whiter than the snow. Before the washing comes the stripping. All pride and self-sufficiency laid aside (Acts 2. 37). *He* loved us, and washed us from our sins in His own Blood.

2. Clothed. "Moses put coats upon them" (v. 13). It is suggested to us that this also was done *for* them. Adam and Eve were reckoned naked until God made coats of skin and *covered* them (Gen. 3. 21). The wedding garment was not bought, it was *put on* as a gift. Covered with the robe of His righteousness.

3. Girded. "Moses girded them with girdles." The girdle speaks of *service*. The putting on of the girdle was their call to a life of activity in the work of the Lord (John 13. 4). Let your loins be girded. Ye serve the Lord Christ. The girdle of many of God's people seem to hang very loosely—off and on.

4. Separated. "Moses put the blood upon their *ears, hands, feet*, and upon the *altar*" (v. 24). Indicating that, as the ear, hand, and foot were connected by the blood with the altar, they were separated for God. The blood-tipped members are as much the property of God as the altar is. The blood on the ear, &c., meant the same as the blood on the altar. God always claims for Himself those whom He hath washed, clothed, and girded (Heb. 13. 12).

5. Supplied. "The offering was put upon his sons' hands" (vs. 26, 27). The separated one is sure to get his hands filled with and for service. He never sends us a warfare on our own charges. This is the true thought of consecration. Cleansed and clothed, and the *hands filled* with acceptable offerings unto God. Who then is willing to *fill his hands* this day? (see 1 Chron. 29. 5, margin). No man, saith the Lord, shall come BEFORE ME empty handed.

Empty-handed service is the cause of so much failure in Christian work.

6. Anointed. "Moses took the anointing oil and sanctified his sons and his sons' garments" (v. 30). This anointing oil is doubtless typical of the Holy Spirit, and teaches us the secret of holiness, how the *garments* of our outer everyday life may be "Holiness unto the Lord." To be holy is to be *whole* within (Rom. 8. 29), and blameless without. This anointing answers to Pentecost after the atoning and cleansing Blood of the Cross. Have you received this same anointing which teacheth you all things? (1 John 2. 27).

7. Commissioned. "Therefore shall ye keep the charge of the Lord" (v. 35). The charge of the Lord is: "Preach the Gospel to every creature" (Mark 16. 15). Ye shall be witnesses unto Me. We have been saved to serve (Acts 9. 15, 16). In keeping this charge the sons of Aaron had to be obedient to the moving of the Pillar of Cloud (Num. 9. 19). "A charge to keep I have." "Lord, as Thou art able to keep that which I have committed unto Thee, may I be enabled to keep that which Thou hast committed unto me." _____

THE GLORY OF THE LORD.
Leviticus 9.

WE have seen that in the previous chapters there is much said about various offerings and sacrifices, all of which indicate, in one way or other, the opening up of a way whereby man as a sinner may approach God and find His favour. What could be more graciously beautiful than the promise of God's glory revealed after all the sacrifices have been made, and that this revelation of Himself should be associated with the *eighth* day? (v. 1). The *eighth* day is always the beginning, or the *first day* of a new week, and so brings us into remembrance of the resurrection day of our

Lord and Saviour, and of the manifestation of His glory, the glory of His power, after the great sacrifice had been made.

1. The glorious promise. "The glory of the Lord shall appear unto you" (v. 6). It has always been His desire to manifest Himself to man, and that man should know Him. For this great end Christ came. He could say, "The glory which Thou hast given Me, I have given them." This glory includes the glory of His long-suffering mercy and self-sacrificing love.

2. The needful preparation. Before the Lord in His glory could appear the people must have for themselves—

1. A HOLY MEDIATOR. Aaron as a priest must first make an atonement for himself (v. 7). He who would come between God and man must himself be accepted by God. Christ is our Priest, *ordained for men* in things pertaining to God (Heb. 5. 1-3).

2. A PERFECT SACRIFICE. It is not without due significance that the four special sacrifices aforementioned (chaps. 1, 2, 3, 4) should all be offered on that day in which the Lord was to appear (vs. 1-4). As we have already observed, all these offerings taken together present one full view of the perfect moral character and precious atoning death of God's beloved Son. The glory of God can only be revealed to those who have a true appreciation of the Saviour's sufferings. I beseech of thee show me Thy glory.

3. The grand result. This may be summed up in the following expressive words—

1. BLESSING. "Aaron lifted up his hands, and blessed them" (v. 22). This implied the consciousness of forgiveness. Accepted through the offering. Hath He not blessed us with all blessing in the heavenlies in Christ?

2. GLORY. "The glory of the Lord appeared unto all the people" (v. 23). This also shall be our portion when

He appears. We shall see Him as He is, and we shall be glorified together. We have got the *blessing* now through His great atoning death; we shall see this glory when we are changed and translated into His presence.

3. JUDGMENT. " There came a fire out from the Lord," &c. This *consuming fire* coming out in the presence of the people suggests the terrible judgment of God, whether it falls on the altar or on the sinner. Our God, the God of glory, is also a consuming fire. This is the judgment that will come upon the wicked whom He shall destroy with the *brightness* of His coming (2 Thess. 2. 8). Solemn words—think of them.

4. ADORATION. " All the people fell on their faces" (v. 24). What could be more fitting? As the glory of His power is manifested we can only bow our faces and worship. Salvation through Christ leads to being glorified together. The glory of His grace and justice leads to the shout of praise and the bowing down of an adoring heart (2 Chron. 7. 1-3). Let us each ask, Has the Lord respect unto *my* offering?

NADAB AND ABIHU.
Leviticus 10. 1-5.

MIRACLES are not sufficient to convince men of sin, and to put them in a right attitude for worshipping God acceptably. Nadab and his priestly brother had just a little ago seen the glory of God, and the miraculous fire falling from Heaven consuming the sacrifice upon the altar, and would be among those who reverently bowed and worshipped (see chap. 9), yet because of their pride and irreverence they were smitten with judgment. Surely there is a solemn warning here for all the people of God. We notice—

1. A great privilege. They were the " sons of Aaron." They had a—

1. GODLY FATHER. To be the son of a saint is a priceless

boon, but a man may be the son of a divine and yet be the servant of the devil.

2. RELIGIOUS UPBRINGING. From their infancy they were familiar with holy things, and had been trained up in the admonition of the Lord.

3. GOOD PROFESSION. They were recognised by others as the *servants* of God. It is possible to bear the name of Christian, to take part in Christian work, and yet in spirit to know not the holiness of God or the awfulness of sin.

2. A presumptuous act. "They offered strange fire before the Lord." They—

1. OFFERED FIRE OF THEIR OWN MAKING. This the Lord had forbidden (v. 1). Their offering was like the prayer of the Pharisee (Luke 18. 11), or like the sacrifice of Cain. Only a manifestation of self-conceit and rebellion.

2. REJECTED THE GIFT OF GOD. The fire that burned on the altar was the gift of God. This they should have used, but this they despised (chap. 16. 12). How much better are those who seek the favour of God on the ground of their own goodness, and utterly reject Christ as the gift of God? They seek to establish their *own* righteousness, but have not submitted themselves to the *righteousness of God*.

3. An unexpected doom. "There went out fire from the Lord and devoured them." *Waxen* professors have need to beware of the fire. They—

1. PERISHED AT THE HAND OF HIM WHOM THEY PROFESSED TO SERVE. This is an early version of the story of Ananias and Sapphira (Acts 5). Not zeal without knowledge so much as presumption without fear.

2. PERISHED BY THAT WHICH THEY REJECTED. *Fire* from the Lord. The rejected stone shall grind to powder (Luke 20. 17, 18). Christ Jesus, the gift of God, is now appointed Judge of all. To reject Him now as offered to

us on the altar of the Cross will be to meet Him then as a consuming fire.

4. A solemn sight. They died *before* the Lord. " Blessed are the dead that die *in* the Lord.'' They—

1. WERE CARRIED OUT. They were able of themselves to go in, but unable of themselves to come out. There is no atonement for the sin of presumption (Num. 15. 30). He that being often reproved hardeneth his neck shall perish without remedy.

2. WERE CARRIED OUT IN THEIR COATS. Their priestly garbs did not protect them. *Coats* of profession will not save. "I saw the *wicked* buried, who had *come and gone* from the place of the holy'' (Eccles. 8. 10). The man who builds his house on the sand is sure to perish on the ruin of it. If our religion is only in our *coats* it will certainly be buried with us.

5. An important lesson. It is the gracious purpose of God to be—

1. SANCTIFIED IN US. " I will be sanctified *in them* that come *nigh Me*." Sanctify therefore the Lord in your heart, for He looketh not upon the *outward* appearance, but upon the heart (1 Sam. 16. 7). Without holiness no man shall see the Lord. The pure *in heart* shall see God.

2. GLORIFIED THROUGH US. " Before the people will I be glorified." It is ours to be *still and know* that He is God, that He may be exalted among the heathen (Psa. 46. 10). Let us magnify the Lord together. Glorify Thou Thy Son in me. _____

YE SHALL BE HOLY.
Leviticus 11.

HOLINESS, or separation from the unclean, is the burden of this chapter. After a full atonement has been made, and the Lord has revealed Himself to His people, as we have seen in chapter 9, it surely becomes His redeemed ones to be imitators of God as dear children (Eph. 5. 1). This is the desire of His heart, "Ye shall be holy, for I am holy." We cannot be followers of the Holy One and take pleasure in those things which are unclean in His sight.

We shall look at—

1. **The warning given.** "They are unclean to *you*, they are an abomination unto *you*." Other people may eat of those unclean animals, but it shall not be so with *you*. Ye are My people, redeemed by blood, and separated for My Name's glory, so your manner of living must not be after the indiscriminating fashion of the ungodly. The lesson for us is plain.

2. **The distinctions made.** God Himself distinguishes what is clean or unclean for His people. The clean animals are known by their *feet* and *mouth*, they part the hoof and chew the cud. What God hath cleansed, that call not common or unclean (Acts 10. 12). The feet and mouth marks point to our *walk* and *word* as evidence of our being clean before the Lord. Many professing Christians are sorely troubled with the "foot and mouth disease," they delight not to walk in His ways or to speak in His Name. "All *fowls* (flying things) that *creep* shall be an abomination unto you" (v. 20). All those who have power to *rise up into the heavenly places,* and who spend their time in *crawling* on the earth, are in an unclean state, and are abominable in the sight of God. "I would that thou wert cold or hot; because thou art neither cold nor hot I will spue thee out of My mouth" (Rev. 3. 15, 16). "Thou shalt not *eat* or become a partaker of any abominable thing" (Deut. 14. 3). Those gifted with the wings of faith become unclean when they get among the "*creeping things.*"

3. **The reasons urged.** There are several powerful arguments here given why we as God's redeemed people should live a separated life. Because of—

1. His sovereign claim over us. "I am the Lord *your* God" (v. 44). This is a blessed revelation indeed. "I am *your* God." Did not the risen Saviour say, "I ascend unto My Father and *your* Father, unto My God and *your* God?" When ye pray, say, "*Our* Father."

2. What He hath done for us. "I am the Lord that *bringeth you up out* of the land of Egypt" (v. 45). We have been delivered out of the hand of our enemies that we might serve Him without fear in holiness (Luke 1. 74, 75). Redeemed by His Blood, and the dominion of sin over us and in us broken up.

3. His immaculate character. "I am holy" (v. 45). He is perfect in holiness. The *wholeness* of His character is eternally and unchangeably complete in all His attributes and works.

4. Our relationship to Him. "I am your God, *ye shall therefore be holy*, for I am holy" (v. 45). "Ye shall *therefore* sanctify yourselves" (v. 44). How can two walk together except they be agreed? "What communion hath light with darkness? Ye are the temple of the living God. As God hath said﹀I will dwell in them, and walk in them; and I will be their God, and they shall be My people. *Wherefore* come out from among them, and be ye *separate*, saith the Lord, and touch not the unclean thing; and I will receive you, and be a Father unto you, and ye shall be My sons and daughters, saith the Lord Almighty. Having therefore these promises, dearly beloved, let us cleanse ourselves, and perfect holiness in the fear of God" (2 Cor. 6. 14-18).

THE CLEANSING OF THE LEPER.
Leviticus 13; 14. 1.

Leprosy, as a type, brings out the terrible nature of sin. Its seat is deep down, not only in the head where it *appears*, but in the hidden man of the heart. Making the whole life barren and unfruitful, like the spring at Jericho (2 Kings 2. 19). Sin, like leprosy, afflicts the *person* himself, the *garments* he wears, and the *house* where he lives. These aptly suggest spirit, soul, and body—

1. The inner PERSON, of the heart.

2. The outer GARMENTS, of the life.

3. The common HOUSE, of our daily associations.

Let us look at the disease and the cure—

1. The character of the disease. "It is a plague of leprosy." It—

1. MAKES UNCLEAN. He is a leprous man, he is unclean (chap. 13. 44). One spot was enough to make him *utterly* unclean. Sin is such an awful thing that to offend in *one point* is to be guilty of all. If we have not *continued in all things* we are under the curse (Gal. 3. 10). If the disease was only skin deep it was not reckoned uncleanness. *Infirmities* are not sins.

2. BRINGS JUDGMENT. "The priest shall *pronounce* him utterly unclean" (chap. 13. 44). *Condemnation* came by the Word of God's representative. He that believeth not is condemned already. From the judgment of the priest there was no appeal. God's pronouncement is always associated with sin. No man can alter it.

3. BRINGS SEPARATION. "He shall dwell *alone* without the camp" (chap. 13. 46). *Outside* the camp meant outside the sphere of Divine fellowship. As long as he is a *leper* he can have no communion with God or His people (Eph. 2. 12). Uncleanness of heart unfits for the enjoyment of His presence. The pure in heart shall see God. What a picture of one *dead* in sin, dead while he lives, dead to God, dead to the enjoyment of holy things, dead to a life of usefulness!

2. It must be confessed. There were four things by

which a leper was known, and which reveal the true condition of a sinner before God. His—

1. CLOTHES WERE RENT. This indicated misery and nakedness.

2. HEAD WAS BARE. He was defenceless and exposed. No covering from the vengeance of a burning sun.

3. LIP WAS COVERED. Indicating that his breath was polluted, and that his mouth was stopped as far as self-justification was concerned.

4. CRY WAS " UNCLEAN." The priest pronounced him unclean. He believed him, and confessed that it was true. He accepted his condemnation and took his proper place. Go thou and do likewise.

3. The manner of restoration. As the leprosy shows the sin, so the *way of restoration* reveals the Divine method of salvation. Note the various acts. The—

1. OUT-GOING OF THE PRIEST. " The priest shall go forth" (chap. 14. 3). The leper cannot come *in*, so the mediator goes *out*. The sinner cannot of himself find his way back into the presence of God, but Jesus Christ, our great High Priest, *went forth* to seek and to save. The Shepherd goes out to seek the lost sheep.

2. OFFERING MADE. " Then shall the priest command to take *for* him two birds" (chap. 14. 4-6). The priest goes forth, then the sacrifice is made. Christ came out from the presence of the Father, then gave Himself a ransom for all. The killing of the one bird, and the dipping of the other in its blood, and letting it fly to the heavens is sublimely typical of Christ's death and resurrection, and of His ascending into Heaven by His own Blood. A new and *living* way.

3. SPRINKLING OF THE BLOOD. " He shall sprinkle upon him that is to be cleansed from the leprosy seven times" (chap. 14. 7). The leper must come into personal contact

with the sacrifice made for him. The *blood* denotes the value of the life offered; this being sprinkled by the priest signifies that the application of Christ's death to the sinner is God's work. I will sprinkle you, and ye shall be clean. He who imputed our sins to Christ can alone impute righteousness to us.

4. WORD OF THE PRIEST. " The priest shall *pronounce* him clean." He alone who pronounced the leper unclean can pronounce him clean. He who condemns the unbeliever, justifies the believer in Jesus. It is God that justifieth. When the poor leper had the justifying *word* of the priest, it mattered nothing to him what the opinions of others or his own feelings were.

5. PERSONAL CLEANSING. "He that is cleansed shall wash his clothes and shave off his hair," &c. (chap. 14. 8). The cleansing through the Blood of Jesus should lead us to put away all filthiness of the flesh and spirit. Those justified before God by *faith* should justify themselves by their *works*.

6. RESTORATION. " After that he shall come into the camp" (chap. 14. 8). After what? After the *sprinkling*, the *washing*, and the *shaving*. It is our uncleanness that keeps us out of the camp of communion. What fellowship hath light with darkness? When cleansed from sin there is nothing to hinder our drawing nigh unto God.

7. CONSECRATION (vs. 14-18). The *blood* and the *oil* put upon the ear, hand, and foot betoken *redemption* and *consecration*. After the blood of atonement (the work of Christ) comes the oil of anointing, the work of the Holy Spirit. That which was bought by the blood is claimed by the Holy Spirit. The rest of the oil was *put upon* his head (v. 29). Indicating that the cleansed one should also have the poured out Spirit *upon* him. The tongues of fire sat *upon* each of them (Acts 2. 3).

THE DAY OF ATONEMENT.

THE WORK OF CHRIST.

Leviticus 16.

THE Day of Atonement was Israel's *great* day. All the vessels and services derived their value from it. It was the most solemn day in all the year to the high priest. The day of Christ's humiliation was the most solemn day in all the history of His eternal existence. In verse 30 we have the key to the whole chapter. There is—

1. The work: " an atonement for you."
2. The worker: " the priest."
3. The time: " on that day."
4. The purpose: " make you *clean before the Lord*."

This great day was the—

1. Day of needful humiliation. The garments of glory and beauty had to be laid aside for the plain " holy linen coat" (v. 4). He could not represent the people *before* God until *atonement* was made. Christ made Himself of no reputation (see Phil. 2. 7, 8). Though in the *form of a servant*, his character was as " holy linen" (Heb. 7. 26).

2. Day of special sacrifice (vs. 5-11). The priest had first to offer a sacrifice *for himself*. His own standing had to be secured before God. Christ being the Son, needed not this (Heb. 7. 27). The *two* goats constituted *one* offering, representing the *two* aspects of Christ's death. The one *went up* (margin 9), the other *went away* (v. 12; John 1. 29)—atonement and substitution.

3. Day of solemn imputation. " Aaron shall confess all their sins, putting them upon the head of the goat" (vs. 21, 22). The goat became a *curse* for them (Gal. 3. 13), was led into a land not inhabited (Mark 15. 34), bearing their iniquities in its body (1 Peter 2. 24; Isa. 53).

4. Day of nearness to God (vs. 12-15). On that day

the vail was opened. Christ's death removed the last barrier (Luke 23. 45). The way into the *holiest* is now manifest (Heb. 9. 8). The blood was sprinkled *upon* and *before* the mercy-seat, signifying—(1) a complete acceptance; (2) a secure standing (Eph. 1. 6, 7).

5. Day of real affliction. "This shall be a statute *for ever*, ye shall *afflict* your souls" (v. 29). SIN is no trifle, neither is ATONEMENT. Frivolous hearts will always treat it lightly. The awful atonement must be accepted with convicted and broken hearts (John 16. 8; Acts 2. 37).

6. Day of perfect rest. "Ye shall do *no work at all*" (v. 29; see chap. 23. 30). On the day of atonement the priest did all the work. Jesus did it all (John 19. 30). Proud man would fain do *something* to help himself to God, but that something can only bring death (Eph. 2. 8).

7. Day of blessed experience. "*Clean* from all your sins *before the Lord*" (v. 30). It is ours to accept by faith what *He has done*, this brings salvation (Acts. 13. 39). And to believe what *He hath said*, this brings assurance (1 John 5. 13). If the death of Christ has not *made us* clean before the Lord it has availed us nothing (John 13. 8).

HOLY LIVING.
Leviticus 19.

"O Lord, I bare an aching heart,
Ease me of sin, whate'er tho smart;
Without, within, I would be pure,
Lord, hear my cry! Lord, work my cure!
I know not all I ask in this,
But give, O give me holiness."

FOR the purpose of practical holiness Christ's sermon on the Mount is not more direct and suitable than the teaching we have in the message recorded in this chapter. It opens with that oft-repeated demand, "Ye shall be holy," coupled with that ever gracious revelation, "For I the Lord *your*

God am holy '' The holy life is the most useful of all lives, the holy man is the most practical of all men. In this portion we have brought before us—

1. The characteristics of a holy life. Here are the features of a holy man. He—

1. HONOURS HIS FATHER AND MOTHER (v. 3). A very needful suggestion to young converts. It has been said that '' Piety begins at home.'' While it should not remain there, yet our Christian character will have little influence if it has not first of all been rooted in the home life.

2. HAS NOTHING TO DO WITH IDOLS (v. 4). Nothing is allowed to take the place of God in his affections. He seeks *first* the kingdom of God, and has more real joy in the presence of God than in company with any one else. As dearly beloved ones, they flee from idolatry (1 Cor. 10. 14).

3. MAKES HIS SACRIFICES WILLINGLY (v. 5). He *willingly* suffers loss for Christ's sake, he delights to do the will of God at any cost. What may be a great hardship to others is a joy to him.

4 REMEMBERS THE POOR (vs. 9, 10). He follows the example of his Master, and preaches the Gospel to the poor. He also realises that the poor have a claim on his possessions, and that he is but a steward of the mercies of God.

5. DEALS HONESTLY WITH HIS FELLOWMEN (v. 11). Even if his business does not succeed he will rather suffer than lie or defraud a neighbour He carries a just balance in his conscience, and will not be guilty of a dishonest silence His service is not mere eye service.

6. WILL NOT DISHONOUR THE NAME OF GOD (v. 12). He is more jealous for the Name of his God than for his own He is willing rather to be made of no reputation than that the honour of his Lord and Master should be tarnished

7. CONSIDERS HIS SERVANTS (v 13) Wages are paid

when due, and paid in a manner that makes the receiver feel that it is a pleasure for him to pay them.

8. WILL NOT TAKE ADVANTAGE OF A WEAKER BROTHER (v. 14). It is so natural to be impatient with the deaf, with those whose faculties of apprehension may be dull, and by our unguarded walk to put a stumbling block in the way of those whose eyesight may not be quite so clear as ours. He remembers (Deut. 27. 18).

9. IS IMPARTIAL IN HIS MANNER. His interest in the Lord's *poor ones* is just as great as in those who occupy the chief seats in the public sanctuary. The impartial love of God is in his heart. He fears God and honours all *men*.

10. IS NO TALE-BEARER (v. 16). The gossip that must enter his ear finds its grave there. Being of a faithful spirit he conceals the matter (Prov. 11. 13). He knows that the tongue is a fire, a world of iniquity, so he bridles it.

11. REBUKES THE ERRING IN LOVE (v. 17). There is no hate in his heart to any brother, or to any mortal. Such murderous feelings have no place in him. Yet at times he speaks sharply, and is faithful in rebuking sin, because he loves the truth and the errring one (2 Tim. 2. 4).

12. DOES NOT AVENGE, OR KEEP UP A GRUDGE (v. 18). He does not recompense evil, but waits on the Lord (Prov. 20. 22). He leaves vengeance to whom it belongs (Rom. 12. 19), and by the grace of God is enabled to bear no grudge to his enemies.

13. DISTINGUISHES BETWEEN THINGS THAT DIFFER (v. 19). He does not practise the mingling of *diverse* kinds. He knows that he cannot serve God and mammon, and that light and darkness will not mix, and that there is no concord between Christ and Belial (2 Cor. 6. 14-16).

14. DISREGARDS UNHOLY METHODS (v. 31). For success in the work of God he depends entirely upon the power and wisdom of the Spirit of God. He has no faith in the

familiar spirits of men or of devils, and will not trust the *wizardly* methods of ungodly worldlings.

2. The great incentive of a holy life. Ye shall be holy, for I the Lord your God am holy (v. 1). I Jehovah your God am holy. Therefore—

1. YE SHALL BE HOLY. "Walk worthy of God in all well-pleasing" (Col. 1. 10; 1 Thess. 2. 12).

2. MY GRACE IS SUFFICIENT FOR THEE. "My God shall supply all your need" (Phil. 4. 19).

3. FEAR NOT IN THE TIME OF TRIAL. "Lo, I am with you alway" (Matt. 28 20).

4. SERVE WITH GLADNESS. "Ye shall receive a reward" (1 Cor. 3. 14)

5. BE IMITATORS OF GOD (Eph 5. 1, R V) "I in them, and thou in Me" (John 17 23)

CHARACTERISTICS OF A SON OF AARON.
Leviticus 21.

THE priesthood of all believers is beautifully and clearly taught in the *sons* of Israel's High Priest. Being *born* of God into the privilege of sonship, they have this liberty of access into His presence as priests. In this chapter we observe some of the marks which distinguish a son of Aaron. Let us see whether we as sons and priests bear these distinctions or not. He is—

1. A chief man among the people (v 4). Not an ordinary man, his birth has separated him from the common herd of humanity. He is acknowledged by all as belonging to a different family, being connected with their great high priest Does our relationship to Christ, the great High Priest, so lift us up into such holy dignity as to be noted among the people as "chief men?" "A man of God."

2. Not distinguished by bodily marks (v. 5). The priests of Rome in this, as in many other things, contradict Scripture by making baldness upon their heads. The marks of a child of God are deeper down in the *meekness* and *lowliness* of Christ. " My sheep *hear* My voice, they *know* Me, and I give unto them *eternal life*" (John 10. 27, 28).

3. One who offers the bread of God (v. 8). This may refer to the *shew bread* that was given to God, and claimed by Him as " His bread," and afterwards given by Him to the priest. So the priest is represented as giving to God that which satisfied Him. Then He satisfies the priest with bread, *the bread of God*. Then as priests we may, through our ministry, give to God that which is the bread of satisfaction.

4. Anointed with oil (vs. 10-12). The crown of the holy oil of his God is upon him. The *anointing* oil is an emblem of the Holy Spirit. To be baptised with the Holy Spirit is to be *crowned* with honour and glory. How many of God's sons and priests are as yet uncrowned because they have not (through their unbelief) received this crowning blessing (Acts 1. 8). Have ye received the Holy Ghost since ye believed? (Acts 19. 2). The *crown* tells of a *kingly* priesthood.

5. Free from profane associations (vs. 13-15). Being a *separated* man, what may be expedient in the case of others is not allowable in his. His life is not governed by his own will, tastes, or feelings, but by the *Word of God*. The purpose of the great High Priest is the ruling motive of his life. "I delight to do Thy will, O God, Thy law is within my heart" (2 Cor. 6. 14-18).

6. Without visible blemish (vs. 17-21). Of course the blemishes here referred to are physical, but suggest certain moral and physical defects that prevent men from having fellowship with God. Unbelief and cold-heartedness are terrible blemishes, those that come to God with them are only mocking Him. A blemished offering He will not accept, it must be perfect to be accepted (Lev. 22. 21). He has made provision whereby the man of God may be *perfect* (2 Tim. 3. 17). That implies being in a perfect *condition* to offer acceptable service unto God. This is a perfection within the reach of every Christian (2 Cor. 13. 9). We are living a *blemished* life if we are not so perfect. Be ye therefore perfect and *entire*, wanting nothing (James 1. 4).

7. One who eats the bread of God (v. 22). His soul is satisfied with God's provision. He *feasts* on holy things which no *stranger* can receive (Lev. 22. 10). Once we were strangers and foreigners, but now fellow-citizens with the saints, and of the *household* of God (Eph. 2. 19). Fellow-priests, are we living up to our holy and blessed calling?

HOLY THINGS FOR HOLY ONES.
Leviticus 22. 1-16.

As Aaron is a type of Christ, so his *sons* represent all who are *born* of God. All God's sons are priests, although all do not live up to their priestly privileges. These "*holy things*," so frequently referred to in this chapter (twelve times), are fit and proper emblems of the "*spiritual things*" freely given us of God, but only fully enjoyed by those who are wholly yielded to God. These "holy things" are God's provision for His holy ones.

There are several important lessons we might learn from what is said about them. That—

1. Dealing with holy things in an unholy fashion brings death (v. 3). The unclean cannot pass over this holy way. The natural man receiveth not the things of the Spirit of God (1 Cor 2. 14) From the worldly-wise and the self-complacent these things are hidden, and our gracious Lord thanked the Father that it was so. The swinish soul cannot appreciate angels' food. Let us take care how we handle spiritual things lest we eat and drink judgment unto ourselves, thus making the *Gospel* a savour of death.

2. **The unclean cannot eat holy things.** "He shall not eat of the holy things until he be clean" (v. 4). We must be cleansed from sin before we can have any appetite or capacity for the enjoyment of heavenly and spiritual things. He will not cast His pearls before swine. Holiness and uncleanness are opposites. He that loveth the darkness hateth the light.

3. **Holy things are the food of the holy.** "He shall eat the holy things because it is his *food*" (v. 7). The holy man can find no *food* in the mere pleasures of the world, the things that enchant the ungodly have no attraction for him; his heart is set on heavenly things. Communion with God is to him more delightful than his daily food, and the salvation of sinners more precious than silver or gold.

4. **No stranger or hired servant could eat these holy things** (v. 10). The *stranger* represents those who know not God, who have not believed in His Son. The *hired* servant denotes that class of professing Christians who desire to make gain out of godliness, who serve the Lord for personal profit. Such religious mercenaries have their reward, but they never taste the HOLY THINGS.

5. **Those bought by the priest, or born into his house, could eat of the holy things** (v. 11). To be *bought* or *born* into the priestly family gave the right to these holy privileges. *Bought* by the blood of Christ, and *born* of God, brings us into the family of God, and gives us the right and fitness for the enjoyment of the unsearchable riches of Christ, those holy things so freely given us of God.

6. Unholy relationships disqualify for eating these holy things (v. 12). An unequal yoke often destroys the appetite for spiritual things. The priest's daughter had a right by birth, but she disqualified herself by marrying a *stranger*. We may be Christians by a new birth, and yet through our worldly and sinful associations be quite unfit to receive the things of Christ as revealed by the Holy Spirit. But by returning to the Father's house the privilege was restored (Luke 15. 18).

7. Eating holy things unwittingly did not profit (v. 14). It is quite possible to read and speak of those great and precious holy things and yet be an utter stranger to the power of them. The truth may be on the heart and never become assimilated with the life, not being mixed with faith. A man is only *unwittingly* dealing with the exceeding great and precious promises of Christ until he proves them, by a personal faith, in his own soul (Psa. 19. 12). ———

THE FREEWILL OFFERING.
Leviticus 22. 17-25.

THE redeemed of the Lord have many opportunities of showing their love for the Lord by their *freewill* offerings to Him. The Lord loveth a cheerful giver. Being saved by grace, this *grace* should find expression in spontaneous acts of sacrifice and thankfulness. Freely ye have received, freely give. Note here that such offerings—

1. Are " expected by the Lord" (v. 18.) Not that He needs the *gift*, but He much desires that condition of heart and mind that chooses to acknowledge Him in this way. The apostle James says, " I will show you my faith by my works." Our *love* to God may be manifested in the same way.

2. Must be "laid on the altar" (v. 18). Being burnt-offerings they were put on the great brazen altar outside the holy place. This altar speaks to us of the Cross of Christ by which we and our offerings are made acceptable to God. Even a freewill offering is not pleasing to Jehovah apart from the person and work of His Son Jesus Christ. The gifts of the ungodly, even for the work of the Church, cannot be said to be laid on the altar. Freewill offerings to men, but not to God. The *love* of Christ is not the constraining motive.

3. Could be made by "any one" in Israel. "Whosoever he be *in Israel*" (v. 18). A man had to be numbered with the people of God before a *freewill* offering could be accepted. No one has a *free* will until he becomes a Son of God through redeeming grace. Till then sin has dominion over the whole nature, being under the law (Rom. 6. 14). Until we are freed from sin by the power of Christ our offerings never reach the altar.

4. Must be made "willingly." "Ye shall offer at *your own will*" (v. 19). It cannot be a *freewill* offering unless it is made willingly, not grudgingly, or of necessity. When God gave His Son up to the death for us, He gave Him *willingly*. Whatsoever *ye do*, do it *heartily* as unto the Lord. The Lord looketh upon the heart.

5. Must be " without blemish." That which hath a blemish " shall not be acceptable for you" (v. 20). Many offer to God what they would not give to an earthly friend, bad money and bad manners. God hath given to us His Firstborn and His Best, and shall we offer Him the blind, the lame, and the worthless? *Odd* coppers and *spare* moments may be given with a *free will*, but they just reveal the small place the Lord has in such hearts and lives. Yield *yourselves* unto God.

6. Must be " perfect to be accepted" (v. 21). We must see that we are not giving to God *because* it is not perfect. *Perfection* is of course a relative term, what may be perfect for one may be far from being perfect in another.

The poor widow's two mites (one farthing) made a perfect offering, your penny may be an insult. Giving as the Lord hath prospered us, with a willing mind, this is good and acceptable in His sight. Freely ye have received, freely give. ————

SEVEN LINKS IN THE CHAIN OF GRACE.
Leviticus 22. 31-33.

" I AM THE LORD." These words occur three times in these three verses, and are as the three seals of the Triune God, set upon these great and precious truths. It is refreshing and assuring to our souls to find how frequently Jehovah reminds them that it was He who brought them out of Egypt God can never forget the great salvation accomplished for His people, and is constantly reminding them that He who *saved them* was still with them and for them. He who gave up His Son for us, how will He not also *with Him* freely give us all things. We need often to be reminded of this.

The different links in this chain of golden grace are—

1. Revelation. " I am the Lord." If God is to be known He must reveal Himself. No man by searching can find out God. This revelation of Himself we have in Christ Jesus. When Philip said to Jesus, "Show us the Father, and it sufficeth us," Jesus answered, " Have I been so long time with you, and yet hast thou not KNOWN ME, Philip? he that hath seen ME, hath seen the Father. The Father that dwelleth IN ME He doeth the works." What a revelation! Have you heard and seen the invisible God in the words and life of Jesus?

2. Salvation. "Brought you out of the land of Egypt." Egypt was the place of bondage, misery, and fruitless toil. Type of the world and our former state. In their helplessness He pitied, and by His great power at the hand of Moses He *brought them out*. Translated from the kingdom of darkness into the kingdom of His dear Son. Saved by grace.

3. Adaptation. " I brought you out *to be your God.*"
Do we in any measure apprehend the infinite goodness of
God as revealed in these few words. He has delivered us
from the oppression of sin that He might manifest
Himself in all the fulness of His grace and glory unto
us. We are to be *to Him* a people taken out by Himself,
and He is to be *to us* a God (Exod. 6. 7). As our God,
He pledges Himself to adapt the riches of His grace and
every attribute of His character to our daily needs, and
to the enriching of our lives for the glory of His own
Name. I have brought you out *to be your God.* Bless
the Lord, O my soul!

4. Sanctification. " I am the Lord which *hallow*
you." This *hallowing* or *setting apart* for Himself is part
of the great salvation. The Israelites were not saved out
of Egypt merely to escape the cruel lash of the taskmaster,
but that they might be a people *unto Himself.* We have not
been saved by Christ merely to be delivered out of the hands
of our enemies, but that we might serve Him without fear
in holiness all the days of our life (Luke 1. 74, 75). I am
the Lord which hallow you. Sanctification is the Lord's
work. Jesus Christ is *made of God* unto us sanctification
(1 Cor. 1. 30).

5. Representation. " *I will be hallowed* among the
children of Israel." The holiness of God is to be seen
in the holiness of His people. Are we faithful and true
representatives of the character of our Lord and Saviour?
As the temple of the living God He desires to dwell in us
and walk in us (2 Cor. 6. 16). If He is to be hallowed
among His people it becomes us to be *imitators* of God
as dear children (Eph. 5. 1).

6. Prohibition. " Neither shall ye profane My Name."
It is easy for those *called by His Name* to profane it by an
unworthy walk (Col. 1. 10). All connected with our

lives that is *outside* the temple of His holy will is profane. We profane His Name by our unbelieving prayers, by our formal lip professions, and even when we are preaching the Gospel, if it is not in the power of the Holy Spirit. Be filled with the Spirit, and ye shall not profane His holy Name, for He will work in you both to will and to do of His good pleasure.

7. Commission. "*Therefore* ye shall keep My commandments *and do them*" (v. 31). Therefore, because I am your God, having redeemed you to Myself, and set you apart for the hallowing of My Name, ye shall make it your delightful business to keep My words and to do My will. Every saved and sanctified one was a commissioned one. No earthly friend knew Jesus better than His mother. Remember then her words to the servants at the marriage in Cana, " Whatsoever He saith unto you, do it." She herself knew the blessedness of faith and obedience.

THE MEMORIAL FEASTS.
SEVEN EXPERIENCES IN THE CHRISTIAN LIFE.
Leviticus 23.

THESE seven feasts were seasons, or joyful solemnities, *appointed* by the Lord. They were holy memorial gatherings or convocations, through which as a means of grace God blessed His people. They have a deep and powerful prophetic voice. Each feast seems to point out some definite experience on the part of His people, and to denote some fresh manifestation of the riches of His grace and purpose toward them. They may also have a dispensational bearing, representing, as I think they do, the different epochs in the history of His ancient people and of the Church of God. Take a glance at them in this connection—

1. PASSOVER. This suggests the day of Jesus Christ's humiliation and death.

2. UNLEAVENED BREAD may indicate the *present-day* experience of God's people as separated ones.

3. FIRSTFRUITS may point to the first resurrection at the coming of the Lord, as predicted in 1 Thessalonians 4. 16.

4. FEAST OF WEEKS, or ingathering: the restoration of the Jews, when all Israel shall be saved.

5. TRUMPETS: the publishing by the Jews of the Gospel of the kingdom.

6. ATONEMENTS: the final adjustment of all things to God in righteousness.

7. TABERNACLES: "God in the midst of them," as when they abode in tents in the wilderness—the millennial reign. Peace on earth and good will among men.

These holy appointments by God are worthy of our closest study, as revealing the Divine programme with regard to "things to come." But we wish to view these feasts in what some might call a more practical light, as touching our individual experience. The—

1. Feast of Passover, or saved by the blood (v. 5). It is the *Lord's Passover* because He passed over them who were sheltered by the sprinkled blood of the lamb in Egypt. Ye have not been redeemed with silver or gold, but with the precious Blood of Christ as of a lamb without blemish (1 Peter 1. 18, 19). As often as ye eat this bread and drink this cup ye do show the *Lord's death* till He come.

2. Feast of Unleavened Bread, or cleansed by the Word (v. 6.) This feast was held just the day after the Passover, teaching us that there is a very close relationship between redemption and cleansing. The *leaven* of sin and hypocrisy must be excluded from the bread of those redeemed to God by the Blood of Christ. Desire the *sincere* milk of the Word that ye may grow; the reading of trashy, unwholesome

literature hinders the growth of many a child of God. Let
not such a thing be seen in all thy quarters (Exod. 13. 6, 7).

3. Feast of Firstfruits, or consecrated to God (vs.
10-12), The *first* sheaf of the harvest presented to Jehovah
is an emphatic type of Christ (1 Cor. 15. 23), who was the
corn of wheat that fell into the ground and *died* that He
might bring forth much fruit (John 12. 24). If the *first-
fruit* be holy the lump is also holy (Rom. 11. 16). The
redeemed from among men are the firstfruits unto God
(Rev 14 4) The *sheaf* and the *lamb* were offered together
(v. 12) We, a kind of firstfruits, are represented, "risen
together" with Christ the Lamb of God. The sheaf represented the firstfruits of a new life, offered to God in
the power of a blameless Lamb Being made alive unto
God, the sheaf of our whole nature should be presented to
Him as the *firstfruits* of a harvest of praise and honour
yet to come through our faithful life for God.

4. Feast of Weeks, or the filling of the Holy Spirit
(vs 15-22). It is called the " feast of weeks" because it
was held seven weeks after the Passover. It was also called
Pentecost, because it was held on the fiftieth day. On this
day the Holy Spirit was poured out (Acts 2. 1-4). It was
the *harvest* or *ingathering* feast. This was beautifully fulfilled on the day of Pentecost, for we read that " the *same
day* there were added unto them about three thousand
souls " Just as *Pentecost* followed the offering of the *firstfruits*, so the filling of the Holy Spirit follows the yielding
up of ourselves unto God, then comes the harvesting or
ingathering of precious souls. This is God's order, and
there is no other successful way As a corn of wheat
we must also fall and die to sin and self if we would
bring forth much fruit unto God It would also seem
from what is here stated that we are not to expect that
the world will be converted or gathered in during this
dispensation, for He says, " Thou shalt not make a clean

riddance of the corners of thy field" (v. 22), although
the time will come when every knee shall bow to Him.

5. Feast of Trumpets, or the publishing of the Gospel
(vs. 23-25). When a man has been filled with the Holy
Ghost he will soon take to trumpeting the Gospel. The
blowing of the trumpet was as holy a work as offering a
sacrifice. It is "an holy convocation." A dead man cannot blow a trumpet, no matter how costly the instrument
may be, it takes the breath of a living man to make it
effectual. The spiritually dead may preach the Gospel,
but there is no joyful sound from Heaven to the souls of
men. The trumpet is there, but the living and life-giving
breath of the Holy Spirit is absent. Alas, that so many
should be content with the *form* without the power. Those
who *know* the joyful sound walk in the light of His countenance (Psa. 89. 15).

6. Feast of Atonements, or the final salvation (vs.
26-32). In the Hebrew the word rendered "atonement"
is in the plural. This solemn season was a memorial, not
only of atonement made for the people, but also for the
vessels, &c., of the sanctuary. Coming as it does between
the feast of trumpets and the feast of tabernacles, we are
led to believe that it has reference to our perfect *redemption*
at the resurrection of the *body*, the vessel of the Spirit.
Even we ourselves, which have the firstfruits of the Spirit,
groan within ourselves, waiting for the adoption, to wit,
the redemption of our body. For we are *saved by hope*
(Rom. 8. 22-24). We have not yet entered into this
salvation, but we *hope* for it. The feast of atonements
appointed by God makes it sure.

7. Feast of Tabernacles, or walking with God (vs.
33-43). This feast was "a solemn assembly," com-
memorating the time when they dwelt in booths in the
wilderness, and when God dwelt in the midst of them in
the cloudy pillar. Times when they literally walked with

God   Has all this not a voice for us, *reminding* us that after the resurrection or the *changing* of the body (of those who are alive when the Lord comes) will come our "for ever with the Lord?" They shall walk with Me in white. Shall not that saying, then, come to pass which is written, "Behold, the tabernacle of God is with men, and He will dwell with them?" (Rev. 21. 3). Then the fruit of that handful of corn in the earth shall shake like Lebanon (Psa. 72. 16-19).

It is to us sublimely touching that it was on the *last day* of this feast that Jesus stood, and cried, " If any man thirst, let him come unto Me and drink " This spake He of the Spirit which they that believe on Him should receive (John 7). To think that these seven feasts practically ended with this loving, gracious, heart-rending cry of our soul-pitying Saviour gives awful emphasis to the two great truths they contain.

1. THIRSTY ones should come to Him and drink.

2. BELIEVING ones should receive the Holy Spirit.

Christ is God's great perfect feast for sinners and for saints.   ———

THE YEAR OF JUBILEE.
Leviticus 25

EVERY fiftieth year was to Israel a holy memorial festival It was a periodical season appointed by God for the re-adjustment of the social affairs of His people, and is a trumpet-toned type of the Gospel of Christ and its power to put men right with God and *with one another*   The year of jubilee was the " accepted time" and the " day of salvation" to many in Israel   The market value of things was regulated by it (vs. 15, 16)   Man's dealings with man were to be ordered according to the appointments of God Business and the Gospel seem in our days to be entirely divorced. But for all that this law abides, that the *real value* of the things of this life depend on their relationship to Christ and His Gospel. The sound of the jubilee trumpet was the sound of—

1. Atonement. "In the day of atonement shall ye make the trumpet sound" (v. 9). There can be no *joyful* sound to *sinful* man apart from atoning blood. The trumpet needs a living man to blow it, and he must have God's *authority* before it can be a Divine message to those who hear it. Christ died for our sins, and rose again for our justification, therefore the great trumpet of atonement is being blown, and its sound reacheth unto the ends of the earth.

2. Liberty. "Ye shall proclaim liberty throughout the land unto *all the inhabitants*" (v. 10). On the ground of Christ's atonement God proclaims liberty to every captive. The sounding of the trumpet at the *lips* of God's holy ones was the publishing of this glad news. This deliverance for the bond slave was *immediate* and *complete* on the hearing and *believing* of the tidings. The *sound* was for the ear, the message was for the heart (Luke 4. 18).

3. Forgiveness. "If thy brother be poor, thou shalt relieve him" (v. 35). Even the *debt* and *poverty* of a man did not hinder him from enjoying the *grace* of the jubilee, but made him just the more a fit subject for it. To the poor the Gospel is preached. While we were yet sinners Christ died for us, He came not to call the righteous but sinners to repentance.

4. Rest. "It is a year of rest" (v. 5). It was kept as a Sabbath unto the Lord. The Gospel of Christ proclaims rest to the weary and heavy laden (Matt. 11. 28). Not rest in their works, but rest from them. It was the Sabbath of the Lord, therefore God's rest. It was, and is, an entering into His rest. Rest in the Lord (Psa. 116. 7). We which have *believed* do enter into rest (Heb. 4. 1-3).

5. Plenty. "Ye shall eat your fill, and dwell in safety" (v. 19). What a Gospel! Made safe in the place of plenty.

Lying down in green pastures. The unsearchable riches of Christ is our holy land of promise. Into this fulness by His grace, we who believe have been brought. All are yours, for ye are Christ's, and Christ is God's. Be careful for nothing. Take the water of life freely.

6. Restoration. '' Ye shall return every man into his possession'' (v. 13). All that was lost through failure and sin was restored through the jubilee Gospel. All that was lost in Adam is restored in Christ, and the glorious Gospel of the blessed God declares it. *Made nigh* by the Blood of Christ. Poor Mephibosheth heard such a Gospel and enjoyed such a restoration (2 Sam. 9). He restoreth my soul. Heirs of God and joint-heirs with Jesus Christ.

7. Brotherly love. ''Ye shall not oppress one another, but fear the Lord thy God'' (**v. 17**). By this shall all men know that ye are *My* disciples if ye have love one to another. We must love unworthy ones as we unworthy ones have been loved, and forgive as we have been forgiven. The *forgiven* servant who took his fellow-worker by the throat was evidently courageous enough to deal with him face to face, but he was utterly destitute of the grace and compassion of his master (Matt. 18. 28). Thou shalt love thy neighbour as thyself. Freely ye have received, freely give. Be ye imitators of God as dear children (Eph. 5. 1).

THE PATH OF OBEDIENCE.
Leviticus 26. 1-13.

Two paths are opened up before us in this chapter, the one of obedience and blessing, the other of disobedience and misery. The narrow and the broad way of life and destruction.

In looking at the first of these we shall comment on the—

1. Characteristics of the obedient. As seen in the verses referred to above, they—

1. WILL HAVE NO IDOLS (v. 1). No idol or image will have *standing* ground in their thoughts or minds. They will not bow and worship the gods of the world.

2. REVERENCE THE APPOINTMENTS OF GOD (v. 2). They will not turn the Sabbath into a day of selfish pleasure, or the sanctuary into a theatre or showhouse, or the pulpit into a puppet box.

3. ARE GUIDED BY HIS WORDS (v. 3). They walk in the *statutes* of the Lord, and not in the light of the *sparks* of their own kindling (Isa. 50. 11). To them the Word of God, like the sun, is settled in Heaven (Psa. 119. 89).

4. DELIGHT TO DO HIS WILL (v. 3). The Word of God is to be *kept*, not as the miser keeps his gold, hoarded to be *useless*, but as the warrior keeps his sword. Not he that heareth, but he that *doeth His sayings* is wise (Matt. 7. 24).

2. Blessings that accompany obedience. The path of obedience is the path of—

1. FRUITFULNESS. " *Then* I will give you rain in due season, and fruit" (v. 4). " Then," you see this promise is conditional. Fruitfulness depends on our relationship to God, from whence all fruit is found. Out of the vine comes the fruit-producing sap into the branch. He knows when the *season is due*. " In *due* season ye shall reap" (Isa. 44. 3). The *rain* of His blessed Spirit from Heaven precedes the time of ingathering.

2. PEACE AND REST. "I will give you *peace*, and ye shall *lie down*" (v. 6). The secret of fruitfulness and restfulness lies in being calmly obedient to His holy will. As we follow He will make and give. Instead of worry and weariness there is peace and rest (Psa. 23. 2). We take His yoke, and without any secret yearning after popularity find rest to our souls (Matt. 11. 29).

3. DELIVERANCE FROM EVIL THINGS. "I will rid evil

beasts out of the land" (v. 6). There are many "beast-like" evils from which even the Christian needs deliverance. Strong drink, love of money, lovers of pleasure more than lovers of God, pride, impatience self-assertion. These are evil beasts that are often seen in the land of God's inheritance, but from which He is able to rid us. He only can do the riddance. See the whole menagerie exhibited in Galatians 5. 19-21.

4. POWER TO OVERCOME. "Five of you shall chase an hundred" (vs. 7, 8). In this spiritual warfare it is not a question of numbers or of experience, but of "holiness unto the Lord." It is *weak* but *clean* things God uses (1 Cor. 1. 26-31). The sword of His Word is mighty to the demolishing of every refuge of lies. "*Five* of you." Not many, but entirely *agreed*. If *two* of you shall agree as touching anything that ye shall ask in My Name, it shall be done.

5. DISTINGUISHING FAVOUR. " I will have respect unto you" (v. 9). The obedient ones have the eye of His special grace continually upon them (Rom. 8. 28). The Lord will make a difference, so that they need not beg or borrow the favour of the ungodly princes of this world. He hath said, so that we may boldly say, I will not fear (Heb. 13. 5, 6).

6. ABUNDANT PROVISION. " Ye shall bring forth the old because of the new" (v. 10). Old blessings will not be hoarded because of the number and greatness of the new. The old corn of our spiritual experiences will be liberally used because of the plentifulness of the new. This indicates a very healthy state of soul, it is the path of the just that shineth more and more. The old corn of salvation should be brought out because of the new baptism of the Holy Ghost. Let us also bring out the *old* corn of theology because of the *new*, which is broadness *versus* shallowness.

7. DIVINE FELLOWSHIP. " I will walk among you" (v. 12). His presence with us is the pledge of prosperity.

progress, protection, purity, and power. That soul or life possessed by God's Holy Spirit will never fail to find delight in an obedient walk. The testimony of that life will never be silenced by terror or smitten with consumption (v. 16). Greater is the Spirit of Christ in us than the spirit of antichrist which is in the world (1 John 4. 4).

THE PATH OF DISOBEDIENCE.
Leviticus 26. 14-45.

As we have already seen, the blessings which follow obedience are clearly indicated in the first part of this chapter. In this division the events that follow dis- obedience are as emphatically pronounced. In the first we see the narrow way that leads to life; here we have the broad way that leads to destruction. Let us look then at the—

1. **Evils that follow disobedience.** " If ye will not hearken unto Me, and will not do these commandments," then there will be—

1. GREAT FEARFULNESS. " I will appoint over you terror" (v. 16). When a Church has begun to backslide it will soon be in terror about the collections, innovations, and everything but worldliness and sin. A soul out of fellowship with God is in terror of special evangelistic meetings. Disobedience brings cowardliness in the ser- vice of God. The fear of man brings a snare.

2. SURE DECLINE. " I will appoint over you consump- tion" (v. 16). Organs, images, paid choirs, painted windows, or popular entertainments will not check this disease. The wound is greater than the plaster, and deeper than any unbelieving quack can reach. Disobedience as a malady is rottenness in the bones. The *appearance* of health and soundness may be kept up for a time, just as you may paint the face of a consumptive, while there is nothing but weakness and disorder within.

3. UNHEALTHY ACTIVITY. This is described in verse 16 as " the burning ague," and suggests the idea of periodical spasms of *feverish* effort. These spasms may sometimes take the form of " worldly concerts, Sunday evenings for the people, short sermons, popular topics," &c. Such activity in the Name of Christ resembles the *breathless* excitement of the dry bones in the valley of vision. Like the convulsive movements of a skeleton under the power of a galvanic battery.

4. FRUITLESS WORK. " Ye shall sow your seed in vain" (v. 16). " Your strength shall be spent in vain" (v. 20). There may be much earnestness, but as long as there is *heart* rebellion it is only like beating the air (1 Sam. 15. 22). You may sow your seed as a preacher, but it will be in vain as long as your life is unconsecrated to the Lord. You are only spending your strength in vain when you are striving by your culture and eloquence to bring forth fruit unto God in the conversion of sinners, or the upbuilding of the Lord's people. Fruitbearing depends on what we *are* more than on what we *do*.

5. SLAVISH COWARDLINESS. " They that hate you shall rule over you, and ye shall flee when none pursueth you" (v. 17). To disobey God is to come under the tyranny of the world, the flesh, and the devil. Then comes the fleeing before a phantom foe, because there is an evil heart of unbelief within, a conscience not void of offence.

6. UNANSWERED PRAYER. " I will make your Heaven as iron" (v. 19). An *iron* Heaven is an *unyielding* one. Unanswered prayer is unheard prayer. Our prayers prevail just as *we* and *they* are right with God (James 5. 16). Prayers framed for the ear of men instead of the ear of the Lord of Sabaoth will never pierce an iron Heaven. If the heavens are as brass to us it is an evidence that we ourselves are not right with God.

7. SORROWFUL LOSS. " I will send wild beasts among

you, which will rob you of your children'' (v. 22). The wild beasts of infidelity, scepticism, contempt, and indifference has already robbed the disobedient Church of many of her children. A sham religion will neither save nor keep the rising generation. The cause of this lapse is not primarily the want of *interest* without, but the want of *reality* within.

8. INTERNAL DIVISIONS. " They shall fall one upon another" (v. 37). " Devouring one another" is about the last stage of this spiritual consumption. Empty seats, backsliding members, fault finding elders, and ironical preachers are but the natural consequences of a backsliding and disobedient Church.

2. Remedy for all this misery. It will be found in—

1. CONFESSION (v. 40). Not blaming one another, but every man smiting *his own* breast (Psa. 32. 5).

2. HUMILIATION (v. 41). If there is a true consciousness of sin, there will be a real *rending* of the heart.

3. FAITH (vs. 42-45). Unwavering trust in His sure word of promise. When sin is confessed, the place of humility taken, the attitude of faith maintained, then the mighty power of Divine grace will be displayed, the blighting curses of the disobedient life will be rolled away, and the happy fruits of obedience will speedily appear.

THE LEVITES AS A PECULIAR PEOPLE.
Numbers 1. 47-54.

THE Levites were a peculiar people among the thousands of Israel. Their peculiarities, like the Christians, lay in their relationship to God Himself. To be closely associated with Him will always make us peculiar in the eyes of others. Think of their—

1. Separation. They were—

1. NOT NUMBERED with the others (v. 47). God always makes a difference between the ordinary believer and those *wholly devoted* to Himself.

2. CHOSEN BY GOD (chap. 3. 12). He took *them* instead of the firstborn in Israel, so that each had a representative character. Every *firstborn* not represented by a Levite had to be redeemed (chap. 3. 46-48). Ye see your calling, brethren, ye who belong to the inner circle of His chosen ones. In *Christ's stead*, who is the Firstborn of every creature.

3. GIVEN TO AARON (chap. 3. 9). So are we, as His elect, given to Christ. Jesus revealed this thought when He said, "I have manifested Thy Name unto the men which *Thou gavest Me* out of the world." All that the Father hath given Me shall come unto Me.

4. CLAIMED BY GOD. "The Levites shall be Mine" (chap. 3. 12). Peter, James, and John were the peculiar three among the Twelve, they seemed to drink most deeply of the Spirit of Jesus their Master, and so were owned by Him not so much as historians as *teachers*. Covet earnestly the best gifts.

2. Occupation. The work of the Levites was manifold. In these verses something of this variety is apparent. We see them as—

1. OVERSEERS. "Thou shalt appoint the Levites over the tabernacle, over the vessels, and over all things" (v. 50). The chosen servants of God ought to take a general interest in *everything* connected with the work and worship of God. We must have a sympathetic concern for all that has to do with the service and honour of God.

2. BEARERS. "They shall bear the tabernacle" (v. 50). The carrying of the things of the tabernacle was to them the "burden of the Lord." Not every professed follower of Christ is a burden-bearer. Paul

understood this experimentally when he said, '' I could wish myself accursed for my brethren's sake.''

3. MINISTERS. '' They shall minister unto Me'' (v. 50). They were not the servants of the tabernacle, but of God. It is quite possible to be the willing servants of a Church, and yet not be ministering unto the Lord.

4. DEMOLISHERS. '' The Levites shall take it down'' (v. 51). When the pillar moved it was theirs to take the tabernacle to pieces. Those whose office it is to handle Divine things should know how to open up and rightly *divide* the Word of Truth. Dissection does not mean destruction in this case.

5. BUILDERS. '' The Levites shall set it up'' (v. 51). They had at times to take the house board from board, but they could and did put it up again. They were no type of those destructive critics who can only pull down, but cannot build up. Those who cannot set the things of God's house in order had better let them alone.

6. MEDIATORS. '' The Levites shall pitch *round about* the tabernacle that there be *no wrath* upon the congregation'' (v. 53). According to their *position* they were a channel of blessing or of curse to the people. Such are they who occupy the position of public teachers of the Word and will of God. Taking our true place before God and the people we may save many from the wrath to come. Ye are the salt of the earth. Ours should be the position of *devoted ones*.

7. KEEPERS. '' The Levites shall keep the charge of the tabernacle'' (v. 53). They were custodians of the Lord's treasure. At their hands He required every vessel and curtain, every board, pillar, and pin. Are we as His servants faithfully keeping all that the Lord has committed unto us. Hath He not committed unto us the word of reconciliation? (2 Cor. 5. 19). Paul, almost

with his dying breath, said, "O Timothy, keep what is committed to thee." "I have kept the faith" (2 Tim. 4. 6-8). ———

THE STANDARDS OF ISRAEL.
Numbers 2.

THE hosts of Israel were divided by Jehovah into four camps, and every camp had its own standard. The *order* in which they were to march when the pillar of cloud moved was also distinctly specified by the Lord. This arrangement has doubtless a deeply moral significance. The order was neither by birth nor according to numbers. Judah, who went first, was the *fourth* son of Jacob, and the camp that was to go last was the second largest of all. Just as all the vessels and sacrifices were full of spiritual meaning, so the *various positions* in the grand march of obedience to the call of God has likewise its spiritual lessons for us who are pilgrims and sojourners with Him. Perhaps the meaning of the names of the different camps and their moral connection with one another will afford us a clue into a truth, which to us may be profitable. The—

1. Standard of Judah. Judah went *first* (vs. 3-9). *Judah* means "Praise the Lord." It is surely meet that the praising camp should lead the way. Praise is perhaps the *first* sign of a soul truly right with God. It is only when we have apprehended our own needy and guilty state, and by faith laid hold on the mercy and all-sufficiency of Christ that we can praise the Lord with a sincere heart. Can we ever make progress in the Divine life if we have not first of all taken our stand beneath the banner of praise? Judah was made head of his brethren, and from him kings were to descend (Gen. 49. 8-10). Praising Christians will always be princes among the people. The sceptre of power shall not depart from them. Praise ye the Lord.

2. Standard of Reuben. This camp came immediately after Judah. *Reuben* means, "Behold a son."

Behold one in the full enjoyment of sonship.   Reuben as a son sought to save the life of Joseph (Gen. 37. 21), and offered his two sons as security for Benjamin.   After praise comes the testimony of true sonship, '' Behold a son.' Who will believe that we are the sons of God if our lives are not bright with His praise? If the spirit of praise and adoration fills your heart, then may you expect others to take knowledge, saying, '' Behold a son.''   Moreover, the great and blessed privileges of sonship can only be entered into and enjoyed by a *thankful*, trusting heart. Begin to praise and your testimony as a son will be felt and acknowledged by others. It becometh the sons of God to shout for joy.

3. Standard of Ephraim (vs. 18-24).   *Ephraim* means '' double fruitfulness.''   Abundant fruit is sure to *come after* praise and the perfect life of sonship. We praise not the Lord because we are not fruitful, instead of praising Him that we may be made fruitful.   Under Jehoshaphat the people of Judah '' began to sing and to praise,'' *then* the Lord set ambushments and gave them the victory (2 Chron. 20. 22). In our unbelief we will not bless the Lord until we *see*, although the Lord has said, '' Believe, and thou shalt see.'' But the way into '' *double fruitfulness*'' lies through the full appreciation of our privileges as the sons of God. The branch must receive from the vine a *branch's* portion.   Fruitfulness always implies fulness.

4. Standard of Dan (vs. 25-31). The meaning of *Dan* is *judging*. A judge is one seated in authority. The camp of Dan '' shall go hindmost'' (v. 31). The privilege of judging comes last of all. Is it not written that '' the *saints* shall judge the world?'' Are they not to '' reign with Christ a thousand years?'' Are we not to be made *kings* as well as priests unto God? And is it not said that '' we shall *reign* on the earth? Yes, after Ephraim comes Dan, after fruitfulness comes exaltation and reward (Luke 19. 17).

1. AS SINNERS. Praise Him for the great things He hath done for us.

2. AS SONS. Receive the great things He is offering to us.

3. AS SERVANTS. Be fruitful in the work He has given us.

4. AS JUDGES. Expect the honour promised us.

These four standards are also suggestive of—

1. Christ's birth, with its angelic songs.

2. Christ's life, '' Behold the Man.''

3. Christ's death and resurrection. Double fruitfulness.

4. Christ's coming again. Judging His people.

THREE CLASSES OF WORKERS.
Numbers 4.

IN the transporting of the tabernacle and all its belongings from place to place there was great division of labour. As we would think, the work of the Gershonites, looking after the curtains, &c., could have easily been done by a score of men, but for this task alone 2630 were set apart. This teaches us that no work done for God is small or trifling. The packing up of the holy vessels was done by Aaron and his sons (vs. 5-15). Consecrated hands must set in order holy things. The bearers of the tabernacle and its furniture were three families of the Levites, the sons of Kohath, of Gershon, and of Merari. Their work was—

1. Varied.

1. The sons of *Merari* had charge of the FOUNDATION THINGS. ''Sockets, pillars, boards, bars, and pins'' (vs. 31, 32). In setting up the tabernacle the sockets and pillars would be needed first. Foundation truths should always go first. This is the work of the *evangelist*. '' Other foundation can no man lay than that is laid, Jesus Christ.'' The silver sockets speak of redemption, because they were made of the *ransom* price given for the souls of the people (Exod. 30. 15). Yes, the redeeming Blood *first*.

2. The sons of *Gershon* had charge of the UNITING THINGS. "Coverings, curtains, and hangings" (vs. 24-27). The sockets and pillars may be strong, but they are naked and bare without the coverings and curtains, in fact, it was no *tabernacle* without the coverings. These may represent the work of the *pastor*, binding all together and beautifying with the coverings and hangings of order and doctrine. The coverings, &c., brought every pillar and board into *union* with one another. This is the work of the pastor making *manifest* the truth. "All one in Christ Jesus."

3. The sons of *Kohath* had charge of the APPROACH THINGS. "All the *vessels* of the sanctuary" (v. 15). The vessels placed in position indicate the *way to God*. No *service* could be done in the tabernacle without them. All was *powerless* till the work of the Kohathites was finished. This is the office of the *teacher*. These three gifts belong to the Church just as really as they belonged to the tabernacle. "He gave some evangelists, some pastors, and teachers for the perfecting of the saints, for the work of the ministry, for the edifying of the body of Christ" (Eph. 4. 11, 12). The office of a teacher is not only to expound the truth, but to do it in such a way as to *lead into the very presence of God*, and to maintain a holy life. Imparting the knowledge that puffeth up is not fulfilling the work of a teacher. The true spiritual teacher not only points the way, but by the power of the Holy Ghost, through the truth and a holy example, leads into it.

2. **Appointed them by the Lord** (vs. 1-4). No man taketh this work upon him, but he that is *called of God*, as was Aaron. Could you imagine others making other sockets, coverings, and vessels, and setting up *another* tabernacle. The whole thing could only be a sham and a mockery. Why? Because they would not be God's sockets, coverings, and vessels, and servants. What better are the evangelists, pastors, and teachers who run without

being sent, and who lay *other* foundations, and *add to them-selves* teachers having itching ears, who will not endure sound doctrine? From such turn away. It is to *His own* servants the Lord delivers *His goods* (Matt. 25. 14). Those *occupying* till He come, trade with *His pound* (Luke 19).

3. United. The Gershonites had no jealousy at all, although the sons of Merari commenced work before them, and took possession of the spot before they came. They all wrought under one guiding will, and for the honour and glory of one Lord. Their *burdens* were different, but their *aim* was one. "There are diversities of gifts, but the same Spirit, it is the same God which worketh in all" (1 Cor. 12. 4-6). They sought the good of the Lord's house always. By each one using the gift entrusted to them as stewards we show the *manifold* grace of God (1 Peter. 4. 10).

4. Rewarded. The Lord became to them their portion and inheritance (Deut. 18. 1, 2). "I am their possession" saith the Lord (Ezek. 44. 28). Those who consecrate themselves to the work of the Lord will find their all in Him. "They that wait at the altar are partakers *with the altar*" (1 Cor. 9. 13). They that wait on the Lord are partakers with the Lord of His grace, mercy, and strength. "Well done, good and faithful servant, enter thou into the *joy of thy Lord*." Partakers of His life, of His work, then of His joy.

NAZARITESHIP.
A CONSECRATED LIFE.
Numbers 6. 1-12.

NAZARETH means separated or sanctified. Can any good thing come out of Nazareth? Is there any profit in *con-secrating* one's life to the service of the Lord? There are still many sceptics, even among the Lord's people, as to any good thing coming out of the Nazareth of a *separated* life.

They seem to think that the better way is to sanctify the pleasures of the world instead of themselves. "O fools, and slow of heart to believe." There is much that we might learn from the vow of the Nazarite. It—

1. Was voluntary. "When either a man or woman shall *separate themselves*" (v. 2). The Lord does not *compel* us to consecrate ourselves to His service. Having saved us by His Blood, He leaves us to *choose* whom we will serve. But through the apostle the Holy Ghost *beseeches* us by the *mercies of God* to present our bodies a living sacrifice unto God (Rom. 12. 1).

2. Was entire. There can be no acceptable consecration to God that is not complete. It was a separation: 1. *From all the fruit of the vine*, "from the kernels to the husk" (v. 4). "Strong drink" is twice mentioned as if there were a double danger of his consecration being ruined through it. This warning is urgently needed to-day. 2. *From the fashion of men.* "No razor shall come upon his head" (v. 5). It is a *shame* for a man to have long hair (1 Cor. 11. 14), but he must just bear the shame. The separated man has nothing to be ashamed of. He will be peculiar, but he walks not as men. 3. *From the presence of the dead* (v. 6). The *dead* belong to another world, he must not pollute himself with any deadening thing. "They are not of the world, even as I am not of the world."

3. Was unto the Lord. "All the days of his separation he is holy unto the Lord" (v. 8). It was not to make himself odd, or to be talked about among his fellowmen. He willingly gave himself that he might be wholly for the Lord. Through it was he not seeking a deeper acquaintanceship with God? Was he not acting on the principle taught in 2 Corinthians 6. 17, 18, "Touch not the unclean, and I will receive you and be a Father unto you?" Paul was a Nazarite unto the Gospel of God (Rom. 1. 1).

4. Implies an open profession. " No razor shall come upon his head." His hair was a public testimony as to his character. The Nazarite could not be hidden. The consecrated life is a light which cannot be put under a bushel. LOVE is an open mark by which we are known as His disciples. No Christian is ashamed of his consecration any more than a sheep is ashamed of its owner's marks. The scissors of Delilah made havoc of Samson's Nazariteship.

5. Involves great self-denial (v. 7). The fruit of the vine may be very sweet, but he must not touch it. Even if his father, or his mother, or his brother, or sister die, he cannot go near to see them or to bury them. His *natural* inclinations must give place to the Word of God. These things were lawful for others, but not expedient for him. The separated life means, " Not *my* will, but *Thine* be done." "If any man will follow Me, let him *deny himself* and take up his cross." It is a sacrifice, but it is well-pleasing unto God.

6. Meant a life of holiness. " All the days of his separation he is holy" (v. 8). While he lived a separated life he had this testimony, that he pleased God. Holiness then is a condition more than an attainment. Those who have separated themselves from forbidden things, and have yielded themselves into His hands to do His will are holy. When the separating vow is broken we cease to be in a state of holiness unto the Lord. Our consecration is defiled, and our Nazarite testimony is gone. " Be ye holy, for I am holy."

7. Was easily marred. " If a man die suddenly by him, he hath defiled his consecration" (vs. 9-12). Coming into contact with the dead, even by accident, was enough to pollute his holiness in the sight of God. Do we realise how easily the crown of consecration honour may fall from

our heads? How easily the Holy Spirit may be grieved,
and the power of our testimony perish? It is in vain we
go about with our unshorn locks in the sight of men, if in
His holy eyes we have defiled ourselves. Ichabod may be
written over our lives. Take heed unto thyself (1 Tim.
4. 16).　　　　　———

THE PRIESTLY BLESSING.
Numbers 6. 22-27.

JUST as the blue of Heaven is bigger than the clouds of
earth, so the riches of His blessing is greater than our
need. But a very small cloud may hide the blue. The
clouds rise from earth, and are changing and fleeting, the
blue is eternal. His blessing, it maketh rich.

1. The giving of the blessing. God has always plenty
to give. It was given—

1. THROUGH A MEDIATOR. " God spake unto Moses,
saying" (v. 22). Moses was to the people what Christ is
to us, the medium of Divine blessing. There is none other
Name under Heaven.

2. AFTER ATONEMENT HAD BEEN MADE (see Lev. **9).**
He cannot bless us until we have been reconciled through
the death of His Son. We must be *born* of God before we
can receive the children's portion. First the Blood, then
the blessing.

3. RICHLY. The name Jehovah is repeated *three* times,
indicating that it was the blessing of the *Triune* God. This
threefold blessing appears in the apostolic benediction—

1. The grace of the *Lord Jesus Christ.*
2. The love of *God.*
3. The communion of the *Holy Ghost.*

God the Father the source of it, God the Son the channel
of it, God the Spirit the imparter of it. Bless the Lord, O
my soul!

2. The nature of the blessing. It is infinitely deep and full. It implies—

1. INTIMACY. " The Lord bless *thee*." It was very personal, and suggests the knowledge of individual need. He commands his blessing, even life for evermore (Psa. 133. 3). He knoweth thy need.

2. KEEPING. " Keep thee." What a blessing to be kept from sin, from the fear of man and the dominion of the devil. Kept in nearness to Himself and in the power of His Spirit. The Lord is thy Keeper (Psa. 121. 3-5). Remember the Redeemer's prayer (John 17. 11).

3. LIGHT. " The Lord make His face to. *shine upon thee*." The light of His face is a glorious light, we see it in the face of Jesus. David prayed, " Make Thy face to shine upon Thy servant" (Psa. 31. 16). In His light we see light clearly (2 Cor. 4. 4).

4. FAVOUR. " Be *gracious* unto thee." If we have the grace of God, we have within our reach the wealth of God. Having given us His Son, how will He not also with Him freely give us all things? Who has ever used to the full the favour offered in Christ Jesus?

5. FELLOWSHIP. " The Lord lift up His countenance upon thee." His own countenance upon thee means the conscious enjoyment of His own personal presence. Blessed are all they, O Lord, that walk in the light of Thy countenance. O to have the face of God ever beaming upon us; how it would blind our eyes to the attractions and alluring things of earth.

6. PEACE. " And give thee peace." Not only peace *with* God, this we have through atoning Blood, but the peace *of* God. God's own peace ruling and garrisoning our hearts, the peace of God which passeth all understanding (Phil. 4. 6, 7). "MY peace I give unto you, let not your heart be troubled."

7. LIKENESS. "Put My Name upon the children" (v. 27). To put His Name upon us means to put His *nature* within us. The Name of *Christ*, the anointed One, is put upon us when we receive the anointing of the Holy Spirit. The filling of the Spirit is the door into the fulness of the blessing. "I will put My Name upon them, and I will bless them." Blessed with all spiritual blessings in Christ Jesus (Eph. 1. 3-5; Luke 24. 50).

1. Jehovah the Father bless thee and keep thee.

2. Jehovah the Son make His face shine upon thee, and be gracious unto thee.

3. Jehovah the Spirit lift up His countenance upon thee, and give thee peace.   ———

THE CALL OF THE LEVITES.
Numbers 8. 1-14.

"Choose Thou for me, and make Thy choosing mine,
Whate'er Thy love may unto me assign;
What work for Thee to do, where shall I go?
O my Lord, order Thou, I do not know;
I fear to choose self-pleasing scenes and things—
Choose for me, Lord, and give the peace it brings."

THE Levites were the descendants of Levi, and were chosen by the Lord, instead of the firstborn, to do the service of the sanctuary. Let us look at what they were—

1. By nature. When the dying Jacob called his sons together to leave his last message with them he characterised Simeon and Levi as "cruel and *self-willed*" (Gen. 49. 5-7). The best of saints God can make out of such rough and unpromising material. Such were some of us. "Walking according to the course of the world" (Eph. 2. 2). While we were yet sinners Christ died for us. He came not to call the righteous.

2. By grace. The same grace of God which brought salvation to us appeared unto them. By grace they were saved through faith. They were—

1. **CALLED.** "Take the Levites *from among* the children of Israel" (v. 6). They were *outcalled* from among the others as every Christian is. The calling out of the Church of God may be here prefigured. "The men which Thou hast given Me *out of* the world." The elect according to grace.

2. **CLEANSED.** "And cleanse them" (v. 6). "Such were some of you, but ye are *washed*" (1 Cor. 6. 11). Washing implies uncleanness. It is the first necessity to fellowship and service. This washing was done for them (Heb. 9. 13, 14).

3. **SANCTIFIED.** "Let them shave all their flesh, and let them wash their clothes, and *make themselves* clean" (v. 7). After we have been cleansed by the Blood of Christ, and justified freely by His grace, we are called upon to cleanse *ourselves* from all filthiness of the flesh. Shave off every unbecoming habit, and wash the spots of the world out of the clothes of our daily life, and walk worthy of the Lord, in all well-pleasing.

4. **ATONED FOR.** "Make an atonement for the Levites" (v. 12). Here they were taught that it was through *substitution* that the grace of God and the privileges of the believer comes. A sin-offering must be made, and could only be made through the sacrifice of *life*. Christ gave Himself for us, His *soul* was made an offering for sin (Isa. 53. 10).

5. **CONSECRATED.** "Set the Levites and *offer them* an offering unto the Lord" (v. 13). After an offering had been presented to God *for* them, they *themselves* had to be presented to Him. Having been redeemed by His Blood, we are called upon to yield ourselves unto God (Rom. 12. 1, 2). Ye are *not your own* for ye are bought with a price.

6. **OWNED BY THE LORD.** "The Levites shall be Mine." They were His by choice. by grace and by

blood; by love, favour, and life.   A threefold cord not
easily broken.   Who shall lay anything to the charge
of God's elect?   It is God that justifieth.   Who is he
that condemneth?   Chosen by the grace of the Father,
redeemed by the Blood of the Son, claimed by the
power of the Spirit.   They shall be Mine.   They shall
be My sons to love Me, My *servants* to serve Me, My
saints to worship Me.   _____

THIRTY DAYS OF GRACE.
Numbers 9. 6-14.

In this chapter we see grace upon grace.   The Passover
was to be kept on the fourteenth day of the *first* month, but
the question here is raised: If a man was not in a condition
to observe that feast on the day appointed, was he to be
debarred for a whole year?   Some men found in this
position were heard saying, "Wherefore are we kept
back?" (v. 7).   This was a new difficulty, and Moses
deals with it as we should deal with all such when they
suddenly spring up before us.   He took it to the Lord.
If any man lack wisdom, let him ask of God who giveth
to all liberally.   The answer was plainly given.   A
special Passover feast was to be held on the fourteenth
day of the *second* month.   It was a special provision to
meet a special case.   Such is the riches of His grace,
grace sufficient for *every* need.

Here the way of salvation is clearly taught.

1. **Unfitness**.   "Certain men were defiled that they
could not keep the Passover on that day" (v. 6).   The
cause of their unfitness to profit by the provision made by
God on the fourteenth day of the first month was their
uncleanness.   They were not in a state to receive it.   Such
was man's condition at the giving of the law—God's *first*
provision.   Being already sinners, the law could not save
them, but only help to show their sinfulness.   By the

law is the knowledge of sin. Unbelief unfits a man from receiving the benefits of Christ's redeeming death. The defilement was of their own making.

2. Confession. "Those men said, We are defiled" (v. 7). They confessed their unfitness, and sought not to justify themselves. They presented themselves as ones disqualified because of their defilement, and begged for the mercy and grace that might reach their need and satisfy their souls. The grace of God, like a river, flows *down* into every *open* crevice, or like the light of the sun, it never refuses to enter, no matter how dark or dirty the corner may be, if only there is an *opening* toward it. If *any man* open the door, I will come in to him. Confession is the opening of the door. "If we confess our sins, He is faithful and just to forgive us" (1 John 1. 9).

3. Provision. "Ye shall keep the Passover on the fourteenth day of the *second* month" (vs. 9-11). Between the first and second Passover there were thirty days. These were days of grace. After that there was no possibility of receiving a Passover blessing for that year. This little Passover, instituted for the benefit of those who were disabled, is a beautiful little picture of the grace of God devising a plan of salvation for helpless sinful man. To help these men *Moses* was utterly helpless. He could only say, "Stand still, and I will hear what the Lord will command concerning you" (v. 8). Salvation is of the Lord. The *law* was given by Moses, but *grace* and truth came by Jesus Christ. It is suggestive that this provision of special grace was for the *defiled*, or the man that was "afar off" on a journey, and so could not keep the great feast of Passover. The Gospel of His grace offers cleansing to the defiled, and to bring *nigh* to God those who were afar off (Eph. 2. 12, 13).

4. Warning. "But the man that forbeareth to keep the Passover shall be cut off from among the people" (v. 13).

The Passover speaks of redemption: "Christ our Passover was sacrificed for us." To those who wilfully neglect this there is nothing for them but a fearful looking for of judgment. It is counting the blood of the covenant an unholy thing, and doing despite unto the Spirit of grace (Heb. 10: 26-31). To despise or *neglect* grace is to choose death. How shall ye escape if ye neglect so great salvation?

5. Invitation. "If a *stranger* will keep the Passover, so shall he do" (v. 14). Any stranger sojourning with them may become a participant of the blessing of this memorable feast. As it denotes, redemption by the Blood of the Lamb is offered to all who will come into the camp. How fitting all this is, as typical of the great salvation, through the Blood of the Lamb of God. "Let him that is athirst come, and whosoever will, let him take" (Rev. 22. 17). After you have come and taken *your part* of this God-offered grace, you will be no more *strangers*, but fellow-citizens with the saints and of the household of God (Eph. 2. 17-19).

THE HOLY CLOUD.
Numbers 9. 15-23.

" He leads round, but He leads right,
All the way is in His sight;
Be it rough, or be it long,
Void of joy, or set to song,
Bringing much, or mite by mite,
He leads round, but He leads right.

He leads round, but He leads right,
Cloud by day and fire by night;
Morn by morn, let God arise,
Scattering all our enemies;
And will sing with evening light,
He leads round, but He leads right."

IT did look like infinite madness that the children of Israel should be led " about by the way of the wilderness by the

Red Sea." It was indeed a roundabout way, but it was the right way, for God in the pillar of cloud led them. This holy, because divinely possessed, cloud was both a standing and a moving miracle, and a witness to the stability and mobility of God's dealings with His people. No storm could shake it, yet it moved as a guiding lamp for the feet of the pilgrims. Let us think for a little of its—

1. Origin. Of how this cloud was formed we have no account. Like the *body* of Jesus, it had a common appearance, yet there was a great mystery about it. God was in it. It was to the Israelites the *visible* body of the invisible God. Great is the mystery of godliness, God manifest *in the flesh*. The flesh of Jesus Christ was the visible body in which the invisible Father spoke and wrought. "The Father that dwelleth *in Me*, He doeth the works" (John 17. 9, 10). Know ye not that your body is the temple of God, and that God dwelleth in you?

2. Coming. "On *the day* that the tabernacle was reared up the cloud covered it" (v. 15). When all had been set in order, and everything yielded up for the service of God, *then* the cloud rested on it and took possession of it. It is so still with regard to our individual lives. When all is surrendered to Him for His glory He will find a dwelling place in us, and use us for His own Name's sake.

3. Character. "The cloud covered the tabernacle" (v. 15). This *covering* signified *protection* as well as possession. His presence is a covering presence. The same thought is here that we have in the *atonement*—covering. Covered by the wings of the Almighty. The Lord thy keeper, the Lord thy shade, hidden in His pavilion.

4. Significance. "The cloud covered the tent of the *testimony*" (v. 15). The tent, or tabernacle, was a testimony for God *after* it was *covered* with the cloud of His presence. We have only the *form* without the power till we are covered with the Holy Anointing One. It is *His presence* that makes the tent of our life a *testimony* for Him. Cloudless tents are very common, but very useless as witnesses for God.

5. Appearance. " The cloud covered it by day, and the appearance of fire by night" (v. 16). It had the appearance of fire *until* the morning (v. 15). During the absence of the sun the symbol of the Divine Presence took the likeness of fire. Is it not so now? During the absence of the Son of God the Holy Ghost takes the appearance of tongues of fire. This holy fire during the night of this world's unbelief is indispensable until the morning of His appearing. Ye shall be baptised with the Holy Ghost and with fire (Acts 1. 5).

6. Authority. The moving of the cloud is called "The command of the Lord" (vs. 17-20). A most impressive symbol of the Holy Spirit.

1. WHERE IT ABODE THEY ABODE (v. 17). Their communion with God depended on their keeping in touch with the pillar of cloud. Walk in the Spirit, and abide in Him, then your fellowship will be unbroken.

2. WHEN IT MOVED THEY MOVED (v. 21). As they followed the moving pillar, so we must be ready to follow the guiding Spirit. To be *led* by the Spirit of God is an evidence of sonship (Rom. 8. 14).

3. AS LONG AS IT TARRIED THEY TARRIED (v. 22). It was not theirs to decide how long they should stay in a place. To move without the cloud was just to move into a godless condition. To go into a new sphere without the Spirit of God leading is to get into a state of spiritual powerlessness and disobedience. Christian worker, remember that the moving of the Holy Spirit is the *commandment* of the Lord. Grieve Him not by impatience or fearfulness.

THE SILVER TRUMPETS.

THE GOSPEL OF GOD.

Numbers 10. 1-10.

" Broken in heart ! broken in heart !
He bindeth up our wounds;
My God, how tender is Thine art,
Thy word how sweet it sounds !
A broken heart, O trifle small
Beside the radiant skies !
Yet Thou, God, for my heart dost call,
When I myself despise ''

THE blowing of the trumpets was, as it were, the voice of God to the people of Israel. He that hath ears to hear let him hear.

1. The trumpets, or the Gospel. Blessed are they that know the joyful sound. Note their—

1. NUMBER. " Make thee *two* trumpets of silver." These two trumpets remind us of the Old and New Testaments, through which God has been pleased to speak to His people, and by which His call is still heard.

2. NATURE. " Trumpets of *silver*." They were precious and sweet toned. The best of other books are but copper and tin compared with the Bible.

3. UNITY. "Of a *whole piece* shalt thou make them" (v. 2). This is a most assuring characteristic of the Bible. Although both the Old and New Testaments are written by different authors at different times and circumstances, they are each of a whole piece. The One Spirit breathes through all.

2. The trumpeters, or preachers of the Gospel. "The sons of Aaron shall blow the trumpets" (v. 8). In the eighth chapter we see them—

1. CALLED (chap. 8. 6). The first preachers of the Gospel were all called and chosen by the Master. No man can take this honour to himself (Rom. 10. 15).

2. PURIFIED (chap. 8. 7). They must be clean that bear the vessels of the Lord.

3. CONSECRATED (chap. 8. 10). His choosing us should be followed with our complete self-abnegation for His sake. " I have chosen you and ordained you."

4. COMMISSIONED (chap. 8. 15). " Go ye into all the world and preach the Gospel to every creature." This is the trumpeter's great commission.

3. The trumpeting, or preaching of the Gospel. No matter how good the trumpet may be, it takes the breath of a living man to sound it. The preaching of the Gospel in the power of the Holy Ghost is the voice and call of God to the hearer. There may be a great noise where there is no voice or message from Heaven. The blowing of these silver trumpets had various degrees of significance. Through them we hear the following calls—

1. ATONEMENT. " Ye shall blow with the trumpets over the sacrifices" (v. 10). How important this is. The preaching that is not connected with the atoning sacrifice of Jesus Christ is not the preaching that He bids. It is vain blowing apart from the reconciling Blood of the Lamb.

2. INVITATION. " When ye shall blow with them, all the assembly shall assemble themselves at the door" (v. 3). Thus the trumpet call invited to the "*door* of the tabernacle." So the Gospel invitation is to all, and that they all might come to Him who is the Door of the sheep and the Way to the Father. "Come unto Me, and I will give you rest" (Matt. 11. 28). "Unto you, O men, I call."

3. PROGRESS. " When ye blow an alarm then the camps shall *go forward*" (v. 5). The call of the Gospel is not only to salvation, but to advancement in the knowledge of God and growth in grace. "I press on toward the mark," says the apostle of the Gentiles. This note of the Gospel trumpet is greatly needed to-day. Let

us go forward in a fresh consecration of ourselves, and in a new faith in God. Launch out into the deep.

4. CONFLICT. " If you go to war ye shall blow an alarm, and ye shall be saved from your enemies'' (v. 9). With the progress of indifference and scepticism should come this sounding of the alarm, that we may ''be remembered before the Lord,'' and fight the good fight of FAITH. Put on the whole armour of God, that ye may be able to stand. To us the *armour of God* means being *invested* by Christ. '' Abide in Me.''

5. GLADNESS. " Also in the day of your gladness ye shall blow with the trumpets'' (v. 10). It is a blessed work to preach the Gospel with a glad heart. The joy of the Lord is your strength. The weakness of many Gospel trumpeters is that they have no real *gladness* in the service of God. Their gladness comes when their work for Christ is over for the day. . The testimony of such can only be as sounding brass and tinkling cymbals. The power of love is lacking. Restore unto us the joy of Thy salvation.

> '' The trumpet of Christ ne'er sounds a retreat,
> All bloodless His battles, yet by blood made meet:
> Or be it danger, or be it defeat,
> The trumpet of Christ ne'er sounds a retreat.''

A PILGRIM'S INVITATION.
Numbers 10. 29-32.

> '' The past now lies behind us,
> On it be pardon seal'd;
> The present is around us,
> The future unrevealed.
>
> Or long, or short our lives be,
> We place us in Thy hand;
> O Jesus, guide and guard us
> Unto Thy blessed Land.''

MOSES said to Hobab, his father-in-law, who had come from Median to visit him in the wilderness, '' We are journeying unto the place of which the Lord said, ' I will

give it you.' Come thou with us, and we will do thee good.''
Those who by faith see that city whose Builder and Maker
is God desire others to come and share the blessedness.

The Christian life, as a pilgrimage, may be aptly
illustrated from this incident as we see them—

1. Pilgrims. '' We are journeying.'' 1. *Where from?*
From the house of bondage, from the slavery of sin and
the dominion of the devil, from a life of misery and
fruitlessness. 2. *Where through?* Through the wilderness
of this world, still lying in the lap of the wicked one.
The experience of each individual pilgrim may be vastly
different, but all *going on.*

2. Pilgrims journeying to a land of promise. The
Christian's land of promise is Christ Himself. All the
promises of God are in Him. The Holy Spirit takes the
things of Christ and shows them unto us. May our spiritual
life grow up and journey on into an ever increasing likeness
to Him, whom having not seen, yet we love. Heirs
together with Christ. '' I go to prepare a place for you.''

3. Pilgrims animated by faith. '' The Lord said,
I will give it you.'' They believe *His word* and press on.
The way may be rough or smooth, their feelings may be
happy or wretched, but His word of assurance changeth not.
We walk by faith, not by sight. Believe, and thou shalt
see. Faith is the evidence of things not seen. By faith
Abraham sojourned (Heb. 11. 8, 9).

4. Pilgrims anxious for others to come with them.
'' Come thou with us.'' This is a day of glad tidings, we
do not well if we hold our peace (2 Kings 7. 8-10). The
coming of others into the joy of salvation does not curtail
but enlarges our own inheritance of blessing. There are
many like Hobab, who are only *friendly visitors*, they
attend Church, &c., but are not decided followers of the
Lord. Bid them come. That Church or Christian is in a

sad condition that has ceased to say, COME. "Let him
that heareth say, Come" (Rev. 22. 17).

5. Pilgrims willing to help others. "We will do thee
good." The Christian Church is a brotherhood, a family,
the "*Household* of God." O how attractive it would be
to those sin-sick, miserable, heart-broken onlookers if
they could but see the love of God yearning in us for their
good. It takes the love of Christ so to constrain us.

6. Pilgrims willing to be helped by others. "Thou
mayest be to us instead of eyes." Hobab had an intimate
geographical knowledge of the whole country that might
have been helpful to the strangers. Many men of the world
might be a great help to the Church if only brought into
full sympathy with the Lord and His people. In seeking
to win souls for Christ let us not attempt to belittle the
gifts of those who may not yet see as we do. It may be
helpful to point out to them, as Moses did, how their
attainments and experiences could be helpful to the cause
of God, and thus attain their highest value.

7. Pilgrims who often meet with refusals. "He
said, I will not go, but I will depart to mine own land."
Mine own land is often preferred to God's land of promise.
Mine own little plot, self, to the great kingdom of our
God and His Christ. The excuses for not going are very
numerous and varied: "I don't like your company," "I
intend to go some day, but not now," "I would go if So-
and-so would go with me," "I am afraid that I could not
hold on," "I am satisfied where I am," "I have married
a wife, &c., I cannot come." Well, we *are going* whether
you come or not. ———

THE ARK OF THE COVENANT.
Numbers 10. 33-36.

IT is of the Lord's mercy that we should have any *visible*
token of His great spiritual presence with His people.
Look at its—

1. Character. It was—

1. AN ARK. A small box, roughly speaking about four feet long, two feet wide, and two feet deep, made of shittim wood (incorruptible), and overlaid with pure gold. Type of Christ in His twofold nature, incorruptible humanity and pure divinity. The ark, like Christ, *kept* the law and covered up all its requirements. Its lid, like the work of Christ, forming a seat of mercy for Jehovah in His dealings with the people.

2. THE ARK OF THE COVENANT. Because the *law*, God's covenant with the people, which they had broken, was here safely kept and greatly honoured. Then His covenant with them was in the ark, now His covenant with us is in Christ. All have sinned, but all that the Father hath *given Him* shall come to Him. The honour of God is safe in the keeping of His beloved Son.

2. Position. "It went before them." While it rested it stood right in the midst of the camp, when it moved it went before them. The Good Shepherd goeth before His sheep (John 10. 3, 4). He hath gone before us through death into resurrection, "*a three days' journey*," from the mount of the broken law into the resurrection life. "The ark went before them in a three days' journey." The first day—*yielding up* all to God. The second day—*death of self*. The third day—*rising in newness* of life. 1. Consecration. 2. Crucifixion. 3. Resurrection.

3. Purpose. "To search out a resting place." Divine wisdom was needed to search out a resting place for man. Man by searching could never find this out. Christ's great self-sacrificing work was the searching out and the finding of a place where we can rest in peace *before God*. A *resting place* is man's great need. Weary, heavy-laden soul, here is a place where ye can be relieved of your burdens, the place called Calvary. Come unto Me, and I will give you rest. Enter into My rest (Heb. 4. 5). Where the ark rested they rested. Where Christ has rested in the Father's word and will here also we can find rest unto our souls.

4. Power. " When the ark set forward Moses said, Rise up, Lord. When it rested he said, Return O Lord" (vs. 35, 36). The ark was the symbol of—

1. The presence of God. Without His presence it was only so much dead weight. What are all our forms of worship without the power? (Heb. 13. 5, 6).

2. Victory. " Let thine enemies be scattered." When Christ, the ark of His strength, is with us the power of the enemy is broken. Greater is He that is with us than all that can be against us.

3. Blessing. " There I will commune with you" (Exod. 25. 22). Resting where He rested means fellowship with Him and with one another. " My presence shall go with thee, and I will give thee rest." Abiding with the ark the pillar of cloud overshadowed them (v. 34). Blessed with protection and with *provision*, for the manna accompanied the cloud. In His presence is fulness of joy, both now and evermore. _____

THE GRAVES OF LUST.
Numbers 11.

" The scene was more beautiful far to my eye
    Than if day in its pride had array'd it;
The land breeze blew mild, and the azure-arched sky
    Looked pure as the Spirit that made it.

A *murmur* arose, as I silently gazed
    On the shadowy waves' playful motion,
From the dim distant isle till the *beacon-fire blazed*
    Like a star in the midst of the ocean."

The grave of a sinner is always nearer than he thinks. When the mixed multitude began to *lust* it was the breaking open of the chasm of destruction. The fire of the Lord burning among *them* (v. 3) is the blazing of a beacon-fire for *us*. The steps from the place of privilege down to the pit of doom may be very few (Num. 16. 32).

1. The sin of lusting. Unforbidden desires after forbidden things. Observe—

1. WHO THEY WERE. "*Mixed* multitude" (v. 4). A crowd of different peoples and tongues among the Israelites. Mixing with the world of ungodliness is sure to lead to *lusting* after the things of the world. While in the world we are to be *kept from* the evil of it (John 17. 15).

2. WHEN THEY LUSTED. "We remember the fish, &c., which we did eat in Egypt" (v. 5). *Thinking* about the pleasures of the world will ripen into *lusting* when spiritual things are not so precious as before. "*Hearken* unto Me, and eat ye that which is good." "Open thy mouth wide, and I will fill it" (Psa. 81. 10-13).

2. The effect of lusting. Longing for the things of Egypt created in them—

1. A LOATHING TOWARD GOD'S PROVISION. "*Now* our soul is dried away, there is nothing at all beside this manna" (v. 6). Although the manna from Heaven had saved their lives, it now becomes a thing despised as *dry* and common. When the gifts of God (Christ and His Word) become dry and uninteresting it is a powerful evidence that the heart is not right with God. *Love* of the world makes many cold. The manna tasted like *fresh oil* (v. 8). The Word of God in the power of the Holy Spirit is always *fresh*.

2. A DISCOURAGING OF GOD'S SERVANT. "Moses said, they weep unto me, saying, Give us flesh to eat. I am not able to bear this people alone" (chapter 11. 15). The great honour put upon Moses by the Lord is now felt to be a *burden*. God's servants are but human, and the worldliness of professing Christians makes their high position burdensome at times. Perhaps it was a little

weakness on the part of Moses, for the meekest man on earth may at times fail (chap. 12. 3). But that does not lessen the guilt of those grumblers that so grieved him. Mercy is given to the one, while judgment is meted out to the other.

3. The promise of God. He promises in answer to prayer—

1. TO RELIEVE THE BURDEN OF HIS SERVANT. " I will take of the Spirit which is upon thee, and will put it upon them, and they shall bear the burden with thee" (vs. 16, 17). Although seventy men were added to share the responsibilities of oversight it does not appear that any addition of spiritual power was given. No more was needed, because the spirit of wisdom and power given to Moses was enough. But note that every man added had to be endued with the Spirit. "Tarry until ye be endued with power from on high" (Luke 24. 49).

2. TO GRANT THE PETITION OF THE REBELS. " Ye shall eat flesh until it come out at your nostrils and be loathsome unto you" (vs. 18-20). God's blessings will never be meted out to suit the palate of lust. They got what they asked to such a degree that it became a curse. Those who lust after gold or pleasure may get and get to such an extent that they are devoured by them. The answer of their own prayers punish them. We may have good cause in eternity to praise God for unanswered prayers.

4. The terrible consequences.

1. THE WRATH OF GOD. " While the flesh was between their teeth the wrath of the Lord was kindled" (v. 33). Having abundance of good things in this life is no evidence of the *grace of God* (Luke 16. 25). It would appear from Psalm 78. 30, 31 that many of them had grown fat eating the flesh of lust, but their *fatness* only marked them for the slaughter. My soul, grieve not at the prosperity of the

wicked. Let me be now and ever satisfied with Christ, the true bread from Heaven.

2. THE GRAVES OF LUST. They called the name of the place Kibroth-hattaavah (graves of the lust). Every unholy lust is the digging of a grave. Lust brings forth sin, and sin when it is finished bringeth forth *death*. The grave is God's appointed place for lust. The *flesh* lusteth against the Spirit, let it be crucified and buried with Christ. May the grave of Jesus become also the Kibroth-hattaavah of the flesh.

SPIRIT-POSSESSED MEN.
Numbers 11. 24-30.

" O Comforter, the Holy Ghost!
  Before Thee mortal may not boast;
  I grasp Thy Name of Paraclete,
  But find Thee strong as well as sweet;
  But more—Thy presence felt so near,
  The eyes of faith makes bright and clear;
      My glad heart bursts into song,
      By Thy presence still kept strong."

THE Lord does not deal with all in the same way. Moses prayed that he might be relieved from the " burden of all the people," and the Lord granted him according to his request (vs. 11-17). Paul prayed that the thorn in the flesh might be taken away, but instead of that he got grace sufficient to *bear* it (2 Cor. 12. 7-10), and to glory in it. In the one case Moses was the loser (v. 17), in the other Paul was the gainer. Let us take good heed how we treat our thorns and our burdens. From this portion we may learn—

1. The possibilites of a believer's life. On Moses there rested a spiritual influence enough for seventy men (vs. 24, 25). Is there any limit as to the measure of wisdom and power God is able to communicate to a meek and faithful servant ? The Spirit was given to Christ, our great High Priest, *without* measure, so that this

holy anointing oil might flow down to the skirts of
His garments—the whole body of His people.

2. Spirit-possessed men are separated men.
" Gather the seventy and *set them* round about the tabernacle" (v. 24). These men were *called* out, set aside,
and their names written (v. 26) before the Holy Spirit
was put upon them. The one hundred and twenty in the
upper room were separated and set aside for this definite
purpose before they were all filled with the Spirit. Come
ye yourselves apart at God's bidding, and ye shall receive
the power of the Holy Ghost coming upon you.

3. There are degrees of Spirit filling. " The Lord
took the Spirit that was upon Moses, and gave unto the
elders" (v. 25). After this Moses would not have the same
measure of the Spirit upon him. This was not needed,
because he had not the same amount of work to do. The
measure of our Spirit-filling depends much upon the
measure of our faith and *service* for the Lord. The Lord
does not give His penny to idlers in the market place.
Carey's motto was good, "Attempt much for God, and
expect much from God."

4. Spirit-possessed men cannot be hid. " Eldad
and Medad prophesied in the camp, and there ran a young
man and told Moses" (vs. 26, 27). The power of the Holy
Spirit is fire from Heaven, it cannot be hid. If it is put
under a bushel, then so much the worse for the bushel.
Christ could not be hid. When He lives in us by the Holy
Ghost there is no hiding of Him. When those who have
hitherto been dumb for Christ begin to prophesy it is sure
to create some excitement. " There ran a young man and
said Eldad and Medad do prophesy." There is nothing
like the mighty power of the Holy Spirit to make *young
men* run, and to waken them up out of the sloth of spiritual
indifference. When a man gets endued with the Spirit
his life will tell.

5. Spirit-possessed men are not to be hindered.
"Joshua said, my lord Moses forbids them; Moses said,
Would God that all the Lord's people were prophets"
(vs. 28, 29). Perhaps Joshua himself was that young man
who was so suddenly startled by this innovation as to run
with the tidings of it. Such men are needed, and Moses'
gladness at the hearing of it shows the largeness and
meekness of his unenvious heart. Every Spirit-filled
man rejoices in others being endued with power from on
high for Christ and His kingdom's sake. "Would God
that all the Lord's people were prophets," as all might
be (1 Cor. 14. 5). The Holy Ghost has been given that
every believer might have this power, and the command
is, "Be filled with the Spirit" (Eph. 5. 18).

JEALOUSY AMONG THE LORD'S SERVANTS.
Numbers 12.

"Save me, O my God, from fretting,
Sin of all other sins begetting;
Grant that I may understand
All is 'neath Thy ruling hand.
Save me, O my God, from fretting,
Subtle weaver of sin's netting;
Others may be great, I low,
Grace give to Thy will to bow."

JEALOUSY is cruel as the grave. It is a sad sight to see the
Lord's people looking on one another with the self-conceited
eyes of envy. Godliness with *contentment* is great gain.
See here its—

1. Origin. "Because Moses had married an Ethiopian
woman" (v. 1). In this connection it is significant that
Miriam's name is mentioned first, as she doubtless first
kindled this fire of sedition. The *Ethiopian* woman being
raised to a place of great honour seemed to stir up her
envy. Does it make us fretful when some brother of low
degree is lifted into prominence in the cause of Christ?
Are we more ready to find fault than bless God for it?

2. Form. " Hath the Lord spoken only by Moses? hath He not spoken also by us?" (v. 2). This was a question as to the receiving of the favour of God, and their fitness to take the lead in His word. When there is pride and discontent in the heart it will soon break out in fault-finding. Am I not the servant of God as well as he? A sparrow is under the same care as an angel, but their character and the purpose of their lives are very different. A geologist knows the difference between granite and sandstone, so may any schoolboy, but that does not make him a geologist.

3. Subject. " They spake against Moses. Now the man Moses was very meek, above all the men which are upon the face of the earth" (v. 3). Moses makes no attempt to vindicate his own name. He is conscious that his commission is from God, and he leaves Him to deal with the offenders. What can be more cruel than jealousy? It is so terribly soul-blinding that it will charge the meekest men on earth with vanity and presumption. Dissatisfied and envious Christian workers are not infrequently found throwing such stones at those who are more used of God than they are. Take heed to yourself.

4. Treatment. " The Lord spake suddenly unto Moses, Aaron, and Miriam, Come out ye three, and hear now My words" (vs. 4-8). *Suddenly* the Lord appears for the defence of His servant Moses. He honours and justifies him before their faces as more than an ordinary prophet, as one to whom He could speak mouth to mouth and face to face (Exod. 33. 11). God will always compensate His tried servants for their faithful *silence*. The way into *open* reward is through a *shut* door (Matt. 6. 6).

5. Guilt. " The anger of the Lord was kindled against them" (v. 9). Those who are jealous of others in the Lord's work should be reminded that they have a jealous

God to deal with (Nah. 1. 2). He will avenge the wrongs
done to those who abide in the secret of His presence. The
Lord looketh upon the heart. Is thy heart right with God
in this respect? Be sure *this sin* will find you out.

6. Results. The evidence of His wrath upon them is
seen in that it—

1. PRODUCED UNCLEANNESS. "Miriam became leprous" (v. 10). The sin of the heart soon manifested
itself in outward uncleanness. Fault-finders and back-
biters will soon be found *outside* the service of God.
When Christian workers become envious and ambitious,
look out for an outbreak.

2. INTERRUPTED FELLOWSHIP. "Let her be shut out
from the camp seven days" (v. 14). The spirit of jealousy
quickly withers up the spirit of communion. It is an
uncleanness within that unfits for fellowship with God and
with His people. This is a law that is unalterable. The
lack of *brotherly* love grieves the Holy Ghost, and so the
spirit of prayer and worship is lost, and the soul has to
go outside the enjoyment of all holy things. Beware
how ye speak about the Lord's servants. This is a
solemn question asked by Jehovah, "Were ye not afraid
to speak against My servant?" (v. 8). To his own master
he stands or falls.

3. HINDERED PROGRESS. "The people journeyed not
till Miriam was brought in again" (v. 15). The whole
camp was kept back through her sin. Those who sin in
the high places of the Church are great hindrances to the
advancement of the cause of Christ. One fly may spoil the
ointment, one Achan may cause defeat to the whole army
of God, one sin will hinder growth in grace, mar the
testimony, and make the life unfruitful. "Search me,
O God, and try me, and see if there be any wicked way in
me, and lead me in the way everlasting" (Psa. 139. 23).

THE FOLLY OF UNBELIEF.
Numbers 13 and 14.

THE carnal mind is enmity against God, and until the mind is changed toward God His grace and faithfulness will never be appreciated. They may spy the beautiful land, but it is only with blinded eyes. They may hear of its goodness and glory, but only with deaf ears. Until the *heart* is right with God all is wrong. Unbelief toward God as naturally flows out of the carnal heart as waters down the hill. No amount of evidence in itself (for the Israelites had abundance) will ever change the human mind. '' It is the Spirit that quickeneth.'' Unbelief—

1. Measures difficulties by human strength. '' We be not able, for they are stronger than *we*'' (v. 31). '' Grasshoppers in their sight'' (**v. 33**). Those who go to work without God have only an arm of flesh to lean on, in face of terrible obstacles in the way to their possessing Divine blessings. How can a *helpless* sinner ever overcome all the giants of evil within, and all the walls of habit that has been built about them? Measure these by your own powers, and well may you say, ''We be not able'' (Num. 13. 31). It is good when the sinner makes this confession, but sad when Christians do. There are high blessings in God's Word offered to His people: perpetual peace, joy, strength, victory. Like Nehemiah we must measure all difficulties with ''the God of Heaven.'' ''Lo, I am with you always.''

2. Makes void the Word of God. They said '' It is a land that eateth up the inhabitants thereof'' (chap. 13. 32). God had said that it was '' A good land and a large, flowing with milk and honey'' (Exod. 3. 8). Here is a contradiction. Unbelief always contradicts God, because it can only judge by appearance. '' He that believeth not God hath made Him a liar.'' God's Word promises pardon, peace, paradise to all that believe on Jesus. But the unbelieving heart thinks that the religion of Jesus Christ

eateth up the subjects of it, because worldly pleasures are
no more sought after. God says "Look and live."
Unbelief says "Work and live." God's Word says
wisdom's (Christ's) ways are ways of pleasantness. Unbelief says we would need to give up all pleasure to walk
in them (Heb. 4. 2).

3. Despises the provision of God. "They brought
up a slander upon the land" (chap. 14. 36). "Yea they
despised the pleasant land, they believed not His Word"
(Psa. 106. 24). The good and fruitful land was God's
provision for them, but they saw no beauty in it to desire
it. Christ and His precious promises are God's provision
for the sinner, yet how often He is slandered and despised,
wounded also in the house of His friends. You bring a
slander upon the land when you profess to be a Christian,
and walk not accordingly. You despise the pleasant land
when you trust more to your own goodness than to Christ.
You reject God's provision when you pray to be excused
(Luke 14. 18).

4. Dishonours God Himself. "And the Lord said,
How long will it be ere they believe Me?" (chap. 14. 11).
When Eve believed the serpent she discredited the Lord.
When you believe your own evil heart you disbelieve God.
What hath God done for them? "He had forgiven them
from Egypt until now" (v. 9), been gracious to them all
the way, still they doubt His sure Word of promise.
What has God done for you? Where are many that used
to trouble you? Has He not been gracious to you
from the cradle? What are you doing now? Rebelling,
disowning, and dishonouring. Unbelief drove the nails
into His hands and feet. Unbelief pierced His heart.
If you are despising His mercy you are crucifying Him
afresh. What dishonour to doubt Him that cannot lie.
"He that sinneth against Me wrongeth his own soul"
(Prov. 8. 34).

5. Is the source of sin and sorrow. " And all the people wept and murmured'' (chap. 14. 1-4). How readily man believes an evil report, how slow to let '' God be true.'' Those who disbelieve God will weep and wail. Unbelief excludes God, and so prefers darkness to light, sorrow and misery to peace and joy. Have faith in God, and He will wipe away all sad tears. Unbelief shuts out the guiding Spirit, and cries, '' Make us a captain'' (v. 4). O how foolish when man refuses to be blessed of God! Jesus said to the disciples, '' Why are ye sad?'' Just because they ''believed not the Scriptures.'' Why so much sadness in the world? Because God is not believed. The young man went away sorrowful. These shall go away into everlasting punishment. Beware of false reporters.

6. Presumes to succeed without God. "They presumed to go up, nevertheless the ark of the Lord departed not'' (vs. 40-45). The foolish virgins came knocking when the door was shut. Samson said ''I will go and shake myself, and he wist not that the Lord was departed from him'' (Judges 16. 20). I called and ye refused, now I will laugh at your calamity. This is the presumption of almost every unbelieving sinner; they hope to get the blessed possession in the end, although they do not believe God's Word. But if they will not take salvation in God's way they will never possess it in their own. Some went to gather manna on the *seventh* day and found none (Exod. 16. 27). Too late.

7. Incurs the sentence of death. "As I live, saith the Lord, your carcases shall fall in this wilderness'' (chap. 14. 28, 29). How awfully solemn. '' He that believeth not shall not see life,'' &c. (John 5. 56). '' The day thou eatest thereof thou shalt surely die.'' They could not enter in because of unbelief. Take heed lest ye fall after the same example of unbelief. '' He that believeth not shall be damned.'' God is merciful, but God is not to be trifled with. The punishment of the unbelieving is as certain as the blessedness of the believing (Matt. 25. 46).

THE TRIUMPHS OF FAITH.
Numbers 13 and 14.

IF we believe that God hath spoken, then we should believe all He says. But, alas! this is not so. Many say they believe the Bible to be all it pretends to be, and yet how few of its offers are accepted, how few of its promises believed. '' I will show you my faith *by* my *works*.'' Can you show me yours without them? Without faith it is impossible to please God. God is better pleased with faith than works. In truth, faith is a work. '' This is the *work* of God that ye *believe*.''

We notice here seven actions of faith. It—

1. Confirms the promise of God. '' We came to the land, and surely it floweth with milk and honey'' (chap. 13. 27). This is just what God had said about it. '' Faith sets to its seal that God is true.'' Those who prove His Word will find it faithful. God promises peace in believing, and also rest. If you cannot say that you have found these you dare not say you believe God, else you make Him a liar. The submissive will and God's Word can never differ, they are always and altogether at one. Although our *experience* has not yet attained, faith must ever keep far ahead of experience. When Christ is believed, God is honoured, because the soul being justified justifies God.

2. Exhibits the proofs of God's faithfulness. "They went and showed them the fruit of the land" (chap. 13. 26). They brought into the wilderness (v. 3) that which the wilderness could not produce. Every believer ought to manifest to the world fruits that are contrary to it. When they saw the boldness of Peter and John they acknowledged that they had been with Jesus. Every believer's life ought to be a witness to the truth of God's Word. The grace of God can turn barrenness into marvellous fruitfulness. Every Christian whose life manifests the fruits of God's promises condemns the unbelieving. "The fruit of the Spirit is love, joy, peace, longsuffering, gentleness, goodness, faith, meekness, temperance" (Gal. 6. 22). These make a wonderful cluster from the heavenly Eshcol, but, alas! how few seem to carry them.

3. Advocates present possession. " Let us go up at *once* and possess it" (chap. 13. 30). Unbelief always puts off for a more convenient season. If God has made us a promise, why should that promise not be ours at once? God's desire that we should possess it is seen *in the promise* He makes. This is the promise which He hath promised— *eternal life*, present possession. Lay hold of it at once. He promises rest *from* labour, and rest *in* labour (Matt. 11. 28, 29). Not only in Heaven, but now. Are you enjoying it? If not, go up at once and possess it. The land of promise is there before you. If you have *faith* you will possess. Faith values the present, because it knows *future* blessedness depends upon it.

4. Laments the folly of unbelief. " Joshua and Caleb rent their clothes" (chap. 14. 6). Jesus who had all power to save, weeps over impenitent Jerusalem. When a man has discovered the infinite grace of God the unbelief of others seems awful madness. Those whose eyes are opened to spiritual and eternal things are those whose eyes must often weep for others. Those whose hearts have been broken by the love of God will have their hearts often pierced by those who despise Him. Only those who believe God can know the folly and sin of doubting Him. When faith is low sorrow for sin will be shallow, whether in the Church or the individual. If we had the faith of Christ, then we would have somewhat of His sympathy.

5. Rests exclusively in the Lord. "If the Lord delight in us, then He will bring us into the land, and the Lord is with us, fear them not" (chap. 14. 8, 9). Faith does not overlook the difficulties (chap. 13. 28), but contrasts them with the promise and power of Jehovah. Unbelief excludes God in its reasonings. Faith says is anything too hard *for Him.* Those who trust in Him have sure success, for they have: 1. *His pleasure:* "delight in us." 2. *His promise*: "He will bring us." 3. *His presence*: "with us." 4. *His power*: "He is able." Here we see how the bewildered sinner may have deliverance, not by looking at the great sins, or evil habits, or other huge obstacles, but by accepting His promise and leaving all to Him. By faith Abraham obeyed, by faith Peter walked on the sea, by grace are ye saved *through faith.*

6. Follows God always and everywhere. " Caleb hath followed Me *fully*" (chap. 14. 24). God ever justifies fully, and always, and everywhere, those who *continually trust* in Him. This is the life of faith. Faith in God is an act, but it is the act of a once sealed fountain broken open and flowing on continually, and rejoicing to flow, and reckoning this the work of its existence. It mattered nothing to Caleb how numerous the giants, or how high the walls. His heart was stayed on God. We need fear no evil if indeed we can say "He leadeth me." Those who follow fully will suffer persecution—"stone them" (v. 10), "burn them" (three Hebrew youths), "crucify Him." But greater is He that is for us.

7. Inherits the promises. "Him will I bring into the land" (v. 24). This is the victory that overcometh the world, even our faith. Such are not sent empty away, " To-day shalt thou be with Me in Paradise." " He that honoureth Me I will honour." Faith accepts the promises which are the title deeds of Heaven offered by God to bankrupt sinners. There is much land yet to be possessed — "high lands," "sunny lands," "happy lands." "Believe, and thou shalt see." Here is a sunny slope on the hillside of spiritual privilege. "Thou wilt keep him in *perfect peace* whose mind is stayed on Thee." In Psalm 37 five of Canaan's happy fields are promised to the faithful followers (vs. 3, 4, 5, 7, 11, 34). God is faithful. ——

THE SIN OF PRESUMPTION.
Numbers 14. 39-45.

" Deep is the sea, and deep is Hell, but pride mineth deeper;
  It is coiled as a poisonous worm about the foundations of the soul.
  If thou expose it in thy motives, and track in thy springs of thought,
  Complacent in its own detection, it will seem *indignant* virtue."

IT has been said that " Wise men presume nothing, but hope for the best; presumption is hope out of her wits." In this portion of Scripture we have a solemn example of the foolhardiness of attempting to do work for the Lord without His presence with us.

1. Who they were.

1. PILGRIMS from Egypt who had been saved by the power of God.

2. FOLLOWERS of the Divine pillar, who had again and again witnessed the wonder working of Him who dwelt therein.

3. MURMURERS who had refused to accept the report of the two faithful spies, and who desired to make themselves a captain and return to Egypt (v. 4).

2. What they did.
When they heard that the Lord had, because of their unbelief, sentenced them to forty years wanderings in the wilderness (v. 34), they said, " Lo, we be here, and *we will go up*." In doing so they went—

1. AGAINST THE WORD OF GOD. "Wherefore do ye now

trespass? It shall not prosper" (v. 41). What was their duty and privilege yesterday becomes disobedience to-day. God had said, " In this wilderness they shall die." They said, "We will go up." But now it was in their own strength. Vain effort.

2. PRESUMING ON THE PAST MERCIES OF GOD. " Lo, we be *here.*" We have been preserved and brought through to this point. " We will go up." It is in vain we lean on past favours and experiences when by our sin we have grieved the Holy Ghost. Murmuring is sure to lead to failure.

3. WITHOUT THE PRESENCE OF GOD. " They presumed to go up, nevertheless the ark of the Lord departed not out of the camp" (v. 44). If we go contrary to God's Word we must go without His presence. Without Me ye can do nothing. The Lord is with you while you be *with Him* in His will and purposes (2 Chron. 15. 2). Except Thy presence go with us, carry us not up hence.

4. THINKING THAT A FORMAL CONFESSION WOULD SATISFY GOD. " We will go up, for *we have sinned*" (v. 40). Confession without the submission of the will to the mind of God is ardent hypocrisy. Sin may be felt, yet not forsaken. Unless the moth has been hopelessly scorched with the flame at its first contact it will seek it again.

3. **What they experienced**. " The Amalekites came down and smote them, and discomfited them" (v. 45). In their *self-confident* effort they only gained for themselves—

1. DISAPPOINTMENT. They did not reach the place which the Lord had promised. They had built their hopes on a foundation of sand.

2. DEFEAT. The enemy overcame them. The foes of the soul are numerous and powerful. He that trusteth his

own heart is a fool. Without the armour of God we cannot withstand the wiles of the devil.

3. DISGRACE. I use this word advisedly, "*Out of favour.*" Conscious of having lost the favour and presence of God. This is a most alarming discovery to a true child of God. Out of favour with God means also dishonoured among men. Miserable backslider.

4. DEATH. Many were smitten. In a spiritual sense presumption is always accompanied by the smiting blight of death. Pride goeth before a fall. "Uzziah was marvellously helped till he was strong"—strong in self-confidence. The wages of the sin of *self-trust* is death to all fruitfulness for Christ.

4. What they teach us. These things which happened to them are ensamples to us (1 Cor. 10. 11). There is here a solemn warning to the—

1. CHRISTIAN WORKER. Beware of godless effort, of hoping to succeed in Christ's work without the presence and power of the Holy Spirit with you and in you. Except the Lord build the city they labour in vain who build it.

2. SELF-RIGHTEOUS. Beware of seeking the heavenly inheritance, the land of promise, without first making sure that God is with you by His Word and promise.

3. FORMALIST. Beware of trusting formal prayers and confessions while the *revealed* will of God stands opposed to your character and purposes (vs. 41, 42).

4. PROCRASTINATING. Beware of depending on a *late* repentance. Those Israelites found that the eleventh hour for them was *too late*. Their *last* effort was a fatal one. The ark did not always rest in Jordan. If one thief was saved at the eleventh hour, the other perished. Here again, "Beware of the sin of presumption." For this sin there was no sacrifice appointed (Heb. 6. 4-6).

THE DESTRUCTION OF KORAH AND HIS COMPANY.

Numbers 16.

" When Thou seest *passion* in me burn,
  Upon me, Lord, Thy meek face turn;
  Such vision, giving me of faith,
  So touching me with Thy soft breath
  That I shall not *impatient* be,
  But find myself conformed to Thee."

PRIDE goeth before a fall. When envy enters the heart it soon becomes a hotbed for the rank weeds of discontent, impatience, and presumption.

1. See the sinners. The three leaders of this rebellion against Moses and Aaron the saint of the Lord (Psa. 106. 16) were Korah, Dathan, and Abiram; their followers were 250 princes, famous men of renown. Great men are not always wise. The voice of the people is frequently the voice of the devil. Korah seems to have been the ringleader. His name means ICE, and he answers to his name. Only a man with an icy, cold heart and frozen feelings could have acted such an ungracious part toward the " meekest man on the face of the earth." Where love is thin faults are thick. When professing Christian workers become icy in their manner, you may soon expect them leading the opposition. Such icebergs are a terrible danger to Gospel ships.

2. See their sin. It was very great, and was the *growth* of time, as all great sins are. A backslider is one who is *sliding* back, slowly it may be, but surely, into the mire of *open* sin. The down grade from uncharitableness leads to the engulfing of the whole character in the pit of iniquity. Its—

1. ROOT WAS UNBELIEF. They had ceased to believe that Moses and Aaron were still the special representatives among the congregation. Take heed lest there be in any

of you an evil heart of unbelief. Begin to doubt God's will, and you begin to fall.

2. BRANCH WAS ENVY. "Wherefore lift ye up yourselves *above the congregation*?" (v. 3). The Lord had lifted Moses and Aaron up, but it was they that were lifting *themselves* up. It was Socrates who said, "Envy is the daughter of pride, the beginner of secret sedition, and the perpetual *tormentor of virtue*." This witness is true.

3. BLOSSOM WAS PRESUMPTION. "Ye take too much upon you, seeing all the congregation are holy, *every one of them*" (v. 3). As if all the people were as gracious and saintly as Moses and Aaron. Their sin is ripening. There is a growing *blindness* to the good in others, and to their own sinfulness.

4. FRUIT WAS DEATH. Lust bringeth forth sin, and sin brings forth death, just as surely as night follows day.

3. See them separated. "Separate yourselves from among this congregation, that I may consume them" (vs. 21-24). It is an ominous sign when the representatives of a government are called out from among a nation. The calling out of Lot meant the destruction of Sodom. The calling up of the Church indicates coming judgments (2 Thess. 1. 7-10; Jer. 51. 6; Rev. 18. 4).

This separating reminds us that—

1. THERE ARE TWO CLASSES. Those *for* God and those *against* Him. The wheat and the tares, growing together now, but must finally be separated.

2. A SEPARATION IS NEEDED. God will not judge the righteous with the wicked. Before God could accomplish His purpose with Sodom Lot had to be dragged outside. Separation is needed now if we, as the followers of Christ, would escape the judgment of the world through lust (2 Cor. 6. 17).

3. GOD IS RIGHTEOUS. In calling for a *separation* He shows His special regard for His own. " Come out of her, *My people.*" Shall not the Judge of all the earth do right? None perish that trust in Him.

4. See them swallowed up. " The earth opened her mouth and swallowed them up" (vs. 31-35). The means of vengeance are always at the hand of God. The powerful opposition is easily overcome when the arm of God is made bare. The judgment of these gainsayers (Jude 11) was—

1. UNEXPECTED. " The ground clave asunder *that was under them*" (v. 31). Their foundation gave way. They have *no standing* in the judgment (Psa. 1. 5). Only the *ground* between them and the pit, instead of the promise of God.

2. SUDDEN. " They went down alive into the pit" (v. 33). He that hardeneth his neck, having been often reproved, shall suddenly perish, and that without remedy. They say, Peace, peace, then suddenly destruction cometh.

3. COMPLETE. " They, and all that appertained to them, went down" (v. 33). God's destroying work is as perfect as His saving work. "How shall ye escape if ye neglect so great salvation?"

_____

THE ROD THAT BUDDED.
Numbers 17.

" O Lord, my God, Thou changest not,
Nor deed of kindness e'er doth blot;
I, too, through Thy so tender ruth,
Have come to know this precious truth.

Thy heaviest rod upon me laid,
To bud and blossom Thou hast made;
And still Thy rod, like growing thing,
Fragrance and fruit from Thee doth bring."

THE rod that budded is a most delightful type of the Lord Jesus Christ.

1. In His calling. Like this rod He was set apart, and the name of the High Priest put upon Him.

2. In His life. Like this rod He was common in appearance, no beauty to be desired, a root out of a dry ground.

3. In His death. Like Aaron's rod, He was *laid up* with others. "On either side one, and Jesus in the midst." Lifted up on the Cross, and also for the *judgment* of God.

4. In His resurrection. Like the rod He budded and blossomed and brought forth fruit.

5. In His ascension. Like the rod He is laid up again *before the Lord* for a testimony. He is in the presence of God *for us*.

There are other lessons that might be learned from this most fruitful theme, truths applicable to the Christian life and testimony, for as He is, so are we. The story of the occasion of these rods may be read in the preceding chapter, in the rebellion of Korah and his company against Moses and Aaron. See here the—

1. Demand of God. "Take twelve rods, write thou every man's name upon his rod, and lay them up, where I will meet with you" (vs. 1-3).

1. This is A call for representatives. Every rod represented a tribe. Is our Lord not pressing His demand to-day for *representatives* when the Korahs and the princes of the world are challenging the ministry and power of the Gospel?

2. Each representative had to be entirely yielded up. Each rod was to be "laid up before the testimony" (v. 4). Put in the holy place, in front of the vail. Those who would have the Divine impersonation stamped upon them must be *wholly yielded* up to Him. Not every one that *saith* Lord, Lord, shall enter into the fulness of blessing exhibited in Aaron's rod.

2. Evidence of being chosen of God. The chosen of God will always be self-evident. "Behold the rod of Aaron budded, blossomed, and yielded almonds" (v. 8). This thing was done *in secret*, but it could not *remain* a secret. Light and *life* manifest themselves. This evidence was twofold.

1. LIFE. This life was the *gift* of God. The gift of God is eternal life. If we have been *made alive* unto God, then we may be assured that we are the *called of God*, as was Aaron. Partakers of the Divine nature.

2. FRUITFULNESS. "It yielded almonds." Fruit is the evidence of *abundance* of life. If we have been *born again* like the rod of Aaron, whose *natural* life had died and given place to his new life, it is that we might bring forth fruit unto God. Did not our Lord say " I have *chosen you* and ordained you to bring forth fruit," and that like the fruit on this rod, "your fruit *should remain?*" (John 15. 16). But you say only one out of the twelve *yielded up* rods were chosen. Yes. But which was chosen? The one with the *High Priest's* name on it (v. 3). It does not matter by what name you consecrate yourself, if it is not in the *Name of Jesus Christ*, the Great High Priest, the *evidences* of God's choice will not be seen in your life. Put *His Name* upon your life, and lay it up before Him for His honour and glory, and as surely as Aaron's rod budded will your life bud and blossom and yield fruit. But note further—

3. Position of testimony for God. It was to be—

1. KEPT IN HIS PRESENCE. "The Lord said, Bring Aaron's rod *again* before the testimony to be *kept*" (v. 10). If its life and fruitfulness are to remain, it must be *kept in nearness* to Him who is the source of its life and fruit-

fulness. The application of this is simple, yet sublime. The branch cannot bear fruit of itself, *no more can ye,* except ye *abide in Me* (John 15. 1-6). The secret of abiding fruitfulness is being *kept* in nearness to the life-giving One. In His presence is fulness of joy.

2. As a WITNESS. "To be kept *for a token* against the rebels" (v. 10). It is so with the living Christ now before the throne of God (Acts 17. 30, 31). It is so with every spiritually resurrected soul. They are witnesses against the rebels who believe not the word of the Gospel. The believer's *life,* like the *works* of Noah, are intended to condemn the world (Heb. 11. 7). As this *living* and *fruitful* rod was an evidence that God had chosen Aaron, so the *life* of the Christian is a token to the ungodly world that the Father hath sent His Son to save it (John 17. 21). Kept in His presence for the enjoyment of His love, kept there for a witness to the power of His grace. He is able to keep that which I have committed unto Him.

AARON AS A REPRESENTATIVE OF CHRIST
Numbers 18.

> "I seek retreat from all this empty noise,
>   Mere human words, in books that have no end;
> In the one Book supreme I still rejoice,
>   O Lord, more mighty fire—touch'd preachers send!
> Send seers who know Thy voice and follow Thee
>   To height and depth, not sham'd of Jesus' Blood.
> O give us, Lord, these more and more to see,
>   Thy words still their predestin'd heavenly food."

IN Aaron we have a deeply impressive type of the priestly character of our Lord and Saviour.

Like Christ he—

1. **Was sent of God as a Revealer.** His name means *"Enlightener."* He was chosen by God to *speak out* His mind and will in the ears of Pharaoh. It was of him the Lord said, "I know that he can speak well"

(Exod. 4. 14). Christ came to reveal the Father's will. He could speak well. "Never man spake like this Man." I am the *Light* of the world.

2. Had charge of all the holy things. "I have given thee charge of Mine offerings, and of all the hallowed things" (v. 8). Christ indeed had charge of the offering and all the hallowed things of God. He came to give Himself an offering and a sacrifice to God. All things are now in His hand, because He is the Son of Man. The keys of Heaven, earth, and Hell are hanging at His girdle.

3. Had a special anointing. "Unto thee have I given them *because of the anointing*" (v. 8). "This precious ointment—symbol of the Holy Spirit—was poured upon his head, and ran down upon the beard, even Aaron's beard, and went down to the skirts of his garments" (Psa. 133). This *running down* of the holy oil indicates an overflowing measure of fulness. The Holy Ghost was given to Christ without measure, and because of this anointing the Lord was able to finish the work given Him to do. He lived and moved and had His being in the Holy Spirit as the *Man* Christ Jesus.

4. Had the privilege of eating in the holy place. "In the holy of holies shalt thou eat it" (v. 10, Heb.). He had meat to eat that others knew nothing of and could not enjoy. In the secret place of God's holy presence His soul was abundantly satisfied. "I *delight* to do Thy will, O God." My *meat* and My *drink* is to do the *will of Him* that sent Me. This is holy food, eaten in the most holy place. O my soul, as one hidden with Christ in God dost thou feed on this hidden manna? The finest of the wheat is found in the secret of His presence.

5. Redeemed the unclean. "The firstborn of man, and the firstling of unclean beasts, shalt thou surely redeem" (v. 15). It is most significant that *man* is classed with *unclean* beasts in need of redemption. The cow or sheep were reckoned holy, not needing to be redeemed (v. 17). Christ hath *redeemed us* from the curse of the law, being made a curse for us. It was not an *example* the unclean needed, but a Redeemer. Redeemed with the precious Blood of Christ (Eph. 1. 7).

6. Had many servants given him. "Behold, I have taken the Levites; to you they are given as a gift for the Lord" **(v. 6).** The Levites were given to Aaron by the Lord as co-workers together with him for the Lord. Many have also been given to Christ by the Father as the fruit of His sufferings, and as co-workers for the honour of His great Name. "Holy Father, keep through Thine own Name those whom *Thou hast given Me*" (John 17. 11).

7. Had his seed blessed in him. " The holy things I have given thee, and to thy seed with thee, in a covenant of salt for ever" (v. 19). All spiritual blessings are ours in Christ Jesus (Eph. 1. 3). "He shall see *His seed*, and the pleasure of the Lord shall prosper in His hands. He shall see the travail of His soul, and shall be satisfied" (Isa. 53. 10, 11). Of His fulness have all we received, and ye are complete in Him (Col. 2. 10). Having delivered Him up for us all, how shall He not *with Him* also freely give us all things? (Rom. 8. 32).

8. Found his part in God Himself. "The Lord spake unto Aaron, saying, I am *thy part* and thine inheritance" (v. 20). Like Aaron Christ had no earthly inheritance among the people. Not where to lay His head, although He was Heir of all. "This is the heir, come let us kill Him." Like Mary, having chosen the better part, the best part was given Him. To our Lord, the Father Himself, was His exceeding great reward. Glorify Thou Me with THINE OWN SELF (John 17. 5). The Lord is my portion saith my soul. Choose the better part, that shall never be taken from you (Psa 73. 26).

THE RED HEIFER.

Numbers 19.

THE ordinance of the heifer was appointed by God (v. 2). Like the plan of salvation it doubtless would be misunderstood by many. The offering must be according to the mind of God. He Himself appoints it. Jesus Christ, the great Sacrifice, was also, after God's own heart, "The Lamb of God." God only has the right to say what and how much He will accept as an atonement for man, or as a cleansing for the defiled. It is not a question of how much a man will give, but what will God accept. His terms are alone just. The whole scene shows us Christ and His salvation.

1. The sacrifice, or the character of Christ. "The heifer was to be without spot or blemish, and one upon which never came yoke" (v. 2). Christ offered Himself without spot unto God, and as a Lamb without blemish (1 Peter 1. 19). Men tried to find a blemish in God's Lamb that they might reject Him, yea they rejected the "Holy One" and "the Just," although they found no fault in the Man. Man in the pride of his heart still tries to get God in a fault. The *yoke* speaks of the *curse*. "Cursed is the ground for thy sake." But the yoke of sin never was on Him as a *bondage*. Sin never fettered His life, though sorrow often filled His heart.

There must be no leaven in the meat-offering. He "was holy, harmless, undefiled, separate from sinners" (Heb. 7. 26).

2. The slaying, or the death of Christ. "Bring her without the camp and slay her" (v. 3). Without spot, and yet without the camp, seems strange. Holy, yet treated as unclean. As a *substitute* it must be dealt with as vile, yet to be accepted of God it must be intrinsically spotless and blameless. So was it with Christ, without spot, yet treated as the vilest, slain without the gate as the chief of sinners. He was despised and rejected of men.

God was well pleased with Him, yet He hid His face from Him without the.city. The great truth here is substitution, the just One suffering for the unjust to bring us to God.

3. The consuming, or the offering of Christ. "Burn the heifer, her skin, her flesh, and her blood" (v. 5). All must be consumed, and all that was burnt was given to and accepted by God. It was a whole burnt-offering, yet in the place of the sin-offering, wholly devoted to God. Here we see Christ offering *Himself*, every part and power of His being are all laid down, and all accepted by God. Sometimes the offerings were flayed (skinned), typifying *outward* imperfection. But Christ's outward and inward life were all pure, and all given to God. We fail in thought, word, and deed, but *He* faileth not. " The cedar, hyssop, and scarlet were cast *into the burning*" (v. 6), implying that the greatest (cedar), the smallest (hyssop), and vilest (scarlet) may be accepted in this offering.

4. The ashes, or the virtues of Christ. The ashes were to be gathered and laid up in a clean place: " It shall be kept, *it* is a purification for sin" (v. 9). The ashes were all that remained. The clean place may have a reference to the " new tomb" in which Jesus was laid. They are spoken of in the singular: it. The result of Christ's death is one whole "purification for sin," the alone remedy, divinely appointed, and on the ground of death. These ashes were to be *kept*, set apart for the unclean. What a gracious provision, what good news for the defiled and unclean! So God is still *keeping* mercy for thousands.

5. The defiled, or the need of Christ. " He that toucheth the dead shall be unclean" (v. 11). Death is the work of sin. Sin, when it is finished, bringeth forth death. Therefore a *touch* was, and is, enough to make a man unclean in *the sight of God*. If a man touches the work of sin he has become unclean. He that offendeth in one point is guilty of all. Who has not touched or come in contact with the fruit of sin? This uncleanness must be met with by the ashes, the fruit of the death of the holy One. All have sinned, all need the purifying merits of Christ's death. Only the defiled had any claim upon the ashes; only sinners have claim on the Saviour. Your uncleanness is your warrant to come to the fountain opened.

6. The sprinkling, or the acceptance of Christ. " The ashes and running water shall be put in a vessel, and sprinkled upon him that touched" (vs. 17, 18). The slaying of the sacrifice or the keeping of the ashes was not enough, there must be *contact*, and that through the water of the Word. The Spirit takes the things of Christ, and shows them, and applies them. The unclean must have faith in the ashes, or in the God who appointed them, or he would not receive them. So must there be faith in the *finished* work of Christ. The sprinkling is the imparting to the sprinkled all that the ashes mean—righteousness, acceptance, and cleansing from all sin The *running water* may represent the *moving* of the Spirit through the Word, revealing and applying the great salvation.

7. The unbelieving, or the neglecters of Christ. " But the man that shall not purify himself shall be cut off" (v. 20). And that man will have himself to blame for it. The effectual provision is free and within the reach of all. In despising or neglecting the ashes he despises God, and "cut off" from all communion and hope will be the doom of every Christ neglecter. "How shall we escape if we neglect so great salvation?" Nothing that defileth shall enter in. The unwashed would defile Heaven. The *neglecters* are " cut off" equally the same as the rejecters, and the "cutting off" is but the consequence of natural unfitness. " All that believe are justified from all things" (Acts 13. 39).

THE SIN OF MOSES, AND ITS FRUITS.

Numbers 20. 1-13.

"Speak gently to an erring one,
E'en if a deed of shame be done;
For else you but exasperate,
Perchance turn anger into hate."

LET him that is without sin cast the first stone. Judge not that ye be not judged. Troubles seem to come in crowds. In this chapter three sad events are recorded: 1, The death of Miriam (v. 1). 2, The transgression of Moses (v. 12). 3, The stripping of Aaron (v. 28). Three results of unbelief. With respect to Moses we shall look at—

1. The circumstances connected with his sin—

1. THE PLACE. Back to *Kadesh* where they had been thirty-nine years ago when they sent to spy the land, where many doubted and brought the doom of forty years wanderings upon them. Beware of old sins and barren places in your experience.

2. THE CONDITION OF THE PEOPLE. Discontented and faultfinding. "They chode with Moses," and murmured against the providence of God (vs. 3-5). This is always a source of intense trial to the faithful man of God.

3. THE HUMILITY OF MOSES. "Moses and Aaron fell upon their faces" (v. 6). Not as before the people, but before the Lord, and His glory appeared unto them, and a way of deliverance was revealed. "Thou shalt bring forth to them water out of the rock" (v. 8). Moses could not make the water, but at his *bidding* it was to come.

2. The nature of his sin. "Thou shalt *speak* unto the rock (v. 8). This was his commission, but instead of *speaking* he *smote the rock twice* (v. 11). When water was to be brought from the rock the *first* time, God

commanded Moses to *smite* the rock (Exod. 17. 6).
That Rock was Christ (1 Cor. 10. 4), and so in the
purpose of God He could only be *smitten* once, "He
suffered *once*." Further blessing or fresh outpourings
of His fulness comes to us by asking: "*Speak* ye unto
the Rock." We have here an incidental evidence of
the carefulness of Jehovah about those things which
were typical of His coming Son. The teaching in the
types is the teaching of the Holy Ghost. These things
are spiritually discerned.

In this sin of the servant of God there was—

1. DISOBEDIENCE. God said *speak*, but he *smote*, and
that twice over, as if there were *impatience* also in the act.
Perhaps he was allowing himself to be guided more by his
past experience than by the fresh Word of God. This is
always a danger to the servants of Christ. The means
used and blessed yesterday may not be the God-appointed
means to-day. Wait on the Lord.

2. SELFISH PASSION. "Hear now, ye rebels." It is
quite true that they were *rebels*, but calling them such
names in these circumstances did not improve matters.
His spirit was provoked, so that he spake unadvisedly with
his lips (Psa. 106. 33). The best of men are but men at
the best. The meekest man on the earth was not proof
against pride. Let him that thinketh he standeth take
heed lest he fall.

3. PRESUMPTION. "Must *we* fetch you water out of
the rock" (v. 10). It is very grieving to God when we
seek *our own* glory while doing His work. Note how
different it was with Peter and John in connection with
the healing of the lame man mentioned in Acts 3. 12.
"Do you wish *me* to show you the way of salvation?"
said a preacher to an anxious soul. Such *me's* are apt
to be magnified by the seeker so as to hide the Master.

Without ME you can do nothing. It is the Spirit that quickeneth.

There are two things that we must not forget in dealing with the sin of Moses: (1) *That he himself tells us of it.* He does not seek to hide from the eyes of others his own failings. For the glory of God and our good it is recorded. (2) That his failure through unbelief (v. 12) *did not alter the faithfulness of God.* "The water came out abundantly" (v. 11). The unbelief of some does not make the faith of God of none effect. As Christians we all come short of what we might be, but He abideth faithful. Bless His Name.

3. The fruit of his sin. It—

1. DISHONOURED THE LORD. " Because ye believed Me not, to *sanctify Me in the eyes* of the children of Israel" (v. 12). The Lord's Name is profaned by the unbelief and self-glorying acts of His people. " I will be sanctified in you before the heathen" (Ezek. 20. 41).

2. SHUT HIM OUT OF THE PROMISED POSSESSION. "Therefore ye shall not bring this congregation into the land which I have given them" (v. 12). Servant of God, one sin may shut you out of the enjoyment of a great privilege, one small cloud may hide from your gaze all the blue of Heaven. This is why many of the Lord's people are hindered from entering into the fulness of blessing and power in their service for Christ, there is sin in the camp. They could not enter in because of unbelief.

3. IS A SOLEMN WARNING TO US. Boast not thyself. It is possible to be calm and clear like the placid pool, and yet not be *clean* at the bottom, so that when the stone of slander or calumny is suddenly cast in the whole may become polluted. Cleanse Thou me from secret faults, and keep me in the hollow of Thy hand.

THE DEATH OF AARON,

PREFIGURING THE DEATH OF CHRIST.

Numbers 20. 23-29.

ON seeing a butterfly just escaping from its chrysalis an anonymous writer has said:

> " Why lovely insect dost thou stand,
>   And wave thy quivering wing;
> As half afraid thou wert aloft
>   On fields of air to spring ?
> But now has reach'd thy slender form
>   A sunbeam warm and bright,
> And instant thou hast upward sprung
>   *Towards the source of light.*"

The Christian never dies, 'tis only a rising up to the source of his life and being, lost in the brightness of His presence. Aaron in his calling and priestly character is a well-known and full-orbed type of Jesus Christ our Great High Priest. It is just what we might expect that he who resembled our Lord so closely in his life and work would also be like Him in the cause and manner of His death. Aaron's death was like Christ's, in that—

1. He knew of it beforehand. The Lord revealed to Aaron that he was to be gathered to his people (vs. 23, 24). Jesus knew the *time* and manner of His death long beforehand. Even the prophets had spoken of it. "My time is not yet." He came not to be ministered unto, but to *give His life* a ransom. On the mount of glory they spake of His decease (Luke 9. 31).

2. It was sudden. Aaron went up Mount Hor for the purpose of dying. No time of sickness is hinted at. It would seem as if he had been *cut off* suddenly. " The Messiah shall be cut off." " They marvelled that He was dead *already*." The soldiers expected Him to linger on for a while in His dying, but reproach *broke His heart* (Psa. 60 20).

3. It was because of sin. Aaron was cut off from entering the promised land "because he rebelled against My Word" (v. 24). Sin was imputed to him, and for sin he died. Christ died for sin, but not His own. The Lord laid upon Him the iniquity of us all. He bore our sins in *His own* body, in His very soul, which was exceedingly sorrowful even unto death, and which He poured out as an offering for sin.

4. He murmured not in prospect of it. It is most significant that through all this trying time Aaron's voice is never heard. Like the great Antitype *he opened not his mouth*. He for the joy that was set before Him endured the cross. No murmur ever escaped the lips or ever found conception in the heart of Jesus. Nevertheless, not My will, but Thine be done.

5. He died on a mount. "Take Aaron and his son and bring them up unto Mount Hor" (v. 25). It was to him a solemn climb, leaving all others behind him, to see their faces no more on earth. Jesus set His face like a flint to *go up* to Jerusalem, although He knew it was to accomplish the decease referred to by Moses and Elijah on the mount of transfiguration. As Moses lifted up the serpent in the wilderness, so must the Son of Man be lifted up. A handful of corn on the top of Mount Calvary, destined to fill the whole earth (Psa. 72. 16).

6. He was stripped. "Moses stripped Aaron of his garments" (v. 28). Christ also was stripped, and even to His shame. "They parted My garments among them, and for My vesture did they cast lots." This they did that the Scripture might be fulfilled, both in type and prophecy.

7. Two were with him in his death. There were only

three on that mount when Aaron died, one that was
exalted through his death and one who was not (v. 28).
On Mount Calvary, when Jesus died, there were *other two
with Him*, Jesus in the midst, and on either side one. One
was also blessed and exalted through His death: " To-day
shalt thou be with Me in Paradise."   It may not be lawful
to compare the other unbelieving thief to Moses, but, like
Moses, he was shut out because of unbelief (v. 12).

8. His work was continued after he was gone.
" His garments were *put upon* Eleazar his son" (v. 28).
His son perpetuated the work begun by his father, and this
by the commandment of the Lord. Aaron's mantle fell
on Eleazar, as afterwards the mantle of Elijah fell on
Elisha, and as further down the course of time the Spirit
that possessed the Lord Jesus Christ fell upon His heirs
in the upper room that they might continue the priestly
work of intercession after His departure. He hath made
us kings and *priests* unto God. Eleazar, the son of Aaron,
ministered *in his stead* (Deut. 10. 6). *We* beseech you in
Christ's stead be ye reconciled to God. This is our
priestly work. May the holy anointing be upon us for it.

THE BRAZEN SERPENT.
Numbers 21. 1-9.

" THE soul of the people was much discouraged because of
the way."   Those who follow the Lord because they know
it right, but *love* Him not, are sure to grow weary. A
rebellious heart makes it hard to follow. Sin always
causes the *compassing* instead of going straight up to
possession. It is the *walk* of life that brings out what we
really are. Dissatisfaction is sure to lead to rebellion.
If the heart is not satisfied in God it will wander elsewhere.
Backsliders, beware. Notice three things about Israel—

1. Their sin. It was threefold. It was a sin against—

1. GOD HIMSELF. They spake against God (v. 5). All sin is against God. We speak against God when we grumble about His providence, when we refuse to submit willingly to His workings. We speak against God when we show more sympathy for the worldling than the Christian, more interest in the things of this life than the life to come. When we prefer the pleasure of the flesh to the profit of the soul. He that is not for Me is against Me.

2. THE SERVANT OF GOD. They spake against Moses (v. 5). Those who hate Christ cannot love His people. "They persecuted Me, they will also persecute you." It is not desirable that *we* should be well spoken of by those who speak against our God. The measure of our oneness with Him will be the measure of our suffering for Him. If the blessings of Christ fall upon us because of our identity with Him, why not His reproaches. If I am spoken against by those who speak against Christ they bare witness that I am like Christ.

3. THE PROVISION OF GOD. "Our soul loatheth this light bread" (v. 5). The heart that is at enmity with God will loathe His bread. Christ is His bread for the world, but the world does loathe Him as light bread, just fit for children and sick people, but not for strong men in the battle of life. Many in their pride treat Christ as not sufficient for them, they want something else, and thus despise the provision of the grace of God.

2. Their sorrow. This sorrow that worketh repentance is seen in their—

1. CONFESSION. They came and said, "We have sinned, for we have spoken against the Lord" (v. 7). True sorrow will lead to true confession. There is little hope for the sinner until he makes this confession, "Father I have sinned." When sin is seen as against the Lord it

makes it exceeding sinful, and when this is believed confession comes easy and natural.   For a man to believe that
he is a sinner against God, and not to confess his guilt, is
just proving his determined enmity against Him.

2. PETITION. " Pray unto the Lord." The despised
servant now becomes the intercessor.   The persecuted
becomes the pleader for the persecutors.   In the evil day
they send for Daniel.   The way of access is still through
Him who is our Leader and Commander.   Without being
asked the Lord Jesus prayed, "Father, forgive them."
Stephen also made intercession for the transgressors.
When men are truly sensible of their guilt, then are they
conscious of their need of a Mediator.

3. AFFLICTION.   It was only when the Lord sent serpents among them (v. 6) that they came to themselves.
The rags and poverty of the prodigal made him think of
his father's home.   The fiery serpents of trial and trouble
have brought many to confession, when these have been sent
of God.   But the venom of the old serpent's bite has gone
deeper down than this, into the veins and arteries of a
sinful humanity.   Man is a poisoned being, his moral
nature even at its best is a polluted and a condemned thing.
For this there is but one remedy.   Regeneration.   Christ
crucified.

3. Their salvation.   It was—

1. DIVINELY APPOINTED.   The Lord said, " Make thee
a serpent," &c. (v. 8).   This provision, like the incarnation and death of Christ, could never have been suggested by man.   Man can invent no remedy for sin any
more than the condemned criminal could invent a plan
whereby the *law* can be set aside and himself justified.   He
that condemns must justify.   Salvation is of the Lord.
By a serpent they have been bitten, by one in the form of
a serpent they must be healed.   Through man came death,

by man also came the justification of life. The Man Christ Jesus who was *made in the likeness* of sinful flesh.

2. DIVINELY SUITABLE. "Set it upon a pole and *every one* that is bitten, when he looketh upon it, shall live" (v. 8). This serpent was lifted up for *every bitten one*. It was within the reach of all. The means of application was possessed by all that had eyes to look. If they had eyes that could see the tents and the hills, then with the same eyes could they see their salvation. If men have faith to believe in others, then with that same faith they can believe unto salvation. Christ has been lifted up high above every one else as the Friend and Saviour of men. "Look unto Me, and be ye saved" (Isa. 45. 22).

3. DIVINELY EFFECTUAL. "*Any man*, when he *beheld* the serpent of brass, he lived" (v. 9). None looked in vain. None perish that trust in Him. "*Any man*." It mattered not how many serpents had bitten him or how few; it mattered not whether he was rich or poor, the promise of God was, "He that looketh shall live." The same God has said, "He that believeth in Him hath everlasting life." And this salvation is as real to-day as the serpent-healing of old. It is not the *means* that saves, but the God of salvation. They believed God and looked, and He healed all their diseases.

> "Rejoice, rejoice, O all the earth,
> And break forth now with holy mirth;
> The serpent old is now, death—wounded,
> Hell's kingdom, lo! Christ's Cross confounded;
> "Whoever" is the embracing word,
> And Thou to it stand'st true, O Lord."

BALAAM'S PARABLE.
THE PRIVILEGES OF GOD'S PEOPLE.
Numbers 23. 18-24.

IT is rather a puzzle to grasp the character of Balaam; his moral nature looks like a tangled skein. He reminds one

of Bunyan's Mr. Face-both-ways. He seems to be typical
of those who have a great deal of spiritual knowledge, but
who are more of a hindrance than a help in the Lord's
work; large-headed but cold-hearted professors, who talk
much religion, but who keep company with the ungodly
(chap. 31. 8). God may use the mouth of a Balaam just
as He may use the mouth of his ass. He who can make an
ass to speak may make a false prophet to discern wondrous
things, and to say much that is most true and precious,
although they themselves are utter aliens to the experience
of them. This second parable of Balaam's opens with a
clear vindication of the *faithfulness of God.* '' God is not
a man that he should lie.'' Then he sees the people of
God as a—

1. Forgiven people. ''He hath not beheld iniquity in
Jacob'' (v. 21). Blessed are they whose sins are forgiven
(Rom. 4. 7, 8). Your sins are forgiven for His Name's
sake (1 John 2. 12). It is God who justifieth (Rom. 8. 33).

2. Delivered people. ''God brought them out of
Egypt'' (v. 22). Out of the house of bondage, out from
the rule of Pharaoh. He hath saved us from the wrath
to come (1 Thess. 1. 10); from the power of darkness
(Col. 1. 13); from sin (Rom. 6. 18); from this present
evil world (Gal. 1. 4).

3. Joyful people. ''God is with them, and the shout
of a king is among them'' (v. 21). Well may we be joyful
in our King. All power in Heaven and earth is His, and
He hath said, Lo, I am with you alway. Rejoice in His
presence, in His light and love, in His power and faithfulness. It will be well with the cause of Christ when the
ungodly hear the shout of the King of Glory in the midst of
His people. When the Gospel is preached in the *power of
the Holy Spirit* there will be heard the unmistakable shout
of the invisible but ever-present King of Saints.

4. Protected people. "There is no enchantment against Jacob" (v. 23). The character of God's people is proof against all gossiping conjurers. The well-springs of the Christian's life and enjoyments cannot be poisoned by the enemy. They live in the presence of Him who will not listen to the envious talebearer. Miriam and Aaron may speak against Moses, but it is only to their own hurt. His goodness is great to them that fear Him (Psa. 31. 19).

5. Witnessing people. "It shall be said of Israel, What hath God wrought?" (v. 23). Their *separated* life was a witness for God. The riches of His grace is seen in His kindness towards us. In turning our captivity He hath filled our mouth with laughter and our tongue with singing. What hath God wrought? He hath done great things for us whereof we are glad (Psa. 126. 1-3).

6. Courageous people. "Behold, the people shall rise up as a great lion" (v. 24). This fearless king of beasts is the chosen emblem of Christian courage. There are many who *crouch* as a lion, but few who *rise up* for the truth as it is in Jesus, and spring upon those evils which are robbing the Church of her life and power. Men after John Bunyan's Mr. Great-Heart are much needed at the front (Prov. 30. 29, 30).

7. Victorious people. "He shall not lie down until he eat of the prey" (v. 24). Behold, the lion of the tribe of Judah hath prevailed, and the lion's whelp shall share the spoil (Gen. 49. 9). We are more than conquerors through Him who loved us. This is the victory that overcometh the world, even our faith. Let not thy soul lie down to rest until ye eat the joy of victory over all your sins and over all your circumstances. All His own shall yet be "more than conquerors" (Rom. 8. 37).

SEEING BUT NOT POSSESSING.

Numbers 27. 12-17.

" As the sunshine in the clouds,
  As the foam-bells in the floods,
  As the fragrance in the flower,
  As the dew-mown grass's dower;
    Thou dost, Lord, in love assuage
    Trouble's sorest, keenest edge.''

THE keen edge was taken off Moses' disappointment when God in love gave him a sight of the land into which he was hindered from entering because of the sin he committed in rebelling against the Word of the Lord. Moses, as representing the law, could not bring the people into the promised land. What the law *could not do*, in that it was weak through the flesh, God hath accomplished in the sending of His Son in the *likeness of sinful flesh* (Rom. 8. 3). The law was given by Moses, grace and truth came by Jesus Christ. We shall take note of his—

1. **Assuring vision.** " The Lord said unto Moses, Get thee up into Mount Abarim, and see the land which I have given'' (v. 12). If Moses could not enter the land, he had his faith confirmed by *sight* that the good and pleasant land was there. It was—

1. A LAND OF BLESSING Often spoken of, but as yet unpossessed, and typical of the exceeding great and precious promises given us in Christ Jesus, of which many Christians have heard much, but how few have taken full possession.

2. A LAND BEYOND. Moses saw it from Mount Abarim. Abarim means *regions beyond*. He had a very clear and greatly enlarged vision afterwards from the top of Pisgah (Deut. 34. 1-3). O how great are the '' regions beyond'' of Christian possibilities in the present life. Truly the land is great, but God was the Giver. All are yours, and ye are Christ's (1 Cor. 3. 22, 23).

2. Melancholy failure. "When thou hast seen it thou shalt be gathered unto thy people, for ye rebelled against My commandment" (vs. 13, 14). He failed because of—

1. UNBELIEF. He rebelled against His *word* by smiting the rock instead of *speaking* to it (Num. 20. 8-12). How often in spirit have we done this same thing? The Lord has said only *believe*, but we have imagined that something more was needed, some worldly wisdom or fleshly energy to give emphasis to His word. Our smiting instead of speaking only serves to reveal our unbelief. There are many blessings into which we cannot enter because of unbelief.

2. GOD-USURPING PRIDE. God charges him with refusing "to sanctify Me before their eyes" (v. 14). Moses said, " Shall *we* fetch water from the rock for you?" For the moment he stepped into the place of the Lord, and robbed Him of His honour before the eyes of the people. All pride and self-exaltation is an attempt to dethrone the Lord. Self-interest will always shut out the Lord from the enjoyments of the fuller Christian life. Ponder deeply the words of our Lord when He said, "Father, I thank Thee that Thou hast *hid* these things from the wise and prudent, and hast revealed them unto babes" (Matt. 11. 25).

3. Magnanimous action. " Moses said, Let the Lord set a man over this congregation, which may lead them, and *bring them in*" (vs. 15-17). If he cannot enter into the land himself he is most anxious that the others should. He is intensely desirous that his successor should be more successful in this matter than himself. This prayer of his reveals—

1. AN ENTIRE SUBMISSION TO THE WILL OF GOD. No grumble escapes his lips. If the honour of leading the people into the possession offered them is not to be his, then "Good is the will of the Lord." He did not fall

into that other common sin of getting *huffy*, a plague that sometimes breaks out among Christian workers, affecting both preachers and people alike.

2. A DEEP INTEREST IN THE PEOPLE OF GOD. He would be thankful to know that others were to inherit more than himself, if the Lord was to be glorified in it. In the good land of promise, the unsearchable riches of Christ, freely given us in Him, there is enough to make a satisfying *lot* for every child of God. O that all Christian leaders were as anxious as Moses to see the people of God entering into their inheritance in the Lord. But, like Moses, we must first at least *see* the land for ourselves before we can be really concerned about the enriching of the children of God with the fulness that is in Christ for them. Yet blessed are they that have not seen, and yet have believed.

CHARACTERISTICS OF A HEAVEN-SENT LEADER.

Numbers 27. 18-23.

" Workman after workman dies,
This Thy Church, Lord, sorely tries,
As in tears she stricken stands,
Sadly missing " vanished hands,"
Wills strenuous, and brave hearts
Ever ready to take their parts.
O God, wilt fresh trust us give?
Workmen die, but Thou dost live;
In deepest desolation
Thou Thy work dost carry on."

MOSES has just had intimation of his removal through death, and the Lord singles out Joshua as the one who was to take his place and fill up his part. God buries His workmen but carries on His work. There are some things mentioned here in connection with the call of Joshua that might help us to search our hearts as preachers or teachers of the Word of God, and to see whether we as the servants of the Lord are after this Divine order. He was—

1. Called by the Lord. The Lord said, "Take thee Joshua, and lay thine hand upon him" (v. 18). This position was not his own choosing until the mind of God was unmistakably plain. It is His to *thrust* out labourers into the field. Pray ye the Lord of the harvest.

2. Filled with the Spirit. He was doubtless one of the seventy who shared the Spirit of power that rested on Moses (Num. 11. 17). But by the laying on of the hands of Moses he was *filled* with the spirit of wisdom (Deut. 34. 9). All Christians have a measure of the Spirit, but all are not filled with the Spirit. In the times of the old dispensation all did not get the offer of this filling, but *now* God wishes none to be without it. "Be ye filled with the Spirit" (Eph. 5. 18).

3. Honoured by the Lord's representative. "Thou shalt put some of thine honour upon him" (v. 20). The honour which God put upon Moses was shared by him. This honour have all the saints. Did not a greater than Moses say, "The glory which Thou gavest Me, I have given them?" (John 17. 22). The spirit of Elijah doth rest on Elisha. *Endued* with the power of the Holy Spirit is the token that we are in the true apostolic succession.

4. Accepted by the Lord's people. "That all the congregation may be obedient" (v. 20). They answered Joshua, saying, "According as we hearkened unto Moses, so will we hearken unto you" (Joshua 1. 16, 17). The power of God by the Spirit means having authority, and such authority that the children of God will recognise as from above. When a man speaks in the power of the Holy Ghost others will be conscious that they are hearkening to the Divine voice. As they would listen to Jesus, so will they listen to such.

5. Guided by Divine light. "He shall stand before Eleazar the priest, who shall ask counsel for him, after the judgment of Urim before the Lord'' (v. 21). The *Urim* signifies "lights," and denotes the wisdom that comes from above (1 Sam. 28. 6). He was emphatically " taught of God.'' This is another mark of a Heaven-sent teacher; he does not depend on the wisdom of men. He is frequently found consulting the Urim of the Holy Scriptures. The strength of his yeas and nays comes from these. His difficulties and all perplexing problems are settled in the light of this Urim.

6. Successful in his work. " They shall come in, both he and all the children of Israel *with him*'' (v. 21). He was called and empowered to bring the people into the land of promise, and he brought them in without fail. His promise was fulfilled. ''As I was with Moses, so will I be with thee'' (Joshua 3. 7). His presence always secures success. If God is to work in us and through us that which is pleasing in His sight, then we must in spirit, soul, and body be perfectly yielded up to Him. The secret of true and lasting success lies in *His will* being *done in us*. There is no higher attainment than this, and it may be yours, and yours continuously.   ———

A CALL FOR UNITED EFFORT.
Numbers 32. 1-33.

'' O Lord, whome'er Thy grace has blessed,
Causing Thy Name to be confessed;
Wilt Thou not quicken them to see
That each one service owes to Thee?
Enkindle in *each* heart such flame
As shall consume all coward shame.
The time is short, and life is flying,
And all around us souls are dying;
Stir up, O Lord, each heart and will,
And with Thine own compassion fill.''

THE children of Reuben and the children of Gad sought their inheritance on *this* side of Jordan. But Moses said, Shall *your brethren* go to war, and shall ye sit here? (v. 6). From this chapter we may learn that—

1. All the Lord's people have a common cause.
Though there were twelve tribes, yet were they all *brethren*
(v. 6). The weakening or strengthening of one was the
weakening or strengthening of the whole. So is it in the
cause of our Lord and Saviour. " I have called you
friends." "Are ye not all brethren?" Ought not each
one to be interested in whatever concerns the kingdom
of God?

**2. Putting self-interest first is a great danger to
the Lord's work.** " The Reubenites said, Let this land
be given thy servants for a possession, and bring us not over
Jordan" (vs. 1-5). They saw that the land of Jazer and
Gilead was just such as they wanted, so they desired there
and then to settle down and let the others look out for
themselves. It is a melancholy sight to see Christians
settling down in the knowledge of salvation, or in the
enjoyment of the doctrine of the higher Christian life, and
falling out of the ranks of aggressive *workers*.

3. Selfish interest discourages others. " Wherefore
discourage ye the heart of the children of Israel from going
over into the land?" (v. 7). There are different ways by
which we may discourage our brethren in the pursuit of
a deeper and more enlarged experience of the fulness of God
in Christ. We may do it by bringing a slander on this
good land through our own unbelief and poverty-stricken
lives as Christians, or by magnifying the difficulties in the
way of entering into the possession of it (Deut. 1. 22-28),
or by our own self-complacent indifference to their
spiritual growth in grace.

**4. Seeking the good of others is helping on the
cause of God.** " Shall your brethren go to war, and shall
ye sit here?" (v. 6). It is a great privilege to be able to
help our brethren into their rightful inheritance in Christ.
In these present days there is an intense longing in the
hearts of multitudes of the Lord's people for an *enlargement*

of the coasts of their spiritual experience. It is a question
if ever there was a time when there was a more crying need
for pure Bible teaching. There may be much sermon
preaching without the commanding power of the revealed
mind of God as contained in the Scripture of truth. As the
days go on it may be that teachers of the Word will be in
greater demand than evangelists.

5. Doing nothing is a sin against the Lord. '' If ye
will not do so, behold, ye have sinned against the Lord,
and be sure your sin will find you out'' (v. 23). The sin
of idleness, or of neglecting to do our part in the great
campaign of the Church's work, is a sin against the
Lord that will be sure to find us out. It betrays itself in
cowardliness, indifference, worldliness, and finally in
open sin. Why stand ye here all the day idle? Do you
say no man hath hired us? Hath not the Lord hired you
in *purchasing* you with His Blood?

**6. Devotion to the interests of the kingdom of God
secures present blessing.** '' If ye will go armed before
the Lord until He hath driven out His enemies, this land
shall be your possession'' (vs. 20-22). The sons of Reuben
and of Gad were to have their possession *this side of Jordan*
on condition that they passed over and helped their
brethren into their lot of inheritance. The reason why
many Christians have not entered into a soul-satisfying
portion in this present life is because they have ceased to
help others. There is no class of the disciples of Jesus so
happy as the *workers*. Those workers, of course, who are
not seeking now their own, but the good of others at the
command of the Lord. '' Bear ye one another's burdens,
and so fulfil the law of Christ'' (Gal. 6. 2).

> '' Pleasure is only half pleasure unshared,
> O, forth then, my brother, share thine!
> Pleasure when shared is a *treasure prepared*,
> Excelling aught drawn from the mine.''

HOW TO INHERIT GOD'S LAND OF PROMISE.
Numbers 33. 50-56.

" The way is long by which I hie,
Flags my spirit wearily;
Let Thy gracious hand me grasp,
Let my trembling hand Thine clasp;
We are tired, my heart and I,
Ah! but, Jesus, Thou art nigh.''

As the children of Israel were often " discouraged because of the way," so there are still many who are weary and tired seeking the better land of promise offered in Jesus Christ His Son. It is a land of rest and refreshing that can only be entered into by faith. Let us think again of—

1. The character of the land. The land of Canaan is not so much a type of Heaven as it is of our present inheritance in Christ Jesus. It was—

1. A LAND OF PLENTY. "The Lord thy God bringeth thee into a good land. A land of brooks, of fountains, and depths. A land of wheat, barley, and vines, of oil, olive, and honey. A land wherein thou shalt eat bread without scarceness, *thou shalt not lack anything in it*" (Deut. 8. 7-9). What a figurative description of the fulness of Christ! O the depths of His riches (Phil. 4. 19).

2. A GOD-GIVEN LAND. " The land which the Lord thy God giveth thee" (Deut. 8. 10). "God so loved the world, that He gave His only begotten Son." He has given us His Son, and in Him all the riches of His grace. The unsearchable riches of Christ. What a gift! "All are yours, and ye are Christ's; and Christ is God's" (1 Cor. 4. 23).

3. A LAND OFFERED TO ALL HIS PEOPLE. The land of *promise* was for every Israelite. There was in it an ample portion for every individual. There is enough in Christ for every Christian, yea, for every creature under Heaven. Whosoever will may take the water of life freely.

2. The way to possess the land. There had to be—

1. A BELIEVING OF THE PROMISE. It is called the land of promise. The promise of God had to be accepted, His word must be trusted. This is the promise which He hath promised us, eternal life, and this life is in His Son. This is the work of God that ye *believe*. They could not enter in because of unbelief.

2. AN ENTERING INTO IT. The land could not be inherited by them until they were *in* it. They had to claim it with their *feet* (Joshua 1.3). We must be *in Christ* before we can become *heirs* of God. We are accepted in Christ, and here Christ is made of God unto us wisdom, righteousness, sanctification, and redemption. Ye are complete in Him, perfectly filled up, abundantly satisfied. "The Lord is my portion," saith my soul. He is the lot of mine inheritance. My cup runneth over (Psa. 16. 15; 23. 6).

3. A DRIVING OUT OF THE ENEMY. "Then shall ye drive out all the inhabitants of the land" (vs. 52, 53). The enemies that would hinder our souls from entering into the full possession of our inheritance in Christ are very numerous and subtle, often feigning to be friendly. No quarter was to be given. Every native had to be driven *out*. Every *thought* must be brought into captivity to Christ, and every desire of the flesh subdued.

3. The warning against failure.

1. FAILURE IS POSSIBLE. "*If ye will not* drive out the inhabitants" (v. 55). It is to be feared that multitudes of the Lord's people fail here. They enter the land, that is, they accept the Lord Jesus Christ as their Saviour, but they fail to drive out the *old man* with his lusts.

2. COMPROMISE IS DANGEROUS. "Those which ye let remain shall be pricks in your eyes, and thorns in your sides" (v. 55). The enemy must have no place in the camp of the saints. Give no heed to the reasoning of the

carnal mind, let not your eye spare thêm. These *questionable* things that at times act as thorns in the conscience, bringing discomfort, or as pricks in the eye, hindering from seeing things in their true light, *drive them out.* Bring out the Agags. Compromising with the evil within, or with the world without, mars the soul from enjoying its possessions in Christ.

3. DISOBEDIENCE IS FATAL. " If ye will not drive them out, moreover it shall come to pass that I shall do *unto you* as I thought to do unto them" (v. 56). That is, if you will not put away every evil thing out of your life, and be obedient to the word and will of the Lord after you have come to Him for justification and life, the joy of salvation and the blessings that are in Christ will lose all their preciousness and attractiveness to you. You will be driven out of the enjoyment of spiritual things in heavenly places. Ye cannot serve God and mammon. If ye be willing and obedient ye shall eat the good of the land, but if ye refuse and rebel ye shall be devoured.

THE CITIES OF REFUGE.
Numbers 35.

`` The child that to its mother clings
Lies not all safely on her breast
Till she her arms around it flings,
Sweetly caressing and caressed.
Ev'n so, my God, Thy mighty arms,
Not aught of mine, shield me from harms."

DOUBTLESS the apostle had these cities of refuge in his mind when he wrote these words in Hebrews 6: " We have a strong consolation who have *fled for refuge* to lay hold upon the hope set before us." So the cities of refuge are typical of the hope *set before us* in Jesus Christ. "*A man* shall be an *hiding place*." As such they were—

1. **Appointed by God.** " The Lord spake unto Moses, saying," &c. (v. 1). Him hath God exalted to be a

Prince and a Saviour (Acts 5. 31). "This is My beloved
Son, in whom I am well pleased." A prophet chosen
out of the people.

2. In charge of the Levites (v. 6). The Levites had
charge of the holy things in connection with the worship
of God, and may represent the ambassadors for Christ,
into whose hands the Gospel of salvation has been committed, as taught in 1 Corinthians 5. 20.

3. Set apart for manslayers. "Which ye shall
appoint for the *man*slayers" (v. 6). O Israel, thou hast
destroyed *thyself*—a manslayer. The man who commits
sin is a manslayer. All have sinned, all are in need of
a place of refuge. How many are killing *themselves*
unwittingly?

4. To be entered in haste. "That he may flee
thither" (v. 6). There is great danger in delay. Death
may overtake the sinner before he reaches the refuge
that is in Christ. Escape for thy life. Behold, *now* is
the accepted time. I flee to Thee to hide me.

5. A protection against a lawful avenger. "Cities
for refuge from the avenger" (v. 12). The avenger of the
murdered one had the authority of God to kill the murderer
outside the cities of refuge. The avenger fitly represents
the law, which cannot save, but has power to kill. By
the deeds of the law shall no flesh be justified.

6. In convenient places. "Three cities on this side
of Jordan, and three in the land of Canaan" (v. 14).
Within easy reach of all, and were located in conspicuous
spots, so that they might be easily seen at the distance.
The Gospel of Christ is to be preached to every creature.
"Wisdom crieth without, she uttereth her voice in
the streets, she crieth in the chief places of concourse"
(Prov. 1. 20-28). "Behold the Lamb of God" (John 1. 29).

7. Open for all. "For *every one* that killeth any person" (v. 15). The stranger as well as the children of Israel had the privilege of the refuge. The salvation of Christ is offered to all. There is room enough in this atoning death for every guilty, trusting soul. If *any man* thirst let him come unto *Me*. By Me if any man enter in he shall be saved.

8. For all those who were sorry for their deeds. These cities afforded no shelter to the *wilful* murderer. " He shall surely be put to death" (v. 16). They were appointed for those who had killed *unawares*, and the man who had killed his neighbour unawares would certainly be a very sorrowful man. The death of Christ, apart from *repentance* and faith, cannot shelter the guilty soul. Repent, and believe the Gospel.

9. Places of justice and judgment. " The congregation shall judge between the slayer and the avenger of blood, according to these judgments" (v. 24). There is a very solemn thought here. To become our refuge Christ must take our place. The just judgments of God were meted out to Him, and the question of sin eternally settled. So that He is now a just God and a Saviour. "I have betrothed thee unto Me *in righteousness*" (Hosea 2. 19).

10. Abiding places for the slayer. " He shall *abide* in it unto the death of the high priest." This is a precious thought. The life of the slayer who had fled to the city for refuge was henceforth *connected* with the life of the high priest, *who was anointed with the holy oil* (v. 25). As long as the high priest lived, he lived in the place of safety. As long as Christ our Great High Priest lives, we shall live by Him. Because I live, ye shall live also. Abide in Me. The language of David is very beautiful in this connection. "Abide thou with me, fear not; for he that seeketh my life, seeketh thy life; but with me thou shalt be in safeguard" (1 Sam. 22. 23).

EXPOSITORY OUTLINES.
New Testament.

WHY TEMPT YE ME?
Mark 12. 13-17.

Tempted Thyself, Lord, Thou dost know
How hard 'tis in *the way* to go;
How foes without and foes within
Still hold us captive unto sin;
How, even with Thy full grace given,
Earth too, too oft vails Thy pure Heaven.
O break our chain, Lord, set us free,
Thou tempted once, us tempted see.''

THE Lord had just spoken a parable that cut some of them to the quick (v. 12). So they sent a few picked Pharisees to '' catch Him in His words,'' but they themselves are caught. The Word of God is quick and powerful, even to catch word-catchers. It is a discerner of the thoughts and intents of the heart. Observe here that even in scorn the truth may be spoken.

1. A truthful confession. These faultfinders unconsciously said what was true as to—

1. HIS CHARACTER. '' We know that Thou art true?'' (v. 14). His words were true. His heart was true. His motives were as pure as light. He is the truth. When Pilate asked, What is truth? the answer might have been given: The life and testimony of Christ. But they loved the darkness (John 3. 19).

2. HIS COURAGE. '' Thou carest for no man, and regardest not the person of men'' (v. 14). He cared not for the power or threatenings of man, but He loved their souls, and cared for the poor, humble, needy. The many waters of hatred and opposition could not quench His zeal to do the will of His Father in Heaven. May such holy boldness be ours.

3. HIS MISSION. " Thou teachest the way of God in truth" (v. 14). Nicodemus confessed that He was a Teacher come from God (John 3. 2). He came from God to teach us the way to God. Never man spake like this Man. His way is God's way, and there is no other. " I am the Way, no man *cometh to the Father* but by Me." Coming any other way is coming to shame and confusion and disappointment, but not to the Father.

2. A critical question. " Is it lawful to give tribute to Caesar, or not?" (v. 14). This was perhaps the most puzzling question that they in their wisdom and hate could devise. If He answers yes, then they will charge Him as a traitor to His nation. If He says no, then they will report Him at once to the Roman tribune as a teacher of sedition. How glad some people would be to get the Lord in a dilemma, but the spirit of wisdom in Christ Jesus is able to quench all the subtle darts of the evil one. It is not ye that speak, but the spirit of your Father which is in you. Greater is He that is in you than he that is in the world.

3. A discerning mind. " But He, *knowing* their hypocrisy, said unto them, Why tempt ye Me?" (v. 15). The eyes of Christ are as Heaven's searchlights, before which nothing can be hid. In coming to Christ as they did, with words of flattery on their lips, they only proved their ignorance of Him whom they professed to know. Had they known that they were standing before the heart-searcher they would certainly have preferred the darkness to such piercing light. Be not deceived, God is not mocked. Let your prayers be honest before Him, or they will prove self-condemning. "The Lord looketh upon the heart" (1 Sam. 16. 7).

4. A suggestive request. " Bring Me a penny that I

may see it.'' If He, who was rich, but for our sakes became
poor, had had a penny in His own possession He would
not likely have asked them to *bring* Him a penny. A
penniless Saviour, yet making many rich. This is not
after the fashion of the world, but there is a world of
consolation in the thought. We may be rich in faith,
bringing glory to God, even when we cannot show a penny.

5. A conclusive answer. ''Whose is this image and
superscription?'' They said, Caesar's. Jesus answered,
'' Render to Caesar the things that are Caesar's, and to
God the things that are God's'' (vs., 16, 17). The *image*
of Caesar on the coin was evidence enough that it was
connected with Caesar. *Likeness* proves relationship.
Those who have the image of the world and the devil
stamped upon their lives declare that they belong to the
world and the devil, and are rendering themselves to
such. Has the image of Christ been stamped upon your
soul? Then render to God the things which are God's.
This is your reasonable service (Rom. 12. 1).

THE FIRST COMMANDMENT.
Mark 12. 28-34.

'' Thy love, Lord, is serene,
   No tumult marks its flow;
Calm as that sea was seen
   When forth Thy Word did go.
O that my love to Thee
   Show'd Thy tranquillity.''

THE love of God is stronger than death, and as calm and
steady as the mountains that are round about Jerusalem.
The Pharisees had come to catch Him in His word (v. 13),
then came the Sadducees to entangle Him in His teaching
of the resurrection (v. 18), then this lawyer comes with the
disputed question as to which was the chiefest among all
the commandments. We certainly are much obliged to
them for their questions, for each one gives the Saviour a

fresh occasion to emphasise some things which we all need to know. In this answer we are forcibly reminded that *love* is the fulfilling of the law.

1. The question asked. "Which is the first commandment of all?" It betrays—

1. SOME CURIOSITY. It seems to have been a disputed point among the scribes as to which of the commandments was the most important. Although it looked like asking which of the ten links of a chain, or which member of the body is of chiefest consequence, yet how graciously the Lord deals with even such.

2. SOME ANXIÉTY. Beneath the mere cavil the Master seems to see in the scribe an earnest desire after *truth*, which brought him to the very door of the kingdom (v. 34). Deal tenderly with questioners. The Holy Spirit may be at work.

2. The answer given. All the Lord's answers to questions are polished shafts from the quiver of the Almighty. In this reply we have a call to—

1. ATTENTION. "Hear, O Israel" (v. 29). The answer is not for this scribe alone, but for all professed seekers after truth. Well may we *hear* when He speaks, who can meet and answer the deepest longings of the human soul. "Hearken diligently unto Me, and eat ye that which is good" (Isa. 55. 2).

2. FAITH IN THE UNITY OF GOD. "The Lord our God is one Lord" (v. 29). The great mystery of the Trinity is clearly revealed, but never explained (2 Cor. 13. 14). Like the mystical union of the Church, and of the individual believer with Himself, it is received by faith. All *one* in Christ.

3. PERFECT SURRENDER. "Thou shalt love the Lord with all thy heart, all thy soul, all thy mind, and with all

thy strength" (v. 3). This is a demand made upon: 1, The whole of our *affections*, "all thy heart." 2, The whole *life*, "all thy soul." 3, The whole realm of *thought*, "all thy mind." 4, The whole *energy* of our being, "all thy strength." A whole burnt-offering unto God. This, the first commandment, is fulfilled in one word: LOVE. That love of God in our hearts that *constrains* us to yield ourselves completely unto Him (1 John 5. 3).

4. BROTHERLY KINDNESS. "The second is *like*, Thou shalt love thy neighbour as thyself" (v. 31). It is very significant that our Lord links the first and second together, making them one commandment of equal importance. The love of God, and love to God, *must* manifest itself in love to others (1 John 4. 11, 12). If a man love not his brother whom he hath seen, how can he love God whom he hath not seen? (1 John 4. 20; Eph. 4. 32).

3. The effect produced. There was—

1. ACQUIESCENCE. "The scribes said, Well, Master, Thou hast said the truth" (v. 32). It is quite possible to admire the wisdom and character of Christ and yet not to enter into the power and blessedness of His life. A mere mental assent to the truth taught by the Saviour is not salvation.

2. COMMENDATION. "When Jesus saw that he answered discreetly, He said unto him, Thou art not far from the kingdom of God" (v. 34). He evidently had an intellectual apprehension of the meaning of the Lord's words. His teaching was so far understood that he had in thought come to the very threshold of the kingdom of God, theoretically near, but experimentally outside. His reason and conscience were both on the side of the truth.

3. A COMING SHORT. "Not far from the kingdom." These are encouraging, yet O how mournful the words! "*Not far*," but not near enough to be inside. The mind

enlightened, but the heart unyielded; the conscience convicted, the reason convinced, but the *will* still stubborn and unsubdued. Ye will not come to Me that ye might have life. He will have a willing people in the day of His power. Not far from the cities of refuge was no guarantee of safety. ———

THINGS TO COME
Mark 13

"O Thou blessed Holy Ghost,
Pleading we dare Thee accost;
Hast Thou not from days of old
Of His second coming told?
Hast Thou not by word and trope,
Given Thy Church this mighty hope
How long till Thou, the Crucified,
Take the world for which Thou'st died."

As Jesus went out of the temple, one of the disciples could not help, as he passed, commenting on the greatness of the stones and of the *buildings*. The Master answered, Seest thou *these* buildings, there shall not be left one stone upon another. And immediately it would seem that the thoughts of the Master went out to other great stones and to other buildings in connection with God's great purposes in the ages to come. Stones more costly and a building more wonderful, from which no stone will ever be thrown down. Ye are God's building, fitly framed together, growing into an holy temple in the Lord. While the disciples sat with Him in the mount having a private talk, they asked these two questions: When shall these things be? What shall be the sign? While the remarks about the temple *originated* these queries, the answers of Christ stretch far beyond the destruction of Jerusalem to the coming of the Son of Man with great power and glory (v. 26). It is impossible to believe that all the signs mentioned here were given before the sack of the city by the Romans (vs. 10, 24-27). The teaching of Christ in this chapter may be taken as a reply to these two questions, *When* shall these things be? and, What shall be the *sign* when all these things shall be fulfilled? (v. 4).

1. What are the signs? Christ speaks of *them* as one continued unbroken sign, extending from the time He spoke right down till the day of His appearing again the second time. There will be—

1. FALSE PROPHETS (vs. 5, 6). Men who will seek to deceive with vain words (Eph. 5. 6). Messengers of Satan.

2. WARS AND RUMOURS OF WARS (v. 7). These we assuredly have always with us, they are a testimony that the King of kings and Prince of Peace is not yet seated on the throne of David.

3. HATED FOR HIS SAKE (vs. 9-13). This hatred to the Lord's people, that leads to imprisonment and terrible trial, is ascribed to the work of the devil (Rev. 2. 10). The Millennium is not yet.

4. NATURAL AFFECTION PERVERTED (v. 12). A man's enemies shall be those of his own household (Micah 7. 6). Because iniquity shall abound, the love of many shall wax cold (Matt. 24. 10, 11).

5. UNPARALLELED AFFLICTION (v. 19). This same time of awful trial is predicted in Daniel 12. 1, repeated in Joel 2. 2, and explained more fully in Luke 21. 24-28.

6. DECEITFUL WONDER-WORKERS (v. 22). Demon-possessed men, claiming the homage of Christ, whose coming is after the working of Satan, with all power and signs and lying wonders, captivating them that perish (1 Thess. 2. 9, 10). The presence of antichrists declare the *absence* of Christ.

7. CHANGES IN THE NATURAL HEAVENS (v. 24). There will be darkness and gloominess, clouds and thick darkness, distress and desolation (Zeph. 1. 14, 15). These are the infallible signs given by Him who is the Truth.

2. When shall these things be? We would note that—

1. THE EXACT DAY CANNOT BE KNOWN (v. 32). As it was in the days of Noah, so shall also the coming of the Son of Man be. The *fact* of the coming flood was revealed, but the moment the *door* would be shut no man could tell.

2. THE CERTAINTY OF HIS COMING CANNOT BE DENIED (vs. 30, 31). He *will* come again, and the generation of the Jewish people shall not pass away as a distinct nationality till all these things be fulfilled. "Ye are My witnesses."

3. THE GOSPEL IS TO BE FIRST PREACHED UNTO ALL NATIONS (v. 10). It is to be preached unto all *nations* for a witness (Matt. 24. 14). It would seem that even in the apostles' day this was accomplished (Rom. 10. 18; Col. 1. 6-23).

4. THE ABOMINATION OF DESOLATION WILL BE SET UP (v. 14). This prediction is found in Daniel 9. 25-27, and must be fulfilled before His appearing.

5. THE FIG TREE MUST FIRST BLOSSOM (vs. 28, 29). The fig tree doubtless denotes the Jewish nation, who are showing remarkable activity in the so-called "Zion movement."

6. THE GREAT CRISIS IS HIS PERSONAL APPEARING. "Then shall ye see the Son of Man" (vs. 26, 27). This *same Jesus* shall so come in like manner as ye have seen Him go (Acts 1. 11; 1 Thess. 4. 16; Rev. 1. 7).

3. What is to be our present attitude? Here the language of the Master is very urgent, condemning thereby the apathy, indifference, and unbelief of many with respect to His coming again. We are to be—

1. TRUSTFUL. "Take heed, behold I have *foretold* you all things" (v. 23). Is it possible for a Christian to continue growing in grace, and in the knowledge of our Lord and Saviour, who wilfully ignores this solemn and timely warning?

2. WATCHFUL. This is urged three times over in verses 33-37. How many are fast asleep with regard to His coming. Watching keeps awake in sleepy times.

3. PRAYERFUL. '' Take heed, watch and pray'' (v. 33). The *watcher* will surely become an intercessor. Faith in His coming will have a wholesome effect on the life.

THE MASTER AND HIS SERVANTS.
Mark 13. 33-37.

''Many men seek themselves in seeking God,
And serve Him, that they may serve themselves of Him.''
       —VENNING.

THE subtleness of self is almost fathomless. Our Lord in closing this outline of coming events sums it up in a little parable concerning Himself, which reveals the present relationship that exists between Him and His servants in view of His coming again. Observe—

1. What He has done.

1. TAKEN A FAR JOURNEY (v. 34). This journey is His going into Heaven. '' If I go away I will come again.'' It was a *far* journey in that it was from weakness and shame to power and glory, from humiliation and death to glorification and resurrection life, from a God-hating earth to a God-honouring Heaven.

2. LEFT HIS HOUSE. The temple was the recognised house of God, but the people know not the day of His visitation. They cast Him out; now He could say, '' Your house is left unto you desolate'' (Matt. 23. 38).

3. GIVEN AUTHORITY TO HIS SERVANTS. This the Master did when He sent down the Holy Spirit from the presence of the Father upon His waiting servants in the upper room on the day of Pentecost. This power every servant must have if he would speak with *authority*, and not like the self-ordained scribes.

4. GIVEN TO EVERY MAN HIS WORK. Every son of God

should be a servant, and every servant may have his work from the Master. To *every man* his work. Is every man doing his Christ-appointed work? If you don't do your God-given work it will remain undone through all eternity, and may be to you an everlasting reproach. "What wilt Thou have me to do?" (Acts 9. 6).

5. COMMANDED THE PORTER TO WATCH. The porter is the Holy Spirit, who opens the door to Jesus as the Shepherd of the sheep, by resting upon Him when baptised in Jordan (John 10. 2, 3). He is *watching* the interests of Jesus Christ on earth, and looking and longing for His coming. "The Spirit and the Bride say, Come" (Rev. 22. 16, 17).

2. What He will do.

1. COME AGAIN (v. 35). He has left His house, but it is only for an indefinite season. "If I go I will come again." As servants we are occupying till He come. At the Lord's Supper we show forth His death *till* He come.

2. COME AS LORD (v. 35, R.V.). Not in the lowly humiliation of His first coming, but as King of kings and Lord of lords, to reward His faithful servants, and take vengeance on them who obey not the Gospel.

3. COME SUDDENLY. "Ye know not when the Master cometh" (v. 35). The very uncertainty of the time of His coming is surely intended to keep our eyes awake and our faces heavenward (Heb. 12. 3).

3. What His servants are expected to do.

1. WATCH. "Watch ye therefore." The meaning is, be *wakeful*. Be alive and all alive, be awake and wide awake, for the good of His cause and the honour of His Name. Watch for souls, and watch for the coming of "His Son from Heaven (1 Thess. 1. 10).

2. PRAY. "Take heed, watch and pray" (v. 33). The manner of our Lord while in this world is a soul-stirring

example of the purpose, power, and privilege of prayer. Looking for His coming will revive the spirit of pleading in us. Looking at persons and things around us, in the light of His coming, will surely humble us at His feet, and keep us near the blood-sprinkled throne of grace.

3. WORK. " He gave to every man his work" (v. 34). Watching and praying will all the more fit us for the work given us to do. Work while it is day. In connection with our individual task let us keep in mind that this is the work of God, that *ye believe* in Him. Let it be the work of *faith*, and then it will be the labour of love, and when He does come may we hear His well done, good and faithful servant. ─────

SHE HATH DONE WHAT SHE COULD.
Mark 14. 1-9.

" The iron is hot for the striking,
  Do, man of God, thy part;
  O weigh not disliking or liking,
  Speak from a burning heart.

Work, for the harvest now whitens,
  Go in, man of God, and reap,
  For he who dark souls enlightens
  Is gathering Christ's lost sheep.''

WHILE the chief priests and scribes were seeking to take Jesus by craft and put Him to death, there was a loving woman seeking a chance to honour Him by pouring the precious spikenard upon His head. In the house of Simon the leper she found this opportunity, and she did what she could, and did it at a time and in a manner which shows her deep insight into the character and purposes of her Lord. Perhaps this great work is the result of her sitting at His feet and learning of Him (Luke 10. 39). All powerful testimony for God has its origin in *secret* communion.

1. The good work. " She hath wrought a good work on Me.'' It was—

1. A WORK OF LOVE. The emptying of the liquid

perfume upon the head of Jesus was an expression of the affection of her heart freely poured out on Him. What is the value of our service if our hearts are not in it? The first commandment is, Thou shalt *love* the Lord.

2. A WORK OF SACRIFICE. " Very precious." The cost of the ointment in our money might be about £9. She did not give to Christ what cost her nothing. We have never really done what we could for Him if our service has not been costly to us. Spare moments and odd coppers are the expressions of a heartless, thankless soul.

3. A WORK OF FAITH. " She is come aforehand to anoint My body to the burying." How did she know that He was so near His death and burial? She had doubtless believed that the Son of Man came not to be ministered unto but to minister, and to *give His life* a ransom for many. May the Lord the Spirit work in us this Christ-refreshing faith. " I will show you my faith by my works."

4. A WORK IN SEASON. Jesus said, " Me ye have not always." She embraced the present passing opportunity. She will be eternally glad that she did so. You may honour Christ *now* by serving Him, but the brief day of privilege will soon be past. How sad to meet the Lord without ever having made one single sacrifice for the glory of His Name! Shall you? Shall I?

2. The different results. There was—

1. THE INDIGNATION OF SOME. Some had indignation, and said, " Why this waste?" This is the language of blind greed and self-interest. In the eyes of such everything is *wasted* that is given to Christ and His cause, only that which is given to themselves is put to a proper use. Small doubting souls reckon it only waste of time to wait on God, but they may be heard sometimes singing:

" Were the whole realm of nature mine,
That were a present far too small."

2. THE APPROVAL OF CHRIST. "She hath done what she could."

(1). He *accepted* the offering. He said, "She hath wrought a good work on *Me*" (v. 6). Done for Him, it is acceptable to Him.

(2). He *justifies* the offerer. "Let her alone." It is God who justifieth; who is he that condemneth? The Lord is our defence in the time of trouble. He careth for you.

(3). He *rewards* the good work. "Throughout the whole world this that she hath done shall be spoken of for a memorial of her" (v. 9). The fragrance of that self-sacrificing act has been felt all down the ages. Everything done for Christ in such a spirit will have an enduring influence. Palestine is called "the glory of all lands" just because of its connection with Him who glorifies all that is associated with Him. In union with Him there is salvation for the sinner, sanctification for the saved, and eternal reward for the self-sacrificing servant.

THE BREAD AND THE CUP.
Mark 14. 22-25.

"On the night of utmost trial,
  When Gethsemane was near;
Traitor's kiss and friend's denial,
  Cross of shame and piercing spear.

Thou didst give these symbols holy
  Of Thy sacrifice and love;
Spread'st a table for most lowly,
  Antepast of bliss above."

THE *acts* of Jesus are as significant as His words, especially those acts in the upper room, while handling the symbols of His own body and Blood the day before His crucifixion. As a dying man He here calls His friends together while He makes His last will and testament.

1. The bread a symbol of His body. "Jesus took

bread, and said, This is My body." The symbol is beautiful, for bread is not more indispensable than the sufferings of Christ for the life and salvation of man. "Except ye eat His flesh, and drink His Blood, ye have no life in you" (John 6. 53).

1. HE TOOK IT. It was His own voluntary act. He took on Him the likeness of sinful flesh. He was God manifest in the flesh. In taking a visible body He was taking that which was to be " life for the world." This He did at His incarnation, a humbling but God-glorifying act.

2. HE BLESSED IT. That is, in the taking of it He sanctified it and made it holy. His body became a holy thing, fit to be offered as a sacrifice unto God. It was blessed by the Holy indwelling Spirit in a life of blameless service to God. Blessed with infinite blessing.

3. HE BRAKE IT. This also was His own doing. Although with wicked hands they crucified Him, yet He could say no man taketh My life from Me, I have power to lay it down, and I have power to take it again, this authority I received of My Father. He *gave Himself* for us. Yes, the breaking of His body was by His own willing consent. This gives additional virtue to His sacrifice.

4. HE GAVE IT. In giving the broken bread to His believing disciples He thus indicated that the bestowing of the saving virtue of His broken body is in His own hands. " I give unto My sheep eternal life." There is none other Name under Heaven. This is My body which is broken *for you*. Substitution is here clearly taught.

2. The cup a symbol of His Blood. The life is in the Blood. In pouring out His Blood He was pouring out His *soul* unto death.

1. HE TOOK THE CUP. The cup of sorrow and suffering put into His hand by His loving and righteous Father.

What it all meant when He said, "If it be possible, let this cup pass from Me; nevertheless not My will, but Thine be done," we cannot tell; into such profound depths we cannot go. This cup meant for Christ infinitely more than it can mean to us; He tasted death for every man.

2. HE GAVE THANKS FOR IT. Selah! Let us pause and think. He gave *thanks* for the cup that was His own appointed symbol of His agony and awful death. O the depths of His grace! Thanking the Father for the privilege of suffering and dying in the sinner's stead. What love! Herein is love. Bless the Lord, O my soul, and forget not all His benefits.

3. HE GAVE IT TO THEM. Paul tells us that it was *after He had supped* that He said "This do ye" (1 Cor. 11. 25). After His atoning death comes the gift of life. The giving of the cup also suggests His desire that we should enter into "the *fellowship* of His suffering, and be made conformable unto His death" (Phil. 3. 10). "Are ye able to drink of the cup that I shall drink of?"

4. THEY ALL DRANK OF IT. "Ye shall drink of the cup that I drink of" (Mark 10. 39). And they did by becoming martyrs for His sake. If any man follow Me, let him take up his cross. He that loseth his life for My sake, and the Gospel's, shall save it. To drink of this cup is to bear about in the body the dying of the Lord Jesus, that the life also of Jesus might be made manifest in the body (2 Cor. 4. 10). I am crucified with Christ, nevertheless I live. The partakers of Christ's sufferings will be made glad when His glory shall be revealed (1 Peter 4. 13).

In observing the Lord's Supper we are not called upon to remember Him as a *Teacher*, nor as an *Example*, but as our SACRIFICE, to show forth His *death* till He come. This is My body *broken* FOR YOU, take, eat. O ye guilty sons of men, take this great atoning work and divide it among yourselves (Luke 22. 17).

BETWEEN THE CUP OF BLESSING AND THE TRAITOR'S KISS.

Mark 14. 26-42.

"Most hidden and most manifest,
Thou the mystery dost invest
With Thy humaneness, O Christ!
Sweetness, tenderness unpriced,
With this grace may we be blest,
Most hidden and most manifest."

THE experiences of our Lord and Saviour between the giving of the cup (v. 23) and the getting of the kiss (v. 45) were numerous, varied, and well defined. A close examination of them reveals the awful intenseness of His life in its closing hours. We select the above portion of Scripture only as an example of how the last days of Christ's life might be studied. Within the compass of these few verses we have the Lord Jesus—

1. Singing. "They sang a hymn" (v. 26). Jesus sang, although the thorn of the cross was at His breast. What if it were the twenty-third Psalm, "Yea, though I walk through the valley of the shadow of death, I will fear no evil."

2. Predicting. "All ye shall be offended because of Me this night" (v. 27). What a sudden change. In a few hours the clear sky of communion will be thick with the dark, ominous clouds of desertion. While He was singing He knew that the Shepherd was about to be smitten and the sheep scattered. The sword was about to *awake* against the Man that was God's fellow (Zech. 13. 7). This sword now sleeps for us.

3. Suffering. "He began to be sore amazed and very heavy" (v. 33). The iniquities of us all were beginning to meet on Him (Isa. 53. 6, margin). Was He *amazed* at the number of them, while He felt the awful burden *very heavy*? May we, like these disciples, "sit here," and see the salvation of God.

4. Sorrowing '' My soul is exceeding sorrowful unto death'' (v. 34). The bearing of our sins by the Holy Son of God was no heartless mechanical process. He could not come into contact with sin and guilt without His spotless soul becoming *"exceeding sorrowful."* In bearing our sins He also experienced the indescribable agony incurred by the guilt of them in His own soul. '' It pleased the Lord to bruise Him, He hath put Him to grief.'' Be still my soul.

5. Praying. '' He went forward and fell on the ground and prayed'' (v. 35). What a prayer! We have never been deep enough in the fires of an *agonising abhorrence at sin* to know what it all means. It was not possible this hour and cup could pass from HIM if guilty men were to be saved by the *grace* of God. Still His prayers with strong crying and tears were heard (Heb. 5. 7, 8).

6. Yielding. '' Nevertheless not what I will, but what Thou wilt'' (v. 36). I came down from Heaven not to do Mine own will, but the will of Him that sent Me (John 5. 30). Why did He shrink from the cup? Would He have been true as a *Son* if He accepted without any expression of dislike that which would break up His fellowship with His Father and turn His Father's ''Beloved'' into a curse? Nevertheless He yielded to be made a curse for us, and became obedient unto death.

7. Exhorting. '' Watch and pray'' (vs. 37, 38). Given at such a time and in such an agony of spirit, we may truly learn our need of this. O how tenderly His sorrowful soul deals with His drowsy disciples! ''The spirit truly is ready, but the flesh is weak.'' He knows the frailty of our frames, He can be touched with a feeling of our infirmities.

8. Confessing. ''Behold, the Son of Man is betrayed *into the hands of sinners*'' (v. 41). What a confession for this Mighty One to make, who could call legions of angels from Heaven. Betrayed by a professed disciple. He knew what was in man. Had He not been already entirely abandoned to the suffering of death He never could have been *betrayed*. He *gave* His life a ransom for all.

9. Commanding. " Rise up, let us go" (v. 42). But, alas, how far off did they follow Him. " Let *us* go." Are we ready to go to death with Him? Is crucifixion not as needful for *us* as for Him if we would know the fellowship of His sufferings. " I am crucified with Christ." He must be crucified that the body of sin might be put away *for* us. Our old man must be crucified that the body of sin might be destroyed *in* us (Rom. 6. 6). O that a sleepy, worldly Church could hear this call, " RISE UP, LET US GO."

THE STEPS IN PETER'S DOWNFALL.
Mark 14. 29-72.

" Speak gently to an erring one,
  E'en if a deed of shame be done;
  We see the deed and instant blame,
  But not how hard it is to tame
  A heart of sin that has not died,
  A rebel will unsanctified."

BACKSLIDING is a process. Eve first saw, then desired, then took, then eat before she gave to Adam. Falling away out of the company and fellowship of Christ is the result of an inward disease preying upon the vitals of our spiritual being. That disease is self-will. Let us follow Peter in his downgrade march step by step. There was—

1. Self-confidence. Peter said, " Although all shall be offended, yet will not I" (v. 29). The "I" here is very self-assertive, comparing himself with the others he believes himself more trustworthy than any. Yet it was written that " He that trusteth in his own heart is a fool" (Prov. 28. 26). "Let him that thinketh he standeth take heed lest he fall" (1 Cor. 10. 12).

2. Proud boasting. "If I should die with Thee, I will

not deny Thee in any wise'' (v. 31). So said they all, but
Peter spoke vehemently. Peter was as yet unbelieving and
ignorant of his own weakness. Had not the Lord said unto
him, ''Whither I go ye cannot follow Me *now?*'' (John
13.36). All self-boasting is a contradiction to His Word.

3. Unwatchfulness. He said unto Peter, '' Simon,
sleepest thou?'' (v. 37). Pride and self-confidence are
sure to lead to unwatchfulness. It is the consciously weak
ones who lean hard. Sleepy souls are easily tempted
(v. 38). By his sleep he became insensible to the sufferings of Christ. The next step down is—

4. Ashamedness. '' Peter followed Him afar off''
(v. 54). Jesus is not so popular now with the multitude.
Peter follows; but far enough off as not to be identified
with Him. A professing Christian is indeed afar off when
he is ashamed of Him and His Word. At this stage the
Word of God is neglected, prayer given up, and the company of those who testify for Christ forsaken.

5. Worldliness. '' Peter sat with the servants, and
warmed himself at the fire'' (v. 54). Having fallen out of
company with Christ, he now finds his company among
those who know him not, and warms himself at the enemy's
fire. While the prodigal was spending his all in the far
country he was just seeking to warm himself with the coals
of the enemy's fire. This is what the backslider is doing in
seeking to find pleasure and comfort in the ways and things
of the ungodly. A Christian must be *cold* indeed when he
turns to the crackling thorns of worldly delights for
heart warmth.

6. Denial. While he was warming himself he was
charged with having been with Jesus. But he denied,
saying, '' I know not'' (vs. 67, 68). When a man has gone
the length of finding *warmth* among the Lord's enemies we
are prepared for the next sad step—denial. This is often

done, if not by lip yet by *wicked works*. The Lord has uttered a solemn warning to such in Matthew 10. 33.

7. Recklessness. " He began to curse and to swear saying, I know not this Man" (v. 71). He had said, " Though all shall be offended, yet will not I," yet he becomes more easily offended than any, and now staggers into the ditch of open profanity. If a backslider be not restored before he goes the length of shameless lip denial the likelihood is that he will soon be found in the ranks of the reckless, the drunken, or some other *open* sin.

8. Repentance. Peter called to mind the word that Jesus said unto him, and when he thought thereon he wept (v. 72). The Lord had not prayed for Judas that his faith fail not, and he went out and hanged himself. It was when the prodigal son *thought* of his father's house that he said, " I will arise and go to my father." It is usually by some word of Christ that the backslider is brought to think of his ways, and to weep the bitter tears of repentance.

PILATE AND JESUS.
Mark 15. 1-15.

" The waves of the world's sea may surge,
But the blue sky above is calm."

THE life and character of Jesus is like the calm blue of Heaven compared with this restless world of troubled human spirits. The calmness of Jesus in the presence of the excited and bewildered Pilate is full of deep significance. A witness to the majesty of truth. Small men are fussy. "Still waters run deep." Pilate's treatment of Jesus is an example of how multitudes to-day treat the Gospel of Christ. Note that he—

1. Had Jesus given to him. "They delivered Him to Pilate" (v. 1). Now was Pilate's opportunity of justifying himself by justifying Jesus. When the Gospel is preached in the power of the spirit it is as it were a delivering up of Jesus for the acceptance or rejection of the hearer. How often has He been brought within your reach? What a solemn privilege!

2. Ascertains His character. "Pilate asked Him, Art Thou the King of the Jews? He answered, Thou sayest it" (v. 2). "To this end was I born" (John 18. 37). He has Christ's own testimony as to His kingly character, although He was of no reputation. Gospel hearer, you know the claims of Jesus, you too are familiar with His poverty and His dignity; yea, more, with His death and resurrection, with His power to save and keep.

3. Marvels at Him. When Jesus answered nothing to the many things charged against Him, Pilate marvelled (v. 5). He whose Name is "Wonderful" must in His manner be marvellous to many. The silent submission of Jesus to such false accusations (for He knew that for envy they had delivered Him) was a revelation. Gospel hearer, have you never been led to marvel at the uniqueness of His character, the profundity of His teaching, or the richness of His grace?

4. Was inclined to favour Him (vs. 9, 10). He found no fault in Him, and was disposed to release Him. Gospel hearer, you must surely confess that you have no fault to find with Jesus. Does not your deeper convictions tell you that He is the Truth? Have you not at times felt inclined to believe Him, and release Him by confessing Him before men? Have you not also, like Pilate's wife, "suffered many things because of Him?"

5. Submits his will to the people regarding Him. "Pilate said, What *will ye* that I shall do unto Him?" (v. 12). His vacillating spirit would deal with Jesus according to the fickle and perverted will of the multitude. Gospel hearer, are you treating Christ according to your better convictions, or in a manner only to please the

Christ-hating world? Is the will of the ungodly to be your guide as to what ye shall do with Jesus? If you judge Christ by the opinions of His enemies you will be verily guilty of the Blood of God's Son.

6. Questions the justice of their judgment concerning Him. "They cried out, Crucify Him. Pilate said, Why, what evil hath He done?" (vs. 13, 14). *Self-righteous* priests and a *wilfully ignorant* and prejudiced people have no need of the Christ, and nothing to give Him but a cross. Gospel hearer, have you not thought that it was unjust and grossly wicked to cast out and crucify the meek and lowly Jesus? Yet by your refusing to receive Him you are deliberately casting Him out of your life, and virtually saying by your unbelief, "Away with Him, I will not have this Man to rule over me."

7. Scourged Him (v. 15). The barbarous thongs, tipped with bones and lead, in the hands of a heathen, ploughed His back and made deep their furrows, making His very bones to stare out. Yet he found no fault in the Man. Gospel hearer, are you scourging the *soul* of Him, whom you know to be faultless, by your love of the world, your indifference to His redeeming Blood, and your unwillingness to submit yourself to Him?

8. Delivered Him up to be crucified. "Pilate, willing to content the people, delivered Jesus" (v. 15). He handed Him over as one who wished to have no more to do with Him. But Pilate shall meet Him again at another tribunal. Gospel hearer, Jesus has been delivered up by God *for* you, and in His Word *to* you. Are you, like Pilate, anxious to get quit of Him, or, like Mary, anxious to have Him? Pilate, with all his great privileges in having Jesus brought near to him, profited nothing, but augmented his guilt. What have you profited by many similar opportunities? What shall ye then do with Jesus?

THE ATTITUDE OF UNBELIEF.

Mark 15. 26-32.

"A cross without a Christ; the heavens dumb;
Oh, who may dare the mystery to plumb?
Or who to such a God will longer come?"

"THRONED upon the awful tree" is how John Ellerton puts it. The crucifixion was the coronation of the Son of God as our Substitute. The immeasurable soul-exalting power of it lies in the fathomless depths of the humiliation of it. This is foolishness in the eyes of men, but it is the wisdom of God. "Let Christ descend from the Cross that we may see and believe" (v. 32). Like modern rationalists, they would prefer a crossless Christ. It was not the nails that held Him to the tree, but His love for the perishing and His determination to finish the work given Him to do. The—

1. Titles given Him. "Christ the King of Israel" (v. 32). This they said in mockery, because they knew He claimed to be—

1. THE CHRIST. The Messiah, the Lord's Anointed. They spoke the truth nevertheless. When Jesus said, "Whom say ye that I am?" Peter said, "Thou art the Christ, the Son of the living God" (Matt. 16. 16).

2. THE KING OF ISRAEL. It was hard for human *reason* to believe that this despised and rejected One was God's appointed Ruler of His ancient people. Wise men, inspired by the message of God, come saying, "Where is He that is *born* KING OF THE JEWS?" Yes, this is His true title.

2. Place appointed Him was a place of—

1. SHAME AND SUFFERING. "They crucify Him, and with Him two thieves." The chosen and anointed One, the One preferred by God above all others, because of His holy devotedness, is classed by religious men with the vilest of the vile. What place has He now, even amongst so-called Christian men?

2. DERISION AND DEATH. "They that passed by railed on Him, and they that were crucified with Him reviled Him" (vs. 29-32; Psa. 22. 7, 8). Yet this is He who cried with a loud voice " Lazarus, come forth," and he that was dead came forth. He who of old " spake and it was done."

3. Proposal made to Him. "Descend from the Cross that we may see and believe" (v. 32). They might as well say let God change His character and purposes that they might see and believe. This presumptuous God-dethroning *we*. " That *we might see*." Why, He could not descend from the Cross because—

1. HE COULD NOT DISOBEY HIS FATHER. He had already said "Not My will, but Thine be done." To die was the will of Him that sent Him.

2. THE SCRIPTURES COULD NOT BE BROKEN. The prophet Daniel had said, " The Messiah shall be cut off, but not for Himself" (chap. 9. 26). Isaiah also by the same Spirit declared that "He would make His grave with the wicked, and be numbered with transgressors" (chap. 53). If He came down from the Cross the Scriptures, as the pillar of truth, would be broken.

3. HE COULD NOT SUFFER MAN TO PERISH. Without shedding of His Blood there was no remission of sin and guilt for us. His love constrained Him to give His life a ransom for many.

4. HE COULD NOT BE UNTRUE TO HIMSELF. The Cross is the evidence of His truthfulness, to His own inner consciousness, as the Redeemer of men, the Saviour of the world. What a revelation of the hidden man of His heart! He abideth faithful.

4. Reasons why some prefer a crossless Christ. Because—

1. THE CROSS REVEALS THEIR GUILT. It is the

manifestation of man's inert hatred to holiness and God-likeness. To have no personal dealings with the Son of God any more than with the dead in their graves is just another way of appointing Christ to the place of death.

2. IT IS GOD'S ONLY WAY OF LIFE. The Cross reveals the need of a *Substitute*, the need of an atonement by the Blood of His Cross, and the only possible way of access unto the Father (John 14. 6; Heb. 10. 19, 20). That we can only be saved *as sinners* through the Blood of His Cross is rather humbling to the pride of man's self-confident and deceitful heart. A crossless Christ can only make life to be a Christless cross. ———

TAUGHT IN THE SEPULCHRE.
Mark 16. 1-8.

"When brighter suns and milder skies
　Proclaim the opening year,
What various sounds of joy arise,
　What prospects bright appear !
Thus like the morning calm and clear,
　That saw the Saviour rise;
The spring of Heaven's eternal year
　Shall dawn on earth and skies."

VERY early in the morning the two Marys came to the sepulchre at *the rising of the sun*, but the Son of God had already risen. He who was before all things rose from the dead before sunrise.

1. **Whom they sought.** " Ye seek Jesus," said the messenger from Heaven to them. They sought Him that they might anoint Him (vs. 1-6). But the living Christ is never found among the dead. Anxious sinners often seek Him where He cannot be found, among their own dead works or in their own unregenerate hearts. He is not here.

2. **When they came.** " *Very early* in the morning, the first day of the week" (v. 2). Although they did not find Him where, and as they expected, yet they found Him

(John 20. 18). " They that seek Me *early* shall find Me." Seek Him early in the morning of life, early in the morning of each day, especially the *first* day of the week. This *first day* of the week was the first new Sabbath of the new creation.

3. Where they went. "And entering *into* the sepulchre" (v. 5). It would appear that they *stooped down* and went right into the grave (John 20. 11). In this place of death they had this great revelation of His resurrection power. Where else can we learn it as an experience but by stooping down into His grave? It is by being made "conformable unto His death" that we are made to know the "power of His resurrection" (Phil. 3. 10). We must stoop down to be crucified with Christ if the risen One is to live in us (Col. 3. 1-3). We stoop to conquer.

4. What they received. They found precious treasure in the tomb of Jesus. It is not death to enter here, but life for evermore. Here they pass from the natural life of sense into the spiritual life of faith. By faith enter the grave of Christ as crucified for you, and ye shall be quickened by resurrection life. They received—

1. A VISION OF THE HEAVENLY ONE. " They saw a young man sitting, clothed in a long white garment" (v. 5). Here in this new tomb, where the Lord Jesus was the only one that ever lay, are they brought into fellowship with a *sent one* from Heaven. As the Holy Ghost was not yet given, because that Jesus Christ was not yet glorified, may we not suppose that this *young man* came as a timely and temporary substitute to take the things of Christ and show them to these early seekers? It is still true that when we put self and self-wisdom in the place of death we shall be taught of God.

2. A WORD OF COMFORT. " He said, Be not affrighted" (v. 6). There is nothing to fear in the grave of your

Redeemer. There is a *living One* there, the ever youthful Spirit of God, waiting to comfort the sorrowful seeker.

3. A PROOF OF HEAVENLY SYMPATHY. '' Ye seek Jesus of Nazareth.'' It must have been a relief to them that this God-sent messenger knew the deeper yearnings of their soul, and was at one with them in their interest. The Holy Spirit is all this and much more to us. '' He helpeth our infirmities and maketh intercession according to the will of God'' (Rom. 8. 26, 27)

4. THE ASSURANCE OF VICTORY. "He saith unto them, He is risen.'' This was exceeding abundantly above all that they asked or thought. He is not stolen; He is *risen*. He died for our sins and *rose again* for our justification. This young man, sitting in the place where Jesus was laid, acts the part of a forerunner of the Holy Spirit in bringing the *assurance* of life to the hearts of these Saviour-loving women. Peter tells what effect this *renewed* hope had (1 Peter 1. 3).

5. AN EVIDENCE OF RESURRECTION. '' He is not here; behold the place where they laid Him.'' The place where they laid Him was empty. The clothes were there, and perhaps lying folded (not doubled up), just as they were when He was in them. The *position* of the linen clothes and the napkin evidently astonished the disciples (John 20. 6-8). Who could doubt the resurrection who have themselves passed from death into life, and ''know Him and the power of His resurrection'' (Phil. 3. 10).

6. A GREAT COMMISSION. '' Go your way, and tell.'' Testimony for Christ must follow the reviving influence of His resurrection life. They received their commission from an angel from Heaven. The Holy Ghost said, ''Separate me Barnabas and Saul for the work whereunto I have called them'' (Acts 13. 2). ''Ye shall be witnesses unto Me . . . to the uttermost part of the earth'' (Acts 1 .8).

7. A PRECIOUS PROMISE. " He goeth before you into Galilee, there *ye shall see Him*." Blessed prospect that is ever before them that GO in His Name. Ye shall *see Him*, and be made like Him (1 John 3. 2). Having been sent " they went out quickly." They were not disobedient to the heavenly vision. Go thou and do likewise, and in the doing of His will *there* ye shall see Him.

RESURRECTION REVELATIONS.
Mark 16. 9-14.

"The Lord is risen indeed,
We say it as a creed:
But O to feel its power
Daily through every hour."

THIS first day of the week was full of *new things* for the disciples of the Lord. A new order of things was now being established. When a soul passes from the old natural life into the new resurrection life in Christ it is a new creature entering into a new kingdom, where all things are made new. It is to such the first day of the first month of the year of their eternal life. There are here what might be called some incidental revelations connected with His resurrection worthy of notice. We have a—

1. **Revelation of His power**. " Jesus was *risen*" (v. 9). He had said " I have power to lay down My life, and I have power to *take it again*." He had now taken again that which He had freely given up for us all. The *taking again* proves how completely His life had been given away. Having power to take it, He has now power to bestow it in its fulness to all who believe.

2. **Revelation of grace**. He appeared *first* to Mary Magdalene, out of whom He had cast seven devils. She who was the greatest sinner among His followers receives first of His resurrection favours. Where sin abounded, grace did much more abound. The mighty, pitying Saviour favours the humble, thankful, trustful follower.

3. Revelation of deep sorrow. " Them that had been with Him mourned and wept" (v. 10). The curtain is lifted, and we get a glimpse of how those that *had been with Him* felt and regarded the crucifixion, *they mourned and wept*. They were like a young motherless family, suddenly bereaved of their wise and loving father, their only real friend on earth. Their tears, though partly caused by unbelief, showed at least the place He had in their affections. Did not the enemies of the Cross make Paul weep? (Phil. 3. 18).

4. Revelation of unbelief. " When they heard that He was alive and had been seen of her they believed not" (v. 11). We don't wonder so much at them not believing Mary as at their failure to remember or believe the words spoken to them by the Lord (see John 16. 20-22). Unbelief always brings disappointment and sorrow. Tears mingled with distrust may be but the tears of wounded pride.

5. Revelation of Divine adaptation. " After that, He appeared in *another form*" (v. 12). The same Saviour in a different form. O the depths of His wisdom and riches. He appeared to Stephen as the glorified One, but to Saul as the persecuted One (Acts 7. 55; 9. 5). It does not matter what our circumstances or condition may be, when He appears it is always as such a One as we need. His grace is always made *suitable* and sufficient.

6. Revelation of His faithfulness. " He upbraided them with their unbelief and hardness of heart" (v. 14). While they mourned and wept they did not *look like* those who were unbelieving and hard at heart. But the Lord looks deeper down than groans and tears, and like a wise and true Physician He lays His finger upon the diseased spot, and tells them plainly what is wrong. This is why many professing Christians are afraid to get into very close quarters with Jesus, lest these hidden things should be revealed, lest the real man of the heart should be unveiled. If we do come near to Him He will be faithful with us.

7. Revelation of the responsibility resting on His witnesses. " He upbraided them, because they believed not *them which had seen Him*" (v. 14). The Lord expected that the testimony of those to whom *He had revealed Himself* would be believed. Those only can be witnesses for Him to whom He hath manifested His saving grace and resurrection power, and those who hear such witness-bearing and yet do not believe are charged with *unbelief* and *hardness* of heart. In our Lord's great priestly prayer, recorded in John 17, He prayed for them who shall believe *through their word*. If the Lord believes and expects that men will believe in Him through our word, how is it that we don't look for *immediate* results when the Word is spoken? Lord, increase our faith. ———

THE GREAT COMMISSION.
Mark 16. 15-20.

"The round world before Him lay,
 For that world this one command:
 ' Go, and I am with you alway,'
 Send it out o'er every land.
 North and south, and east and west,
 At His Cross shall ransom'd rest.
 Mighty charter! Great commission!
 Till this earth be Christ's possession."

A WELL known authority on missions has said, " Christianity is the only religion that is missionary." This call, like a stream of light, has come down through the ages, beckoning weary souls to the harbour of rest.

1. The need. This is summed up in one word, *"World."* " Go into all the world." The world of—

1. SINFUL SELF *within*. This is the devil's nursery, where every evil in the world is germinated, and afterwards transplanted by actual deeds. Into this world the power of Christ must come.

2. FASHION AND PLEASURES *around*. That which ministers to the lust of. the eye, the lust of the flesh, and
the pride of life. That world of custom and habit and
godless living.

3. HEATHEN DARKNESS *beyond*. A world of perishing,
yet immortal souls. A world loved by God, and for which
Christ died (John 3. 16). The whole world lieth in
wickedness. The need is great.

2. The provision. '' The Gospel.'' '' Preach the
Gospel to every creature.'' Just as there are different
elements in air and water, so are there in the Gospel. It
contains good tidings of great joy. There is in it—

1. THE INCARNATION OF THE SON OF GOD. God manifest
in the flesh. His Name shall be called Emmanuel. ''God
with us.'' God with us seeking to save the lost, in the
form of a servant. What news!

2. PROPITIATION BY THE BLOOD OF GOD. '' The Church
of God, which He hath purchased with *His own Blood*''
(Acts 20. 28). '' He is the propitiation for our sins''
(1 John 2. 2). The Blood of His Son is God's great
covering for sin. This has been provided, this is offered.

3. REGENERATION BY THE SPIRIT OF GOD. This is a
recreation of the human spirit after the likeness of God.
Made new creatures (2 Cor. 5. 17).

4. JUSTIFICATION BY THE FAITH OF GOD (Mark 11. 22,
margin). '' Have the faith of God'' is the literal meaning.
It seems a strong expression. But every one who exercises
faith in Jesus Christ is having the faith that God has in
Him. As David showed the *kindness of God* to Mephibosheth (2 Sam. 9. 3).

5. SANCTIFICATION BY THE WORD OF GOD. Thy Word
was found, and I did eat it. Now are ye clean through the
Word which I have spoken unto you. He has given us
exceeding great and precious promises that by these we

might be made partakers of the Divine nature. All the promises of God are in Christ for the support of faith and the strengthening and growth of the new life.

6. RESURRECTION BY THE POWER OF GOD. He shall come in great power and glory. The dead in Christ shall rise first. The mortal shall put on *immortality* (1 Cor. 15. 38).

7. GLORIFICATION BY THE PRESENCE OF GOD. The " Great God, our Saviour, shall appear," and we shall be like Him, for we shall see Him as He is. These seven elements belong to the glorious Gospel of the blessed God, which is His alone remedy for the manifold need of a perishing world.

3. The commission. " Go ye into all the world." Clear, simple, definite.

1. WHO? " Ye." Ye who have believed, and have known the reviving power of His resurrection (1 Peter 1. 3).

2. WHAT? " Go." " As My Father sent Me, so send I you" (John 17. 18). Go. Don't sit down and theorise about it. Go, and make this the chief business of your life.

3. WHERE? "Into all the world." The world loved by God (John 3. 16); the world atoned for by the Son (1 John 2. 2). If you cannot go here or there in person, go in your love and prayers and practical sympathy (Psa. 126. 5, 6).

4. The promise. Lo, I am with you alway. " In My Name shall they cast out devils" (vs. 17, 18).

His presence with us is the pledge of—

1. CONTINUAL FELLOWSHIP. If His sanctifying, soul-soothing presence is not realised or enjoyed, it is not that His promise has failed, but that self or sin has grieved the Holy Ghost, who makes His presence a reality and a power.

2. CONTINUAL VICTORY. Moses said, "If Thy presence

go not with us, carry us not up hence." There can be no
victory over the enemies of God if His presence is not with
us (see Num. 14. 42-45). If devils are to be cast out it
must be by the power of *His Name* (v. 17). His Name
implies all that He is.

5. The fulfilment. " They went forth and preached
everywhere, *the Lord working with them*" (v. 20).

1. THEY WERE OBEDIENT. "They went forth." They
went forth like Abraham, leaning on His Word. Not
waiting till they were burned out, like Lot in Sodom.
In the light of this urgent commission, does it not seem to
savour of unbelief to be still saying, "What wilt Thou
have me to do?"

2. THEY WERE SUCCESSFUL. " The Lord *working with
them*, and confirming the Word with signs following."
If the Lord is not working with us our labour is in vain.
If the Word preached is not confirmed with signs there is no
evidence of the Lord's presence. The Lord will work
with us if we, like them, are wholly yielded to the doing
of His will, preaching the Gospel to every creature.

A FAITH CONFIRMING PROLOGUE.
Luke 1. 1-4.

" Amid the Babel of men's clam'rous speech,
  Lord Jesus, what a ' still small voice' is Thine,
And yet where are there words that men's hearts reach
  Like those of Thee, the human and divine?

How have Thy words, Lord, quicken'd human thought?
  How have they penetrated human lives?
How have they into grandest deeds been wrought,
  And how on their deep lines all progress drives?"

THE voice of Jesus in His Gospel is a very " small voice"
compared with the clamorous speech of political partyism
and the strife of modern ungodly tongues, but like a spring
silently making its way through the rocks it comes to
the surface and refreshes many a thirsty soul. What

Luke says about the things of the Gospel in this brief introduction is worthy of our closest attention. We learn that these things—

1. Were the chief topic in the days of Luke. This we infer from the fact that "*Many* had taken in hand to set them forth in order" (v. 1). The words and deeds of Christ were in everybody's mouth. These things were not done in a corner, many were anxious to have them in a *connected* form, and many had attempted so to put them. But any *spiritual* man, such as Luke, could easily detect distorted representations of the life and character of Jesus Christ.

2. Were delivered by eye-witnesses. "They delivered them unto us, which from the beginning were eye-witnesses" (v. 2). John could say, "That which we have heard, which we have *seen with our eyes*" &c. (1 John 1. 1, 2). "He was seen by five hundred brethren at once." Men of old spake as they were moved by the Holy Ghost, and so the men of the new dispensation spake as they were moved by the living personal Christ among them. The great salvation which at first began to be spoken by the Lord was confirmed unto us by them that heard Him (Heb. 2. 3).

3. Were most surely believed in Luke's days (v. 1). If they were accepted without doubt by multitudes in the time of Christ and in the days immediately following, where is the ground for questioning them now? They did not follow cunningly devised fables in making known the Gospel of Christ (2 Peter 1. 16). These things were tested in the seven times hotter furnace of the days in which they were spoken and wrought. The power and truth of them is being yet proven in the experience of them that believe and do the will of God (John 7. 17).

4. Have been recorded by one who had a perfect

knowledge of them (v. 3). Although Luke's name does not occur among the twelve apostles, yet he was familiar with all that had been done, being intimate with the chosen twelve and a close companion of Paul the great apostle of the Gentiles. The Gospel according to Luke is confessedly the fullest record of all that Jesus began to *do*.

5. Are here written in order (v. 3). Luke professes to give us the *order* in which the events of Christ's life took place. This, to the simple Bible student, is a great blessing, as the very *connection* between the recorded deeds of our Lord is full of deep significance. If not in their mutual relationship, yet in point of contrast.

6. Were written that we might have certainty (v. 4). Luke evidently wrote that the honourable Theophilus might be confirmed in his faith. "These are written that ye might believe that Jesus is the Christ, the Son of God" (John 20. 31). In the written Gospel we have a *sure Word*, wherein we do well to take heed as unto a light that shineth in a dark place. The Gospel offers both Salvation and the certainty of it. Yet how many Gospel hearers there are who have not yet known the certainty of those things wherein they have been instructed. Make your calling and election sure.

ZACHARIAS MADE DUMB THROUGH UNBELIEF.

Luke 1. 5-22.

" O Father, God, to Thee I come !
Rather in mercy hold me dumb
Than that, unto Thee drawing near,
I think of mortal men that hear.
O may I reverence more and more,
And in every deed adore."

NOTHING fetters the hand of God from working like unbelief; nothing grieves the Spirit more readily. But although he was smitten dumb he did not flee from the presence of the holy Smiter. He did not give up his work for the Lord although this sore affliction came upon him. Zacharias would teach us not to be so engrossed with our trials even if they should be most sudden and severe as to neglect our work for Christ. After reflecting on this incident we desire to point out that—

1. Visions may come while doing our ordinary work. "While he executed the priest's office, there appeared unto him an angel of the Lord" (vs. 8, 11). Moses kept the flock of Jethro when the call came through the burning bush (Exod. 3. 1). Gideon was threshing wheat (Judges 6. 11). Elisha was ploughing when the prophetic mantle fell upon him (1 Kings 19. 19). David was in the sheepfolds (Psa. 78. 70). Matthew in his toll-booth. Thy God is sufficient for thee, wait on Him and look up.

2. Our prayers may be answered very unexpectedly (v. 13). When the angel said to him, "Fear not, for thy prayer is heard," it was to him staggering news, although he had been praying many long years that a son might be given them. They were both now "well stricken in years" (v. 7), suggesting that he had continued this prayer long after the expectation had died away. If the Lord lays it on the heart to continue in prayer for any definite thing, is this not in itself an evidence that He desires so to bless us? Believe, and thou shalt see the glory of God. "Ye shall reap if ye faint not" (Gal. 6. 9).

3. The Lord is able to do far above what we ask. He not only would have a son born to him, but that son "would be great in the sight of the Lord, and filled with the Holy Ghost" (vs. 14, 15). A son worthy of the God who gave him. The good old man and his humble, blameless wife were now abundantly rewarded for their many years of praying and waiting. God is not unfaithful.

Wait on the Lord.   Though the vision tarry, wait.   You
long for a revival, let not thy faith fail (Psa. 126. 6).

4. The promises of God test our faith. " Zacharias
said, Whereby shall I know this?'' (v. 18).   It was a big
order he received that day from the Lord (read carefully
vs. 14-17).   It was as if the fountains of the great deep
of God's infinite grace had just opened up and poured
their unspeakable riches at his feet.   Is it not the very
greatness of His grace that staggers our weak faith?   If
you wish to find out the measure of your faith, just try
some one of His great and precious promises. "In My
Name ye shall cast out devils" (Mark 16.17). Try that one.

5. Unbelief fetters the tongue of testimony. " Behold, thou shalt be dumb, because thou believest not My
words'' (v. 20).   What a God-dishonouring thing unbelief
is!   How many tongues among the children of God are
under the condemnation of dumbness because of their
unbelief?   How many of us are dumb with regard to the
Lord's coming, the filling of the Spirit, the consecration
of the life, answered prayer, and the deeper experiences of
the things of God, all because of unbelief?   " Because
thou believest not *My words.*'' According to Grosart he
became a D.D. through unbelief—deaf and dumb.

6. Real contact with the Lord makes men to marvel.
" The people marvelled that he tarried so long in the
temple'' (v. 21).   As for Zacharias, he did not feel the
time long.   Who does when they are in real communion
with God?   A man is sure to get out of the old rut and to
do unprecedented things when his ministry becomes a
living and solemn reality before God.   Zacharias, during
the hours of public service, forgot all about the clock that
day.   He was late in getting through, but the people, when
they did see him, were *convinced* that he had seen a vision
(v. 22).   Short services are not always the best.   Where

a preacher's soul is filled with the vision of God, both time and men have to stand back. There is more blessing through *one day* with God than twenty years without Him. Have faith in God. ———

JOHN THE BAPTIST AND THE HOLY SPIRIT.
Luke 1. 12-17.

"Lord, what is this that Thou hast sent?
My heart, like sea-wave turbulent,
Grieves with strange sweet agony;
O born not of the earth but sky!
Of *sin* Thou seek'st me to *convince*,
And 'neath Thy probing touch I wince."

THERE is a singular resemblance between the work of John and the work of the Holy Spirit. Both came to convince men of sin, to bring them to repentance, and to point them to Christ as the Lamb of God who taketh away sin. The points of likeness are not few—

1. **The coming of both was foretold** (v. 13; John 14. 16). John's birth was predicted by the angel, and Christ promised to send another Comforter. Every event *foretold* by God is a link of connection between earth and Heaven; an evidence of the reality of unseen and eternal things.

2. **At the coming of both many were made to rejoice**. It was said of John "that many shall rejoice at his birth" (v. 14). The advent of the Holy Spirit on the day of Pentecost filled many with joy. Three thousand souls *gladly* received the Word, and did eat their meat with gladness and singleness of heart, praising God (Acts 2. 41-47). The fruit of the Spirit is joy.

3. **Both were to be great in the sight of the Lord** "He shall be great in the sight of the Lord" (v. 15) John's testimony was to glorify the Lord, even though in the sight of men and in his own estimation he was but a *voice* crying in the wilderness. Jesus said of the Holy Spirit, "He shall glorify Me" (John 16. 14). The blessed

Spirit is indeed great in the sight of the Lord, although
men should ignore Him and close their ears to the crying
of His voice. Have you heard this voice crying in the
wilderness of your desolate heart and *fruitless* life?

4. Both were to prepare the way for the Lord. "He
shall go before Him in the spirit and power of Elias" (v. 17).
The Holy Spirit also prepares the way for Christ's salvation
to come to us by "convincing of sin" (John 16. 8). John
prepared the way of the Lord by convincing men of their
need of repentance; the Holy Spirit prepares the way of the
Lord into our hearts by revealing to us our need of salvation.

5. Both were to turn many to the Lord. "Many of
the children of Israel shall he turn to the Lord their God"
(v. 16). This also is the mission of the Holy Ghost. " He
shall testify of Me," said Jesus. "When the Spirit of
grace and supplication is poured out they shall *look upon
Me*" (Zech. 12. 10). The *turning* of men to the Lord is
His overcoming work. It is the Spirit that quickeneth.
There can be no salvation or joy in the Lord without this
turning, for all like sheep have gone astray. Turn ye,
turn ye, for why will ye die?

6. Both came to give knowledge of salvation.
"Thou shalt go before the face of the Lord to give
knowledge of salvation" (vs. 76, 77). John gave the
knowledge of salvation by declaring that the Saviour
was at hand. The Holy Spirit gives the knowledge by
revealing Christ in the heart. He that believeth hath
the witness in himself (1 John 5. 10).

7. Both came to make ready a people for the Lord.
This was the outstanding feature of John's mission (v. 17);
this is pre-eminently the great mission of the Holy Spirit,
calling out a people for His Name, and preparing them for
the coming of the Lord (Acts 15. 14). The Church is the
Lamb's wife, called and comforted, and led by the Spirit,

just as Eliezer made ready Rebekah by giving her the gifts of Isaac, and led her right into the presence of him whom she had not seen yet loved (Gen. 24).

8. Both came to honour the Lord and not them-selves. John kept *himself*, as it were, out of sight, saying, I am a *voice*, one to be heard but not *seen*. So the Spirit, we are told, shall not *speak of Himself*. The mission of the Spirit, like that of John, is to point out Jesus as the Lamb of God. He shall take of Mine and show it unto you (John 16. 13, 14). Those filled with the Spirit will in this respect become like the Spirit, seeking only to glorify Jesus. Their language is: "He must increase; I must decrease" (John 3. 30).

A GREAT CHARACTER.
Luke 1. 15, 16.

"AMONG them that are born of women there hath not risen a greater than John the Baptist." He was a Nazarite unto God, drinking neither wine nor strong drink. Where-in did his greatness consist? He was great—

1. Before the Lord. "He shall be great in the sight of the Lord." This assures us that he must have been in a condition of—

1. RIGHTNESS WITH GOD. No one can be great in the favour of God who is not right with Him. Reconciliation is needed to acceptance.

2. LIKENESS TO GOD. It is possible to be justified before Him and yet not be fully conformed to Him. He made the *first* man after His own likeness. The second Man is the Lord from Heaven, after whose likeness we are now to be created by the same Spirit.

3. READINESS FOR GOD. A man entirely separated for Him, with no interest to come between him and his service for God. He was in no way *entangled*, a free man to do His will. This is *greatness*.

2. In himself. " He was filled with the Holy Ghost." Not the greatness of his own will, or purpose, or goodness, but the greatness of God dwelling in him.   This implies—

1. SELF-ABNEGATION.   He died to himself that God might live and move in him.   Not I, but Christ in me. Man's original greatness was lowered to the dust through sin, and eternally ruined.   The way into greatness in the Divine eyes is not by self-reformation, but by self-abnega- tion.   A going out of the ruined nature into the life of God.   I am crucified with Christ, nevertheless I live.

2. DIVINE POSSESSION.   Filled with the Holy Spirit. Yielded up to the will of God as taught by His Spirit abiding within.   Be not drunk with wine, but be filled with the Spirit.   All true greatness comes from Him who alone is great.   Great in wisdom, holiness, and power.   "Thy gentleness hath made me great" (2 Sam. 22. 36).

3. HEAVENLY WISDOM.   To be filled with the Spirit is to be filled with the *knowledge of His will*, so that every thought and act may be in perfect harmony with the mind of God.   He worketh in us both to will and to do of His good pleasure.   Ye are wise in Christ.

3. Among his fellowmen. " Many of the children of Israel shall he turn to the Lord their God."   This greatness then lies in holiness and *usefulness*.   It is not something given us for our own honour, ease, or aggrandisement, but whereby the power of God may come into contact with others.   If you would have this greatness you must not seek it for yourself.   He will not give His glory to another.   Here we see—

1. GREAT FAITHFULNESS.   His ministry gives abundant evidence of his fearlessness and devotion to the work of God.   Like the apostle of the Gentiles he could say, " This one thing I do" (Phil. 3. 13).

2. GREAT POWER.   Like the greater One who was to

come after him, he spoke with power. His word was sharp, and quick, and powerful, because it was a word that burned in his bones. He was in vital sympathy with his message. It was to him no task committed to memory, but the living truth, blazing in a living soul, and dropping from his glowing tongue like coals of fire.

3. GREAT SUCCESS. "*Many* turned to the Lord." A Holy Ghost ministry is always a success. It is not ye that speak, but the Spirit of your Father which is in you. The Spirit of your Father will never speak without telling effect. The secret of his success lay in his exalting the Lord and not himself. He must increase, and I must decrease. "Go thou and do likewise" (Luke 10. 37).

JESUS AS SAVIOUR AND KING.
Luke 1. 30-33.

"Great disaster of the world,
When *Adam* from his throne was hurled;
When the tempter seem'd to win
Through unfathomable sin.
Ah! but it was only seeming;
Lo! the Christ has come redeeming."

JESUS the Lowly Child, yet the "Mighty God," stripped of His glory, and still glorious in His weakness. Great is the mystery of godliness.

1. His saving Name. "Thou shalt call His Name JESUS." *Jesus* means Saviour. God in measuring the depth of man's need could only meet that need by the gift of His only Son. As a Saviour He saves from—

1. SIN (Matt. 1. 21). From its defiling and condemning power, from the love of it, and from the wrath that is to come because of it (1 Thess. 1. 10). He saves from sin by putting Himself between the sinner and his guilt (Isa. 53).

2. SELF (Gal. 2. 20). The *I* is to be crucified with

Christ that the body of sin might be destroyed (Rom.
6. 6). Self-wisdom, self-effort, and self-righteousness
are all enemies from which we need to be delivered, and
from which we are saved when Jesus reigns within.

3. THIS PRESENT EVIL WORLD (Gal. 1. 4). By being
crucified with Christ we are crucified to the world and the
world to us (Gal. 6. 14). The Cross of Christ comes
between us and our sins, between us and the flesh, and
between us and the world. Did not our Lord pray that
we should be kept from the evil? (John 17. 15). He is
mighty to save.

2. His wonderful character. " He shall be great"
(v. 32).

1. GREAT IN HIS ORIGIN. "Called the Son of the
Highest." As a Child He was *born*, as a Son He was
given (Isa. 9. 6). Being the Son of the HIGHEST, He is
higher than angels, or than any created one. Yet He
who belonged to the Highest descended to the lowest for
us, becoming obedient unto *death*.

2. GREAT IN HIS LOVE. He so loved us that He gave
Himself for us. Being the Son of the Highest His love was
of the highest possible order. Behold what love! Herein
is love (1 John 4. 10). His love was consistent with the
greatness of His character, and was stronger than death.

3. GREAT IN HIS POWER. The power of Christ was the
power of faith. He believed, and therefore spake, and it
was done. There is nothing impossible with Him (v. 37).
All power, He says, is given unto Me. He is able to save
to the uttermost. As many *as touched Him* were made
perfectly whole.

3. His glorious prospect. "Who for the joy that was
set before Him endured the Cross, despising the shame."

1. HE SHALL HAVE A THRONE. "The Lord God *shall
give Him* the throne of His father David" (v. 32). He shall

do it. He has not yet received this throne, for the house of Jacob (v. 33) still despise and reject Him as their Messiah King. Jesus Christ is God's appointed heir to David's throne (Jer. 23. 5; compare Psa. 132. 11 with Rev. 22. 16; see also Isa. 9. 6, 7).

2. HE SHALL REIGN OVER THE HOUSE OF JACOB (v. 33). Would Mary remember this while she stood by and saw Him crucified? Is His promise to come to naught? He as King has been rejected, and His reign over them as a people delayed, but the Word of God cannot be broken. The gifts and callings of God are without repentance. That foretold by Daniel must be fulfilled (chap. 7. 13, 14). He was *born* King of the Jews. God hath given Him the throne of David, and He shall reign over the house of Jacob. To *spiritualise* this at the sacrifice of its literal meaning is to wrest the Scriptures. Render to God the things that are God's.

3. HIS KINGDOM SHALL HAVE NO END (v. 33). The Kingdom of God that is *within* us shall certainly have no end. We shall never cease to be under the rule of Him who is our exalted Redeemer. But the kingdom of this world has not yet become the kingdom of our Lord and of His Christ (Rev. 11. 15). The time has not yet come when the blessed and *only* Potentate, the King of kings and Lord of lords, shall reign over all, blessed for ever. These times cannot come "until the appearing of our Lord Jesus Christ" (1 Tim. 6. 14-16).

MARY'S PRAYER.
Luke 1. 30-38.

"Thou stooped'st over Thy bruised child, O Lord,
And 'mid the dark didst breathe the healing word;
Thou knowest all, and with mild mightiness
Granted'st a mother's kiss in my distress."

WHEN the power of the Highest stooped to overshadow the lowly Mary, it was to her indeed a manifestation of *mild mightiness*. She could truly say, "Thy gentleness hath made me great" (2 Sam. 22. 36).

1. The promise. "Fear not, thou hast found favour with God, and shalt bring forth a Son, and call His Name Jesus" (vs. 30, 31). She *found favour*, not as one who deserved it or bought it. The *grace* of God, which is favour, is never found by those who seek it as wages. The *gift* of God is eternal life.

2. The question. "How shall this be, seeing I know not a man?" (v. 34). To have Christ formed *within us* is to be blessed above all. But how can this be? Hear, O heavens, and give answer, O earth. How shall this be? It is not in man to reason, and in all mere human experience impossible. Who can bring a clean thing out of an unclean? Ye must be born again. How shall this be?

3. The answer. "The Holy Ghost shall come upon thee, and the power of the Highest shall overshadow thee" (v. 35). To Mary's question, How shall this be? God's answer is "The Holy Ghost." How is *His Son to be revealed in me*? (Gal. 1. 16). The Holy Ghost shall come upon thee. It is not of *man*, not of the flesh, not of works, not by might or by power, but by *My Spirit*, saith the Lord. He who *brooded over* the creation of old must *overshadow* thee. It is the Spirit that quickeneth. Let us apply this great thought to—

1. GOD'S WAY OF SALVATION. How shall this be? Well, it must just come to you as this honour came to Mary. As the *favour* of God. You cannot purchase it, and you never shall deserve it. God's answer to your question as to how it is to come into your heart and life is, "The Holy Ghost" (John 3. 5). Like Mary, believe God's Word and rest.

2. GOD'S WAY OF SANCTIFICATION. This, like salvation, and the forming of the new nature within us, is all

of Grace. It is the *favour* of God. It is God who worketh *in us*, both to will and to do of His good pleasure. How shall this be? The Divine answer again is the same: "The Holy Ghost shall come unto thee." The storms and trials of life may *blow* off many withered leaves from an outward character, but there is nothing like the *rising of the new life* for *putting off* the old. Be filled with the Spirit.

3. GOD'S WAY OF SERVICE. To all our questions as to how we shall be made fruitful in the work of the Lord He has but one answer: "The Holy Ghost." From *Me*, saith the Lord, is *thy* fruit found. How shall I glorify God in my body and spirit? The power of the Highest shall overshadow thee. As *vessels*, we are to be *filled* with the Spirit and the knowledge of His will. As *instruments*, we are to be polished, and entirely yielded to His will. As *agents*, we act in His Name and for His sake. "Go ye therefore, and teach all nations, baptising them in the Name of the Father, and of the Son, and of the Holy Ghost" (Matt. 28. 19, 20). "Now then we are ambassadors for Christ" (2 Cor. 5. 20).

4. The prayer. Mary said, "Be it unto me according to Thy word" (v. 38). This is very precious. Mary could not *understand* how the Son of God was to be formed in her, but she *believed* that it was His gracious will that it should be so. And she immediately yielded herself, spirit, soul, and *body*, that the will of God might be done *in* her and *through* her. "Be it unto me according to Thy word." This brief, deep, self-surrendering, God-glorifying prayer breathes the secret of salvation, sanctification, and successful service. Not My will, but Thine be done. Take this as an example of how His gracious words may be received and fulfilled in us. Be ye holy, for I am holy. How shall this be? The Holy Ghost shall come upon thee. Be it unto me according to Thy word.

HOLY JOY.

Luke 1. 46-55.

" Bethlehem and Calvary—
    A human child that God might die;
    This the stupendous mystery.
Bethlehem and Calvary—
    Sweet picture of humility,
    And earth and Hell's hostility."

BETHLEHEM and Calvary are the two poles of Divine grace and human guilt. In the one we see the evidence of God's love to man, in the other the proof of man's hatred to God.

In this chapter we have three holy songs:

1. The song of Elizabeth (vs. 41, 42).

2. The song of Mary (v. 46).

3. The song of Zacharias (v. 67).

It is with the song of Mary that we have now specially to do. It is pleasant to think of Mary as a singer. Did ever mortal voice sing a sweeter song than this? Her joy was holy, deep, Divine. It was—

1. **Spiritual joy.** " My *spirit* hath rejoiced" (v. 47). The tidings of the grace of God, in the gift of His Son, filled her soul with joy and made her spirit sing. The Gospel of God is intended to reach the very *spirit* of man, to touch and revive the innermost spring of His being. The lip songs of the hypocrite and the sentimental songs of the world never penetrate to the needy spirit in man.

2. **Joy in God.** "My spirit hath rejoiced in God" (v. 47). God revealed Himself, and He was known to Mary in the gift of His Son, and so known and believed that her spirit rejoiced in God. It cannot be said of us that we know God if in our spirits we do not rejoice in Him. We joy in God *through our Lord Jesus Christ* (Rom. 5. 11). The joy that is in God is pure and blameless, and may be changeless and eternal.

3. Joy of salvation. " My spirit hath rejoiced in *God my Saviour*" (v. 47). How near the heart of the virgin mother comes to her God in these words, " MY SAVIOUR " Mary needed a Saviour, and she found Him in the Son of the Highest, begotten in her by the power of the Holy Ghost. Where and how else can we find Him? My Lord and my God. Christ dwells in our hearts by faith.

4. Praiseful joy. " My soul doth magnify the Lord" (v. 46). Even the joy of salvation may be a selfish joy, but the joy of *adoration* is God-glorifying. Hannah also knew this double joy. Joy in the salvation of the Lord, and joy in the Lord Himself (1 Sam. 2. 1). O magnify the Lord with me, and let us exalt *His Name* together (Psa. 34. 3).

5. Grateful joy. " For He hath regarded the *low estate* of His handmaiden" (v. 48). She is deeply conscious that she could never *merit* the exceptional honour conferred upon her. No more can ye. Every one who knows God and lives in the light of His presence cannot but be conscious of his or her utter unworthiness of such love and favour. It is when, like Mary, we are in *the low* estate that the Lord will lift us up. Humble thyself and He will honour thee (Psa. 138. 6).

6. Hopeful joy. " Behold, from henceforth all generations shall call me blessed" (v. 48). She was blessed indeed, and blessed down through the generations, all because of her very close relationship to both her Lord and ours. May we not learn from this that it is our *nearness* to Christ that is to tell on our children and the generations yet to come? The memory of the wicked shall rot, rot like a rootless, lifeless tree, but those planted by the river shall never wither (Psa. 1. 3).

7. Reasonable joy. " For He that is mighty hath done to *me great things*" (v. 49). When we are so really conscious that the Lord hath done great things *for* us and *in* us, by the *mighty* operation of His Holy Spirit, the joy becomes, as it were, natural. The fruit of the Spirit is joy. The Lord hath done great things for us, whereof we *are* glad (Psa. 126. 3). Think on these things. He that is mighty is still able to do for us great things (Eph. 3. 20).

8. Joy that constrained to testimony. In the following verses (50-55) Mary testifies to—

1. THE POWER OF GOD. " He scattereth the proud in the *imagination* of their hearts. He hath *put down* the *mighty* from their seats, He hath sent the *rich* empty away. The arm that is strong to save is also strong to smite down everything that exalts itself against God. Those who know the joy of the Lord know this also.

2. THE GRACE OF GOD. " His mercy is on them that *fear Him.*" " He hath exalted them of *low degree.*" " He hath filled the *hungry* with good things." " By grace are ye saved, that not of yourselves, it is the gift of God" (Luke 18. 14). It is the hungry and thirsty that are filled (Matt. 5. 6). Our testimony will be blessed if it is given as Mary gave hers.   _____

DELIVERED TO SERVE.
Luke 1. 74, 75.

"Lord, keep alive my sense of wonder,
    Cent'ring in the living Christ,
Oft placing me, His great throne under,
    To hold with Him a gracious tryst;
The ' old, old story' every new,
    And ever proving itself true."

IT is a great and cruel fallacy toward God and man to believe that we are saved merely to be *satisfied*. Such a debased thought is not worthy of the grace of God. The man who *eats* only to be satisfied is a selfish glutton and a worshipper of his stomach. We eat to live, and love, and labour. The provision of God made for us in Christ is to enable us to *live* before God, to *love* our fellowmen, and labour for Christ and His cause.

1. The great deliverance. " We being delivered out of the hand of our enemies." We are here reminded that this deliverance is—

1. ALL OF GRACE. " That He would *grant us*." It is in reality a Divine grant. It is because of His mercy that we are not consumed. When any board or society allows a *grant* to any one, the idea of merit and desert is often present, but with God's grants there can be no plea of merit, else grace is not grace.

2. FROM THE ENEMY, SIN. Sin is one of the *enemies* out of whose hand we need deliverance. In giving us His Son, God has also given us a grant of freedom from sin (Rom. 6. 18). " Sin shall not have dominion over you, for ye are not under law, but under grace" (Rom. 6. 14). Claim this grant.

3. FROM THE ENEMY, SELF. If sin is not to be allowed to lord it over us, the self-seeking *I* must be put in the place of death. As long as the carnal *I* lives it will be the *servant* of sin. By the atoning Blood the victory is won.

4. FROM THE ENEMY, SATAN. The great ACCUSER is always ready to bring some railing accusation against the Lord, against His Gospel, or against ourselves. We are not ignorant of His devices. " Put on the whole armour of God, that ye may be able to stand" (Eph. 6. 11).

2. The purpose of it. " He hath delivered us that we might *serve* Him." We are saved to serve. We have been freed from sin that we might become *servants to God* (Rom. 6. 18). It is good to be able to say "Thank God, I am saved," but it is better to be able to say "Thank God, I am the *bondslave* of Jesus Christ." That we might—

1. SERVE HIM. One is your Master, even Christ. Lord, what wilt Thou have me to do? Speak, Lord, for Thy servant heareth. *Serve* Him, God first, not the Church, not a cause, not the good principle, but the living Christ, our ever present gracious Lord, *whose we are*.

2. SERVE HIM WITHOUT FEAR. If we *love* the Lord with all our heart this will be the character of our service, for there is no fear in love; perfect love casteth out fear. Having received the Spirit of adoption we are saved from slavish fear and serve in the love of a son (Rom. 8. 15).

3. SERVE HIM IN HOLINESS. As saved ones we are "called with a holy calling" (2 Tim. 1. 9). Called into the holy priesthood, having been washed and clothed with holy robes that we might minister in holy things as we eat the holy meat. They must be clean who bear the vessels of the Lord. He which hath called you is holy, so be ye holy (1 Peter 1. 15).

4. SERVE HIM IN RIGHTEOUSNESS. Our *new man* is created *after God* in righteousness and true holiness (Eph. 4. 24). So the new man is expected to serve God in righteousness as well as in holiness. "In holiness" may refer to the nature of God within us; "in righteousness," to the Word of God before us. His holy nature imparted to us gives us *fitness* for service. His Holy Word gives us righteous principles for *guidance* in service.

5. SERVE BEFORE HIM. Sweet is the service that is rendered in the consciousness of His presence and done as standing before Him. Elijah could speak of " the Lord God of Israel before whom I stand" (1 Kings 17. 1). Abraham walked before God. Serving *before Him* is the remedy for the fear of man, and the secret of deliverance from dishonouring God by presenting eloquent prayers to great audiences.

6. SERVE HIM ALL THE DAYS OF OUR LIFE. There is no discharge in this holy war. The Levite might retire after a limited number of years' service, but those delivered from sin and wrath by the agony and blood of God's

beloved Son are to serve Him all the days of their life. All the days of that life which is Divine and eternal. In the days of bodily infirmity and weakness, when we can do nothing but look, may that *look* be the look of blessed submission and holy trust. Yes, Lord, all the days of my life and of Thy life. _____

THE NIGHT OF THE INCARNATION.
Luke 2. 1-20.

> " O prodigious wonder !
> To be sounded by the thunder—
> Our God on earth a Child.
> But as the light, not lightning,
> Attracting and affright'ning,
> Earth and Heaven reconciled."

THIS is in truth what one has called " The birth supreme 'midst things ajar." The Light of the World was born in the night. Naturally and spiritually the world at His coming was wrapped in sullen, helpless darkness. The cold, chilly mists of form and ceremony are now to melt away before the warmth and brightness of His rising. Thank God that He came as " light, not lightning." Notice the—

1. Preparation. " Joseph and Mary, because they belonged to the house of David, went up to Bethlehem to be taxed" **(vs. 1-5).** God had foretold, through the mouth of His prophet Micah, that Christ the King of Israel was to be born in Bethlehem (Micah 5. 2). The decree of the Roman Emperor helped on the fulfilment of God's Word. Our *circumstances* are in the hand of God as well as our soul.

2. Arrival. " She laid Him in a manger, because there was no room for them in the inn" **(v. 7).** No room in the inn for Him is strangely prophetic of the reception He was to have as the Saviour of men. Other persons and things first. Is it not so still? We are told that there is a place for everything. What place has Jesus Christ in

politics, in business, in society (so-called), in the home,
or in the heart. Like that inn in Bethlehem they are
already *full*. No room for Jesus with regard to the affairs
of daily life. Is it not still true that "the Son of Man
hath not where to lay *His head*?" (Matt. 8. 20).

3. Proclamation (vs. 8-12). It was divinely fitting
that "Christ the Lord" should be heralded by the "angel
of the Lord," and accompanied with the "glory of the
Lord." We have here the gospel of the incarnation,
declaring "good tidings of great joy." Good tidings of
the grace of our Lord Jesus Christ, emptying Himself
unto poverty that He might make many rich (2 Cor. 8. 9).

4. Accompaniment. "Suddenly there was a multitude of the heavenly host praising God" (vs. 13, 14).
If there was indifference among men on earth at the coming
of the Son of God there was no indifference in Heaven at
His going. There is joy in Heaven still over one sinner
repenting and believing in Him (Luke 15. 7).

5. Inquiry. "Let us now go and see this which the
Lord hath made known unto us" (vs. 15, 16). The
shepherds *believed* the Word, and acting on it, they found
Him just as it was told them. Instead of reasoning and
cavilling, would that men had the wisdom of these
shepherds, and just say, "Let us go and see." Put the
Word of God to the test. Believe, and thou shalt see.
Seek, and ye shall find.

6. Testimony, "When they had seen they made
known abroad the saying" (v. 17). They believed, and
therefore they spoke. Those who have proved the power of
God's revealed truth in their own experience are better
able to speak of it to others. They cannot help speaking
it, it is such good tidings of great joy. They make known
the *saying* because it is a faithful one, and worthy of the
acceptation of all (1 Tim. 1. 15),

7. Rejoicing. " They returned glorifying and praising God" (v. 20). We may well question whether we have ever found the Lord if we have no joy in speaking of Him, and not constrained out of a full heart to glorify and praise Him. If the Gospel is not tidings of great joy to us it is clear that we have never yet believed it. The shepherds: 1. Heard; 2. Believed; 3. Obeyed; 4. Received; 5. Testified; 6. Rejoiced; 7. Praised. " They *returned* praising God." Returned to their daily avocation, but with a new vision before their souls, and a new power in their lives. Finding Jesus the Saviour is a very practical discovery.

GOOD TIDINGS OF GREAT JOY.
Luke 2. 8-14.

"I, too, would seek the angels to follow,
Lord of all angels, wilt Thou me hallow?
I fain would emulate their holy zeal,
I fain would their glad obedience feel,
My forehead, like theirs, Thy holiness seal."

IN those broad undulating fields lying around Bethlehem, where Ruth began her mission of gleaning, and where David tended the flock of his father Jesse, shepherds were still keeping watch over their flock by night. But that was a night never to be forgotten. That night a star appeared that was destined to supersede the brightness of the sun, and to fill the whole earth with the glory of the invisible God. Good tidings. Look at—

1. The Preacher. " The angel of the Lord." This is the first herald of the new dispensation. It was a great occasion, but it was not what the wisdom of men would call an eloquent sermon. It was brilliant in its simplicity, though in meaning fathomless as eternity. "Fear not, I bring you good tidings of great joy" (v. 8). It was what all sermons should be—plain, pointed, practical, powerful.

2. The hearers. " Shepherds in the fields." They

were both intelligent and attentive. They were more. They were hungering and thirsting for the tidings which now fell so suddenly upon their startled ears. They were anxious souls, looking and longing for His appearing. Just as the highest hill top catches the first glory beams of the rising sun, so these shepherds, standing on the heights of believing expectation, are first bathed in the glory that was coming to bless a sleeping world. They that honour Me, I will honour.

3. The Gospel. " Behold I bring you *good tidings.*" Let us examine the characteristics of this wonderful *God-spell* that was in the approaching ages to hold so many spellbound amidst all the fascinations of the world and pleasures of sin. It was—

1. MYSTERIOUS. "Unto you is *born* Christ the *Lord.*" Who can by searching find out this? The Lord of glory *born* and lying in a manger, stripped of His ineffable majesty and wrapped in swaddling clothes. This is the sign (v. 12). The sign of infinite grace and compassion. Great is the mystery of godliness. God manifest in the flesh.

2. GOOD. " Good tidings." The voice on the mount at the giving of the law only brought fear and quaking. The law proclaimed was holy, just, and good, but that was no tidings of good to sinful men. The Gospel brings good tidings, because it declares a SAVIOUR born. Without the birth of God's Son, no son could be born of God. He who was to bring sons to glory must be "made perfect through sufferings" (Heb. 2. 10; Isa. 52. 7).

3. JOYFUL. " Good tidings of great joy." Its first note is "Fear not." Fear not the depth of your sinfulness, the number of your sins, your own weakness, or the foes of the soul without, for unto you is born a Saviour. God has laid help on One that is mighty, Christ the Lord. We joy in God through our Lord Jesus Christ (Rom. 5. 11).

4. PERSONAL. " I bring *you* good tidings. For unto

you is born this day." The voice of this heavenly wisdom
is still crying out, " Unto you, O men, I call." The
shepherds could not but believe that this blessed message
from God was for all that *heard* it. Hear, and your soul
shall live. This Gospel is unto *you* first (Acts 3. 26).

5. UNIVERSAL. "Which shall be to all people" (v. 10).
When our Lord lay in His swaddling clothes, or when He
stood before Pilate, He was in the eyes of men a very
insignificant object compared with Pilate and the pagan
Emperor of Rome, but where are they now? The world
for which Christ died shall yet be blessed through
His Name. "All nations shall call Him blessed"
(Psa. 72. 11). Are you blessing Him now?

6. CONFIRMED. " Suddenly a multitude of the heavenly
host, praising God and saying, Glory to God in the highest"
(vs. 13, 14). This thing was not done in a corner.
Those who believe the Gospel will have ample reasons for
cleaving to it, both miraculous and otherwise, the Word
will always be confirmed with signs following. The
Spirit beareth witness with our spirit that we are the
children of God (Rom. 8. 16; 1 Cor. 1. 22).

SIMEON—A HIDDEN ONE.
Luke 2. 25-32.

"My mother's grave my Sinai was,
But light, not lightning, was the cause
That won me from my unbelief,
And staunch'd an ageing father's grief;
Softly my childhood's prayer returned,
And my old faith within me burned."

SIMEON seems to have been one of the Lord's hidden ones,
who, under the guidance of God, calmly and quietly served
Him in *waiting*. But the hidden one is here brought into
light. He has prayed in secret, he is now rewarded openly.

1. **See his holy character.**

1. HE WAS JUST AND DEVOUT (v. 25). Just in his

dealings with men, and devout in his dealings with God. Righteous and holy. These are the two sides of a Christian life, they must be equally honest and true.

2. HE WAITED FOR THE CONSOLATION OF ISRAEL. He waited and prayed because he believed. This dear old man of God had no faith in any other means or efforts to comfort Israel than the coming of the King. This is still Israel's hope, for "the Lord shall comfort Zion" (Isa. 51. 3). His waiting was rewarded; his hope was fulfilled. "They shall not be ashamed that wait for Me" (Isa. 49. 23). Wait on the Lord.

3. HE WAS ENDUED WITH THE SPIRIT. "The Holy Ghost was upon him." There is always a very vital connection between *waiting* on the Lord and being *endued* with power (Acts 2. 1-4). The effect of the Holy Spirit resting upon him was twofold: 1. He was taught. It was *revealed* unto him by the Holy Ghost that he should not see death before he had seen the Lord's Christ. 2. He was *led*. "He came by the Spirit into the temple" (v. 27). Every Spirit-possessed one has the things of Christ revealed to him or her, and will be led by the Spirit. It may simplify the matter to reverse the order here: (1) Be filled with the Spirit, then you will (2) be willing to wait on and for the Lord; and then (3) you will be able to live a just and devout life before God and men, being taught of God and led by the Spirit.

2. Hear his joyful testimony. His is indeed a striking attitude as he stands with the infant Saviour in those arms so long outstretched in prayer and patient waiting. Who can refrain from giving a glowing testimony when the arms of their faith have been filled with the personal Saviour? He blesses God as one whose life had now been fully satisfied with his gift. Crowned with his honour, and ready to depart in peace. Such is always the satisfying power of Jesus Christ when received by faith. He testifies of—

1. CHRIST AS THE SALVATION OF GOD. " Mine eyes have seen Thy salvation" (v. 30). Beautiful is the title thus given to Jesus. "*Thy Salvation.*" God's great love, mercy, and power united to redeem and bless us in the person of His Son. This was the making *bare* of the arm of the Lord for salvation (Isa. 52. 10). This naked arm reveals, if we might so put it, the strong and mighty saving muscle of Jehovah. " O arm of the Lord, awake, awake!" What else but the living Christ in our hearts will ever fit us for departing in peace?

2. CHRIST AS THE LIGHT OF THE GENTILES (v. 32). " As a revelation to the nations" (Newberry). Christ is God's revealed Light to the nations of the earth. With regard to the character of God and the way of salvation there is no other light. All else is but the light of sin-blinded reason, which is only supposition or superstition. " I am the Light of the World." Salvation is a coming out of darkness into His marvellous light. The sparks of our own making will never turn night into day (Isa. 9. 2). No more can our own work save us. The presence of Christ with us and in us is as Heaven's own searchlight turned upon the Father that *we* may see Him, and turned upon ourselves, upon sin, death, and eternity that we might see these, as it were, with His eyes. " Walk in the light" (1 John 1. 7).

3. CHRIST AS THE GLORY OF ISRAEL (v. 32). This is the order revealed by the Holy Ghost to Simeon. Christ was to be *first* a light to the Gentiles, after *that* the glory of His people Israel. Was there another in Israel who believed that the Christ would first bless the Gentile nations before He would be glorified among His own ancient people? The Holy Spirit could make no mistake. The Messiah would be cut off, numbered with transgressors. But He will come again, not as a sin-offering, but as the King of Israel, with great power and glory. They shall mourn because of Him (having crucified Him), but the *glory* of the Lord will then have arisen upon them. Where the glorified One is there will be glory, for glory always dwells in *Immanuel's* land, whether in earth or in Heaven, in Time, or Eternity. Christ is our Salvation; Christ is our Light; Christ is our Glory. To Him be the praise.

CHRIST A SIGN SPOKEN AGAINST.

Luke 2 34, 35.

> "Voiceless, alone, and hunger-bitten,
> Lo! where the scapegoat stands sun-smitten;
> Or now among the sere sedge lying
> Parched, and as by inches dying.
> Thou, O my Saviour, for our sake,
> The antitype Thyself didst make.
> But, ah! on Thee a mightier load,
> Thou God-forsaken Son of God."

As soon as Simeon took the Lord in his arms he became a prophet, being taught of the Holy Ghost (v. 25), he spake with all boldness. Each saying is full of deep and far-reaching significance. Receiving Christ is always a means of opening the eyes to behold the things which are unseen. Observe what he says about the—

1. Mission of Christ. "This Child is set for the *fall* and *rising again* of many in Israel" (v. 34). This—

1. WAS TRUE LOCALLY. In the day of His suffering and shame His disciples forsook Him and fled, they *fell* from Him, but they *rose again* into faith and favour after His resurrection.

2. IS TRUE UNIVERSALLY. All who come to Him must *fall* before Him ere they can be *raised again* in newness of life. Saul *fell* to the earth at His appearing to him on the way to Damascus, but he was raised again, a chosen vessel to bear His Name. Zacchaeus had to *come down* at His call before salvation came to his house (Luke 19. 1-9). We must needs be planted in the likeness of His death before

we can be raised in the likeness of His resurrection (Rom. 6. 5).

3. WILL BE TRUE DISPENSATIONALLY. Israel as a nation has already fallen (Rom. 9. 12), and the Gentiles are being presently enriched thereby, but a *rising again* will yet take place, for all Israel shall be saved when the Deliverer shall come out of Zion and turn away ungodliness (Rom. 9. 26).

2. Character of Christ. "He shall be for a SIGN which shall be spoken against." "A *sign* may be offensive in two ways, either by its bewildering uncertainty or its alarming clearness. It was the unmistakable distinctness of Christ's life and teaching that made Him a stone of stumbling and a rock of offence to many. In Him as a sign we see, as it were, the—

1. RED LIGHT OF DANGER. Lifted up before the eyes of the doubting and the impenitent. If the green tree that stood in our place in the fires of God's judgment had to suffer so, what shall become of the dry?

2. BLUE LIGHT OF CAUTION. To those who would rush past the Cross in their haste to be saved, going about to establish their own righteousness. O that men would consider. Take heed to thyself.

3. WHITE LIGHT OF SAFETY. To the believing and the obedient. Christ the Sign declares that the way is clear to him that trusteth. Press on to the mark. If thy Master was *spoken against*, be thou not offended if many speak against thee (Acts 28. 32).

3. Influence of Christ. "He shall be spoken against, *that the thoughts of many hearts may be revealed*" (v. 35). These are solemn words. O my soul tread softly here. To come into contact with Jesus Christ is to have the *thoughts of the heart revealed*. He is the Living Word, who is a discerner of the thoughts and intents of the heart.

The thoughts of our hearts, with regard to Him, are being
revealed every day by our words and actions. Are they
for Him or against Him? As a man is in Christ's sight,
so is he. Our attitude toward Him determines whether we
shall stand or fall in the judgment, and determines *now*
whether our life is pleasing in His sight. The Lord looketh
upon the heart. Has the sword of suffering that pierced
through the soul of Mary, as she witnessed the agony and
death of her Son and Saviour, pierced through our souls,
because of our deep and real sympathy with Him? And
are the thoughts of many hearts being revealed through
the suffering and rejected Saviour *in* us? May the sword
of His Word pierce through our souls, and may the thoughts
of *His heart* be revealed to us.

A SORROWFUL SEARCH.
Luke 2. 41-51.

" We've trod the maze of error round,
  Long wand'ring in the winding glade;
And now the torch of light is found,
  It only shows us where we strayed."

—GEORGE CRABBE.

IT is extremely melancholy at the end of an anxious, busy
life only to find light enough to show that it has been a
life of error and failure and transgression against God. It
is possible for the saving light of the Gospel to become at
last, through wilful neglect, only the lurid glare that
reveals but a ghastly future. Walk in the light while ye
have the light. Seek the Lord while He may be found.

It was the first eventful day in the life of Jesus when He
went to His first Passover at Jerusalem at the age of
twelve. Even then, as the Great Teacher come from God,
He could not be hid. Let us reflect on the seeking and
the finding of Him by His reputed parents.

1. The discovery. " They went a day's journey, and
when they found Him not they turned back." It is always

a sad discovery to those who know and love Jesus to find that He is not with them. Like Samson, they may shake *themselves*, but it availeth nothing (Judges 16. 20). How had this come about? We read that they—

1. SUPPOSED HIM TO BE IN THE COMPANY. *Supposing* Him to be with us is no evidence that He is with us. Many suppose Christ to be with them who are living Christless lives, supposing that all is right when all is wrong. Then again they—

2. DOUBTLESS WERE TAKEN UP WITH OTHER COMPANY. Not that they *intended* to go without Him, but between their suppositions and the pressure of their kinsfolk and acquaintances He was left behind. Is it not the old story, "While I was busy here and there, He was gone?" It is even possible to be busy with the Lord's work when the Lord Himself is not with us. A missionary going out to his work one morning very sad was caught at the door by his wife, who looked into his face and said, "O Willie, much work and little prayer makes a hard task." There was no visiting that morning, but a work was done in Willie's soul that proved a life-long blessing.

2. The search. One day's journey *without* Jesus incurred three days' sorrowful searching. But observe that they—

1. SOUGHT HIM AT ONCE. They did not attempt to go one step farther without Him. Their love forbade them. We will always make quicker progress by turning back to the place where we have parted company with Christ than by going on without His conscious presence with us. If His presence does not brighten your life, seek His face. Wait on the Lord. Turn back.

2. SOUGHT HIM SORROWING. At first they sought Him where they could not find Him, among their kinsfolk and acquaintances. Are we not all apt to run among our

Christian friends, seeking the light and help that only Christ Himself can give? It is always a *sorrowful* search seeking the Lord. If we feel the need of His presence to satisfy our souls as much as His parents did, the terrible sense of *loss* will constrain us to seek Him in tears.

3. The finding. He that seeketh findeth (Jer. 29. 13). They found Him—

1. WHERE? '' In the temple.'' The temple was the '' house of prayer.'' This fact may help to impress us with the thought that in the secret place of prayer we may surely expect to find Him whom our souls love, and whose presence with us we so much need in our journey homeward. Such blessed company makes the road short.

2. WHEN? '' After three days.'' We cannot resist the conviction that there is a profound truth here for every *seeker after Jesus*. The *three days* seem to remind us of the resurrection. '' Destroy this temple,'' He said, '' and in three days I will raise it up again.'' It is not a dead Christ we seek, but the risen, living One, who *sits in the midst*, in the great temple above.

3. How? '' Sitting in the midst of doctors about His Father's business.'' All who ever sought and found Christ have found Him doing His Father's business. It is the will of God both to save and sanctify. In our receiving Jesus Christ by faith, and abiding in Him, the great business of the Father with respect to our individual lives is being done. Thy will be done in us as in Heaven.

4. The following. Note also that He—

1. WENT DOWN WITH THEM. He had just said to them, Wist ye not that I must be about My Father's business? Yet He went *down with them*. Down into the home, down into all the joys and sorrows and details of their everyday life, and this was also to Him the Father's business. Is it otherwise now? Does He not still go down with those who

have sought Him sorrowing into the sphere of their daily toil, into their every circumstance, that all may be brightened and cheered with His presence?

2. WAS SUBJECT TO THEM. He *adapted* Himself to all their needs and requirements. He placed Himself, as it were, at their disposal, and virtually said, "What will ye that I should do unto you?" Reverently speaking, is it not so still? Has He not offered *Himself* to all who have sought Him? Does He not now adapt Himself as our Saviour to our every condition and requirement? Is He not still, on the ground of His own promise, subject to them that believe? He cannot deny Himself.

THE THOUGHTS OF GOD.
Psalm 139. 17.

God's thoughts are great thoughts. What is the sum of them as revealed in His Word? There is the thought of—

1. CREATION. Made the heavens and the earth.
2. REPRESENTATION. He made man in His own likeness.
3. REDEMPTION. Promised in the seed of the woman.
4. JUDGMENT. Seen in the deluge.
5. ELECTION. In the calling of Abraham.
6. FELLOWSHIP. In His dwelling with His people in the Tabernacle.
7. INCARNATION. In the birth of His Son.
8. SALVATION. By grace through the Gospel.
9. SECOND COMING of Christ as King.
10. RESTORATION of the Jewish nation.
11. MILLENNIAL BLISS during His reign on earth.
12. ETERNAL GLORY in the Kingdom of the Father.

BIBLE READINGS.

The Holy Spirit.

1. HIS NAME AND PERSONALITY.

THE name " Holy Ghost," or " Holy Spirit," occurs in the New Testament ninety-three times. In the Acts alone He is mentioned over fifty times; and in the eighth of Romans there are seventeen references. These facts clearly prove that He occupies a conspicuous place in the present dispensation, which is in truth the dispensation of " the ministration of the Spirit" (2 Cor. 3. 8). In the Gospels we see the ministry of Jesus; in the Acts we have the ministry of the Holy Ghost. Does He receive equal prominence in the acts of the Church to-day? How much we hear about " church work," " evangelistic work," " mission work," &c., but how little about the " Spirit's work." His Name reveals His actual relationship to man redeemed. In the name Father we see the parent from whom we have wandered. In the name Jesus we see the Saviour by whom we are reconciled. In the name Holy Spirit we see the atmosphere in which our spirits are to live, and move, and have their being (Acts 17. 28). He, like the air we breathe, comes into continual and indispensable contact with our inner man, supplying our souls with the life and spirit which were in Christ Jesus (Ezek. 37. 5-10). The name "Holy Spirit" carries with it the idea of a holy, moving, vitalising breath At Pentecost this mighty breath came down like rushing wind, bringing the soul-bracing atmosphere of the very " presence of God" in and around the waiting disciples (Acts 2. 1-4). He comes, too, like the fragrant breath from some beautiful and fruitful garden, that makes us feel the *reality* of much that is yet unseen; and so through hope, satisfying every spiritual sense in the new nature, and giving days of Heaven upon earth. In this light the apostolic benediction (2 Cor. 13. 14) is full of blessed meaning.

1. The **grace** of our Lord Jesus Christ—"Humiliation and death."

2. The **love** of God—"Justification and life."

3. The **communion** of the Holy Ghost—"Assimilation and fellowship."

4. Be with **you all**—"Privilege and responsibility."

Likeness, then, is indispensable to communion. What communion hath light with darkness, or Christ with Belial? None. Because there is no likeness. But by the Holy Ghost we are made like the Father, for we are changed into the same image by the Spirit of God (2 Cor. 3. 18). And so our fellowship is with the Father and with His Son Jesus Christ (1 John 1. 3). The presence of the Holy Spirit is therefore as necessary to our spiritual life as the air is to our physical life. Without this we can no more rejoice in the love of God than we could rejoice in the warmth of the sun without the medium of the atmosphere.

Now, a word about His personality. That the Holy Spirit is a person is commonly believed, but most imperfectly realised. The frequent use of the personal pronoun when He is referred to clearly implies that He is a person (John 16. 13, 14). And all through Scripture acts and attributes are attributed to Him which could not be predicated of any mere influence or emanation (Acts 5. 3). And however unfathomable the mystery, the fact remains that this mighty, holy being, whose presence is as a spiritual soul-moving breath, is a Person. And that Person is called GOD (Acts 5. 3, 4). His individuality ought to be as distinctly recognised as that of the Father or the Son.

The devil knows that so long as this truth is forgotten and neglected the kingdom of Christ will make but slow progress, as He is the direct agent between Christ and the sinful souls of men. As a Person, then, what kind of treatment is He receiving at the hands of men? (Acts 7. 51-53). ———

2. THE SUFFERINGS OF THE SPIRIT.

How, and in what way, does the Holy Spirit suffer at the hands of men? He is being—

1. Blasphemed by the presumption of men (Matt. 12. 31, 32).   If we compare verse 24 with verse 28 the sin here spoken of will be plainly seen. They said, " This fellow casteth out devils by Beelzebub." Jesus said, " I cast out devils by the Spirit of God." Therefore they attributed the Spirit's work to the work of the devil, and so blasphemed the Holy Ghost. And how much better is it to attribute the work of the Holy Ghost to " mere excitement" or the cleverness of a preacher?

2. Insulted by the pride of men.   In Hebrews 10. 29 we read of those who in their pride of heart "have trodden under foot the *Son of God*, and have counted the *blood* of the covenant an unholy thing, and (so) have done despite unto the Spirit of grace." To deny the divinity of Christ and the preciousness of the Blood is to despise the testimony of the Holy Spirit and to insult Him to His face. Those who do without the Blood have to do without the Spirit (1 John 5. 8).

3. Vexed by the disobedience of men. " In love and pity He (God) redeemed them, but they rebelled and vexed His Holy Spirit" (Isa. 63. 9, 10). Think of *redeemed* ones *rebelling* and vexing the Holy One. How often, when He reveals some unexpected ugliness within, instead of being thankful for the discovery, the proud heart rebels and refuses to confess. Thus the Holy

Spirit is vexed, and cannot give the blessing He would because of our stubbornness of will.

4. Resisted by the unbelief of men. " Ye do always resist the Holy Ghost, as your fathers did" (Acts 7. 51). " They could not enter in because of *unbelief*" (Heb. 3. 19). In doubting the Word of God, the Spirit of God is resisted, for the Word is His sword. If the Holy Ghost is to have full possession of the Canaan land of the heart, to make a clear riddance of every evil beast (lust), and all that would pollute the holy mount, then the promises of God must be believed or the Spirit will be resisted.

5. Tempted by the insincerity of men. " How is it that ye have agreed to tempt the Spirit of the Lord?" (Acts 5. 1-9). Ananias and Sapphira in seeking to deceive their brethren, tempted and lied against the Holy Ghost. A man is guilty of this when he pretends to his brethren that he is wholly devoted to God, and at the same time indulging in secret sin. Oh, beware of being more holy before men than you are before God, and of tempting the Holy Ghost—yes, tempting Him to leave you self-deceived. " Create a clean heart within me, O God" (Psa. 51. 10).

6. Quenched by the prejudice of men. " Quench not the Spirit; despise not prophesyings" (1 Thess. 5. 19, 20). It seems to me that what is forbidden here is a very common sin, that of treating with indifference the *message of God*, because perhaps the *messenger* is not exactly after our own heart. This secret prejudice, which is frequently the result of sectarianism, may be unknown to our fellows, but it is known and felt by the Holy Ghost, and hangs like a veil between His influence and the soul.

7. Grieved by the frivolity of men. " Grieve not the Spirit" (Eph. 4. 30). This solemn exhortation lies between these other two: " Let your *communication* be good to the *use of edifying*" (v. 29), and " Let bitterness and

evil speaking be put away'' (v. 31). How often is the Spirit
grieved by the light and unprofitable conversation of
Christians; grieved, because He wishes to teach us to
profit. He cannot join in the unprofitable talk, much less in
the evil speaking. The Holy Ghost cannot afford to trifle.
Why should we? Let a watch be put at the door of our
lips. Men filled with the Holy Spirit are solemn men.

3. THE RECEIVING OF THE SPIRIT.

THE gift of the Spirit is as much a promise of Christ as
salvation is (John 15. 26), and should be as definitely
enjoyed. We receive the adoption of sons (Gal. 4. 5) by
receiving Christ, and believing that He has given us the
right to become sons according to His promise (John 1. 12),
and in the same way He has given us the right to receive
the Holy Ghost, and to become sons endued with power.
Let us notice several conditions indicated in Scripture on
which the Holy Spirit is given and received—

1. Condition of forgiveness. '' Repent and be baptised . . . for the remission of sins, and ye shall receive the
Holy Ghost'' (Acts 2. 38). The Spirit may be received
without being baptised (Acts 10. 47), but not without
being forgiven. This Holy Dove cannot dwell among
unclean birds. Christ's first dealing with the temple
was to cleanse it (Matt. 21. 12); and the Spirit's first
dealing with the sinner is to convince of sin (John 16. 8).

2. Condition of sonship. ''*Because* ye are sons, God
hath sent forth His Spirit into your hearts'' (Gal. 4. 6).
Why this '' *because?*'' Every son should resemble his
father. So He sent forth His Spirit that they might be
changed into His image (2 Cor. 3. 18). It is one thing to
claim the *relationship*, but quite another thing to claim
the *likeness*. And yet the likeness is but the outward
evidence of the relationship.

3. Condition of felt need. I will pour water upon

him that is *thirsty*, and floods upon the *dry* ground
(Isa. 44. 3). He giveth power to the *faint* (Isa. 40. 29).
Upon those who seek the Holy Ghost as men dying of
thirst God will pour Him forth in floods. But those
who can live without Him are not likely to have Him.

4. Condition of faith. This spake He of the Spirit,
which they that *believe* on Him should receive (John 7. 39).
In Galatians 3. 13, 14 we have: (1) *A fact stated*, "Christ
hath redeemed us." (2) *A purpose declared*, "That we
might receive the promise of the Spirit *through faith.*"
How strange that the *fact* is so generally believed, while
the *purpose* is almost wholly ignored.

5. Condition of obedience. "The Holy Ghost, whom
God hath given to them that obey Him" (Acts 5. 32).
According to the measure of our willingness and readiness
to do God's will may we expect the help of the Holy Spirit.
In the matter of *will* every child should be able to say "I
and my father are one." If this is not so, there must be
disobedience in heart.

6. Condition of waiting. "Tarry until ye be endued
with power from on high" (Luke 24. 49). *Wait* for the
promise of the Father (Acts 1. 4). The disciples waited,
and the filling came. There are some that seem to read
these passages: "*Work* until ye be endued;" "*Work*
for the promise of the Father." They are afraid to *wait*
lest all should go wrong, as if God could not do without
their fussy restlessness.

7. Condition of prayer. "Your Heavenly Father will
give the Holy Spirit to them that *ask* Him" (Luke 11. 13).
It was while Jesus *was praying* that the Heaven was opened
and the Holy Ghost descended (Luke 3. 21). It was when
the disciples *had prayed* that they were all filled with the
Holy Ghost (Acts 4. 31). It was when Solomon had
made an *end of praying* that the fire and the glory *filled*
the house (2 Chron. 7. 1).

4. THE INDWELLING OF THE SPIRIT.

DAVID prayed, "Take not Thy Holy Spirit from **me**" (Psa. 51. 11). All who, like David, wish to live wholly for God find that the continual *indwelling* of the Spirit is an indispensable necessity. Without this even a Samson is weak as other men. It is the purpose of Christ not only to give us the Spirit, but that He should *abide* with us for ever (John 14. 16). In the texts which speak of His indwelling, various expressive and suggestive figures are used.

1. As a factor in a house. "If any man have not the Spirit of Christ he is none of His" (Rom. 8. 9). Where the Master is rejected the factor will not dwell. The Spirit takes possession of the heart for Christ, so that Christ dwelleth in our hearts by His Spirit. The Spirit occupies till He comes. And every house (heart) thus occupied is occupied *all* for Christ. He must keep the key of every door. He must have the use of all the furniture. The world knoweth Him not, but ye know Him, for He dwelleth with you, and shall be *in* you (John 14. 17).

2. As a spring in a well. "The water that I shall give shall be *in* him a well of water springing up" (John 4. 14). Man's heart by nature is like a well filled with rottenness. Cleansing must precede usefulness. This living spring within fills and satisfies the whole being. The well is deep, for the spring is in God (Psa. 87. 7).

3. As a river in a fountain. "Out of his inner man shall flow rivers of living water. This spake He of the Spirit" (John 7. 38, 39). The blessing is not confined to the well, but flows out like refreshing streams. The Spirit dwelling in us is to be as an unfailing fountain to others. But the outflow will only be in proportion to the springing up within. Spring up, O well!

4. As the sap in the tree. "He shall also quicken

your mortal bodies by His Spirit which dwelleth in you''
(Rom. 8. 11). It is the upspringing of the vital sap that
quickens the seemingly dead and worthless tree into life
and beauty, making it fat and flourishing. So doth the
Holy Ghost vitalise the whole man. The mortal bodies of
Moses and Stephen were quickened when their faces shone.
Many of God's saints are living witnesses to the proof
of this as a present experience, and as a foretaste of
resurrection glory. '' The trees of the LORD are full of
sap'' (Psa. 104. 16; see John 15).

5. As the waters in the sea. '' Be filled with the
Spirit'' (Eph. 5. 18). The Holy Spirit is to fill our whole
man, as the waters fill the sea. Entering into and filling
every crevice, flooding every gulf and chasm, cleansing
what is filthy, and covering all that is unseemly, so may
He flow into every detail of our life. And just as in the
sea there is room enough for the exercise of every living
thing, so *in the Spirit* there is ample scope for every power
in man.

6. As the strength in the body. '' I am full of power
by the Spirit of the LORD'' (Micah 3. 8). A strong man
does not put off and on his strength as occasions require.
He carries it with him and *in* him. He simply uses it,
and every part of his body is filled with it. He is literally
filled with power. It is the steam that worketh in the
engine to will and to do. ''It is *God* that *worketh in you.*''
A man, no matter how strong he may be intellectually or
morally, who has not the '' power of the Spirit'' is,
spiritually, but as a helpless corpse.

7. As the glory in the temple. '' Know ye not that
ye are the temple of God, and that the Spirit of God
dwelleth in you?'' (1 Cor. 3. 16). '' Your body is the
temple of the Holy Ghost'' (1 Cor. 6. 19). The glory in the
temple was as the treasure in the earthen vessel. Before
the glory came Solomon was everything, but afterwards

he was nothing. The presence of the glory was the symbol of Divine *ownership* and *occupancy*. And so the building became " The Temple of God." Likewise ye are the temple of God, owned and occupied for the glory of His Name. What agreement hath the temple of God with idols? See that ye defile not this temple, " for the temple of God is holy, which temple ye are" (1 Cor. 3. 17)

---

5. IN THE SPIRIT.

HAVING received the Spirit, and having Him indwelling and filling us, our life is now to be lived " in the Spirit." That is, under His guiding, ever present, almighty over-shadowing influence, like the Israelites under the pillar of cloud. From Scripture we observe there are certain privileges and blessings which can only be enjoyed by those who are " IN THE SPIRIT." We mention the following—

1. God is to be worshipped. We worship God in the Spirit (Phil. 3. 3). God is a Spirit, and our spirit must worship Him (John 4. 24). But that is not all, our spirit must worship *in the Spirit of God*, or as in the Revised Version, "Who worship in the Spirit of God." We may be serious and solemn in our worship, and yet not be in the Spirit; and if not in the Spirit, then no acceptable worship is given. All such worshippers, no matter how earnest, worship they know not what. In all the churches as well as in Athens, how many there are of whom it might be said, " They are too superstitious."

2. God's voice is heard and His glory witnessed. 'I was *in the Spirit*, and *heard* behind me a great voice, . . . and *saw* the Son of Man clothed in glory" (Rev. 1. 10-18). Those who are continually in the Spirit are continually enraptured with the glory of the Lord. Those not in the Spirit may talk fluently about the "voice" and the "glory," but to their own hearts it is all unreal. In the Spirit we hear not the still *small voice* only as of one speaking from afar and heard with difficulty, but "a GREAT VOICE as of a trumpet," about which there can be no doubt.

3. Heavenly things are understood. "Come up hither, and I will show you things, . . . and immediately I was in the Spirit" (Rev. 4. 1, 2). We cannot understand the things of God but by the Spirit of God, for they are spiritually discerned. Then if God would show thee, . . . *immediately* you must be in the Spirit. The book of the Revelation of Jesus may be divided into four sections. The first beginning at chap. 1. 10; second at chap. 4. 2; third at chap. 17. 3; fourth at chap. 21. 10. At each of these changes in the scene of Revelation, John reminds us that he was " in the Spirit." How else could he understand the great mysteries? How else can we? Is our not being in the Spirit not the chief reason why " the things to come" are so little understood? Paul undoubtedly understood the unspeakable words he heard in Paradise, although it was impossible for him to utter them (2 Cor. 12. 4). Every one who is in the Spirit is unspeakably above those who are not.

4. Man's helplessness and God's power are seen. " The Lord carried me in the Spirit, and set me in the valley of bones; . . . so I prophesied and they stood up" (Ezek. 37. 1-10). It was while he was *in the Spirit* that he saw how dead and dry the bones were, and when he prophesied so successfully. Those in the Spirit see the need as others cannot, and so have no faith in the mere human remedies, but speak the word *as* God has commanded (vs. 7-10), and so witness the quickening power of the almighty breath.

5. Divine strength and comfort are enjoyed. " Behold I go bound in the Spirit," bonds and afflictions abide me, but none of these things move me (Acts 20. 22-24). When in the Spirit a man is dwelling in the holy calm

and undisturbable element of Heaven, and made strong
in the midst of otherwise crushing circumstances. The
peace of God keeps his heart. '' God is our refuge, we will
not fear though the earth be removed. There is a *river*,
the streams whereof make glad'' (Psa. 46. 1-4).

6. Is the proof of His indwelling in us. '' Ye are in
the Spirit, *if so be* that the Spirit of God dwell in you''
(Rom. 8. 9). If the Spirit of God is not abiding in us we
cannot live in the Spirit. It is easy to preach the theory
of the Spirit's indwelling, but *living in the Spirit* is the
practical manifestation of it. He does not come to dwell
in us as a candle under a bushel, or as a helpless invalid
whose presence cannot be seen or felt outside, but as a
mighty life-quickener and a spiritual wonder-worker,
whose presence cannot be hid.

7. All service is to be rendered. '' Look ye out men
full of the Holy Ghost'' (Acts 6. 3). Even for the work of
an almoner this was needed. Paul's preaching was in
demonstration of the Spirit (1 Cor. 2. 4); '' Apollos
taught, being fervent in the Spirit'' (Acts 18. 25); all
prayer is to be in the Spirit (Eph. 6. 18); to be in the Spirit
is to be in immediate touch with God, and not to be in
direct contact with God is to be out of fellowship, and
consequently fruitless (John 15. 6).

---

6. THE BAPTISM OF THE SPIRIT.

THERE is one Lord, one faith, one baptism (Eph. 4. 5).
Yet the Scriptures clearly teach—

1. A baptism with water (Acts 8. 38).
2. A baptism with the Holy Ghost (Matt. 3. 11).
3. A baptism into Jesus Christ (Rom. 6. 3).

Which is the *one* baptism? The first two without the
latter would be insufficient. Is the *one* baptism not the
baptism into Christ? (Gal. 3. 27). And is not the water

baptism the *earthly* witness, and the Holy Ghost baptism the *heavenly* witness of this great *one* baptism? So that by these two witnesses (human and Divine) the great mystical truth of our spiritual union with Christ is established. By the Spirit we are first baptised *into* Christ, and then by Christ we are baptised *with* the Spirit.

Let us notice for a moment what this baptism into Christ implies—

1. It implies DEATH. "Know ye not that so many of us as were baptised into Jesus Christ were baptised into His death?" (Rom. 6. 3). This is no mere figure of speech, but a solemn spiritual reality. "I am dead, nevertheless I live, yet not I" (Gal. 2. 20).

2. It implies BURIAL. "We are buried with Him by baptism into death" (Rom. 6. 4). This is not only a burial into water, but *into death*, into the death of Christ. The death of self must in reality take place before it will yield to the burial, for so long as it lives it will love to be seen of men.

3. It implies RESURRECTION. "Buried with Him in baptism, *wherein* also ye are risen with Him" (Col. 2. 12). There can be no resurrection without death. To be *risen* with Christ is the proof that we have died in Him. Read Philippians 3. 10 in its reverse order.

4. It implies LIKENESS. "For as many of you as have been baptised into Christ have put on Christ" (Gal. 3. 27). If we have been planted together in the likeness of His death, we shall be also in the likeness of His resurrection. Our likeness to His resurrection will just be according to the measure of our likeness in His death.

5. It implies UNITY. By one Spirit are we all baptised into *one Body*. All baptised into Christ are members of the one Body, and so are all one in Him. We may not readily be one in creed, but all believers are one in Christ.

The baptism of the Holy Spirit, like conversion, is not experienced by all in the same way. To some the assurance has come suddenly, to others it has been a gradual revelation. Some can tell the very day and place when the *power* fell on them like a mantle from Heaven; others can only say, "Once I was weak, now am I strong." And how many more seem to be content to know nothing at all about it as a present, personal, precious possession.

With regard to this baptism we might notice—

1. The Baptiser. "He shall baptise you with the Holy Ghost" (Matt. 3. 11). To *Him* alone we must look for this mighty definite blessing. This great *gift* is the fruit of His humiliation and death. And for the glory of His own Name He is as willing to baptise the saint as to save the sinner.

2. The Promise. "Ye SHALL be baptised with the Holy Ghost" (Acts 1. 5). "Ye shall receive the gift of the Holy Ghost, . . . for the promise is TO YOU" (Acts 2. 38, 39). This promise, "He shall baptise," is just as good, and ought to be as surely experienced as "He shall save." And, moreover, this promise is but the second part of the great salvation. It was not enough that the sons of Aaron were washed, they had also to be anointed.

3. The Fulfilment. "*This is that* which was spoken by the prophet Joel" (Acts 2. 16). Now they were perfectly assured that the great promise was fulfilled in their own experience. Peter testified that the "Holy Ghost fell on them *as on us* at the beginning" (Acts 2. 15). John also writes: "*Ye have* an unction from the Holy One." Paul speaks of the "renewing of the Holy Ghost, which *He shed on us* abundantly" (Titus 3. 6). Every ambassador for Christ should be able to bear witness, like Christ, that "The Spirit of the LORD *is upon me*, because He hath anointed me" (Luke 4. 18).

4. The Necessity. "Have ye received the Holy Ghost *since* ye believed?" (Acts 19. 2). The *need* of this gift, and the necessity of *knowing* that we have received it, are alike plainly implied here. We know that "No man can call Jesus Lord but by the Spirit;" but something very different is evidently meant here, and that something is of vital importance to every believer. "Would God that all the Lord's people were prophets, and that the Lord would put His Spirit upon them." Have you received?

5. The Condition. "Thou *lovest* righteousness and *hatest* wickedness: THEREFORE God, thy God, hath anointed thee" (Psa. 45. 7). This love and hate is the fruit of a perfectly honest heart before God. If God is loved with the whole heart, then sin will be hated with the whole heart. The priests of old had to be cleansed before anointed, and this order has never been changed. If thy head would lack no anointing, then thy heart must harbour no sin. "I will take you *from among* the heathen, and will bring you into your own land; THEN will I sprinkle clean water (typical of the *Holy Ghost*) upon you" (Ezek. 36). Separation and restoration preceded the holy sprinkling.

6. The Evidence. "Approving ourselves as the ministers of God . . . *by the Holy Ghost*" (2 Cor. 6. 4-6). The presence and power of the Holy Ghost is the insignia by which a man is known to be a minister of God. If this is lacking he can only speak as one not having authority. That is like the scribes: "Not he that commendeth himself is approved, but whom the Lord commendeth" (2 Cor. 10. 18).

7. The Result. How marvellous are the results of the baptism of the Holy Ghost, as recorded in the Acts alone, when "they were all filled with the Holy Ghost." Who can reckon the results since the apostles' days? What are the results *without* this enduement?

7. THE BAPTISM OF THE SPIRIT: ITS EFFECTS.

WHEN a man is baptised with the Holy Ghost the effect will be very marked (first) upon the inner experience of the man himself. There will be a deeper humility, because of a deeper sense of helplessness and unworthiness. A more holy sobriety, because there will be a keener consciousness of how easily the Spirit may be grieved. There will be that calm earnestness that flows out of a true and solemn heart, in which the living Word of God burns as a fire. Not the enthusiasm of a pompous harangue of eloquent words, but the glowing respirations of a soul filled with the presence and power of God. This anointing is not put upon man's flesh (the old self-seeking nature), for that would only minister to his pride, but upon the mitred head of the consecrated new creature in Christ Jesus, that no flesh should glory in His presence. The Spirit was not given *until* Christ was glorified, and *until* we are prepared to glorify Him at any cost we need not expect this baptism of the Spirit. And, doubtless, this is the chief reason why so many are without this great gift. Christ is not exalted to the throne of their heart.

The following are a few of the more prominent results that are sure to follow this spiritual baptism—

1. General amazement. "They were all amazed, saying one to another, What meaneth this?" (Acts 2. 7-12). Here was something that they could not deny, yet they could not understand it. The natural man *cannot* discern these things; he is blind to these till born from above by the Spirit of God (1 Cor. 2. 10-16). When a man is baptised with the Holy Ghost his speech and his preaching will not be with enticing words of man's wisdom, but in demonstration of the Spirit and of power. If the Spirit is there He will demonstrate His own presence.

2. Glory to God. "The Spirit of God resteth upon you; on *your part* He is glorified" (1 Peter 4. 14). The reproach of the world is sure to assail when the Spirit of God resteth upon us But let us count it all joy, for God will be glorified. He is always glorified in the case of those who have received this anointing. Before, self was exalted and God dishonoured; now, self has fallen, like Dagon, and God is enthroned. And when He is truly glorified in us He will be surely glorified through us.

3. Continual fellowship. " The anointing which ye have received *abideth in you*" (1 John 2. 27). " He shall abide with you for ever" (John 14. 6). Our fellowship with the Father and the Son will be real and continual if we abide in full communion with the Holy Ghost. But, alas! how often the soul is self-excommunicated from this blessed fellowship through pride and unbelief. Samuel anointed David, and the Spirit of the LORD came upon him *from that day onward* (1 Sam. 16. 12). Is there such a day in your experience?

4. Holy boldness. " When they saw the *boldness* of Peter and John they took knowledge of them that they had been with Jesus" (Acts 4. 13). This clearly implies that Jesus Himself was bold. Did they not say of Him " We know that Thou art true, and carest for no man?" (Mark 12. 14). Gideon was very bold when he went and threw down the altar of Baal. " The *Spirit of the* LORD came upon him, and he blew a trumpet" (Judges 6. 30-34). When a man is baptised with the Spirit he *cannot* but blow the trumpet. Peter and John filled with the Spirit, said: " We *cannot but speak* the things which we have seen and heard" (Acts 4. 20). How does this accord with those who *will not* speak unless they are paid for it?

5. Powerful testimony. " They were all filled with the Holy Ghost, and with *great power* gave the apostles witness" (Acts 4. 31-33). The Spirit of the LORD came upon Jesus, and they wondered at the gracious words that proceeded out of His mouth. " For His word was *with* *power"* (Luke 4. 32). Stephen was full of the Holy Ghost, and they were *not able to resist* the Spirit by which he spake (Acts 6. 5-10). Micah says, " I am full of power by the Spirit of the LORD." What to do? For when God fills a vessel He means to use it. " *To a clare* unto Jacob his transgression, and to Israel his sin" (Micah 3. 8). Oh! how much this power is needed to-day, to declare the whole counsel of God, keeping back nothing. The Holy Ghost Himself is the great witness, and we are to testify *with Him* (John 15. 26, 27; Acts 5. 32). Our power for God then will just be in proportion as we are co-workers together with the Holy Ghost. Having the same motives in view, and acting in the same faithful and unselfish manner (John 16. 13).

6. Mighty works. The Spirit of the LORD came upon Samson, and he rent a lion as he would have rent a kid (Judges 14. 16). When we are filled with the Spirit, the lion difficulties which would have frightened and turned us back before, now become as kids in our hands. Jesus said: " Greater works than these shall ye do because I go unto My Father. If I go not, the Comforter (the Holy Ghost) will not come." But He has gone, and the Holy Ghost has come, and mighty works do show themselves in all who have this baptism, while those who serve without Him keep planning and scheming and beating the air.

7. Silent influence. "God, thy God, hath anointed thee. *All thy garments smell of* myrrh" (Psa. 45. 7, 8). Garments of fragrance cover the anointed ones. This influence is not put on for special occasions. Notice that it is *all thy garments*, so that we are shamefully naked without them. It is good to pray, " Let the beauty of the Lord our God be upon us," but it is surely better just to *put on* thy beautiful garments, O captive daughter of Zion! The Old Testament is filled with what we should *do*, the aim of the New is to show us what we should BE. All fruitfulness and power for God is the result, not of what we do, but of what we *are*.

---

8. THE POWER OF THE SPIRIT.

THIS is the age of *spiritual power*. A Christian or a Church destitute of this is behind the age. When Christ ascended to perpetuate His work in Heaven the Holy Ghost descended to perpetuate His work on earth. And He did not come as a helpless infant. No. The atoning work was done. And so He came at once in all His glorious majesty " as a RUSHING MIGHTY WIND," the symbol of power to any degree. And it is the will of God that the Church should live and abide in this Pentecostal, spiritual storm. But, alas ! how she has spread her snow-white sails to catch the wind of man's favour more than God's, and so she has been bereft of her propelling power. Does it not seem as if the time were at hand when Christianity and Christians will be tested, not by their professions, however great or eloquent, but by their spiritual power alone? The ministerial market may be overstocked with men, but there is no possibility of overstocking the market with this. *Holy Ghost power* is in great demand everywhere, and every Christian should possess it. This power is—

1. Needed. " Tarry ye *until ye be endued* with power" (Luke 24. 49). No use going without it. None knew better than Christ what the disciples really needed to fit them for their life-work. The same work will always need the same fitness, " Not by might, nor by power, but by My Spirit, saith the LORD." By His Spirit's power through the consecrated heart and life must the work be done. Wait on this as the sailor waits for the moving breeze. David had to wait for the moving on the tops of the trees before he could stir. If he stirred before the moving he stirred without God (2 Sam. 5. 24; 1 Cor. 4. 19, 20).

2. Promised. " Ye shall receive the power of the

Holy Ghost coming upon you'' (Acts 1. 8); and we know that the waiting disciples had this promise fulfilled in their experience. Paul also testified to Timothy that '' God *hath given to us* the Spirit of Power'' (2 Tim. 1. 7). What good has Calvary done you unless you have come into personal relationship with that awful death? What power has Pentecost brought you unless you have come into personal relationship with the Holy Ghost? The power of the Spirit ought to be as real to us as the forgiveness of our sins.

3. **Life-giving.** ''The Spirit giveth life'' (2 Cor. 3. 6). ''It is the Spirit that quickeneth'' (John 6. 63). '' You hath He quickened'' (Eph. 2. 1). He not only quickens from the dead, but also gives that '' abundance of life,'' without which no lively testimony can be borne for Christ. It is out of '' the abundance'' of the heart the mouth speaketh. If the heart is not full there will be no running over, and if there is no overflowing it is clear that we have more need to get than to give.

4. **Sufficient.** We must depend upon the power of the Holy Spirit alone for success in work for God, just as we trust exclusively to the Blood of Christ for acceptance with God. The power of the Spirit is sufficient: 1. For our inward life. ''Strengthened with might by His Spirit in the *inner man*'' (Eph. 3. 16). It is the inner or new man that the Holy Ghost daily renews and strengthens, and uses for the glory of God. '' As a man *thinketh in his heart*, so is he'' in reality before God. 2. For our outward testimony. Paul says: '' I was with you in *weakness*, and my preaching was in demonstration of the Spirit and of *power*'' (1 Cor. 2. 3, 4). So that our weakness is our highest fitness for the power of God. '' They spake as the Spirit gave them utterance'' (Acts 2. 4). And they that so speak never speak in vain. It is as true to-day as it was of old that *holy men* speak with power as they are moved by the Holy Ghost (2 Peter 1. 21).

5. Cannot be purchased. Simon offered money, saying, Give me also this power (Acts 8. 18). Doubtless there are many in these days who are earnestly coveting this best gift, but who seem to forget that this power is the *gift* of God, and cannot be purchased with education, or with eloquence, or with earnestness, nor even with much work and prayer. It is to be *received*, but cannot be bought any more than the wind.

6. Cannot be imitated. The anointing oil, which was a type of the Holy Spirit, was not to be imitated. No substitute could ever be accepted for this (Exod. 30. 33). Any amount of zeal or earnestness will never stand instead of the power of the Holy Ghost. It is easy to imitate the earnestness of a man endued with this power, but the power itself none can copy. Men may thunder while yet there is no quickening and searching fire. The tongue of fire is not in the thunder, but in the lightning.

7. May be lost. The power of the Spirit was upon Samson, but he sinned, and slept, and wist not that the Lord was departed from him. And so he "shaked" himself in vain (Judges 16. 20). And what a poor man he was without the power. None seem so utterly helpless as those who were once endued with spiritual power. Without this power a man may shake himself, but it is only himself that he shakes. We have known those whose power used to make thousands tremble, but whose testimony now reminds us of the withered branch. In Numbers 11. 17 we see, in the message of God to His servant Moses, how God may take the Spirit that is upon one and put it upon another. Many a one, as well as Uzziah, has been marvellously helped till he was strong. But when he became strong in his own strength the Spirit of Power departed. And where is the usefulness of a *powerless* Christian? Like savourless salt, they are good for nothing.

9. THE GIFTS OF THE SPIRIT.

JESUS CHRIST is the gift of God to the world (John 3. 16), and in this gift is everything the sinful world can need for acceptance and peace with God. The Holy Ghost is the gift of both Father and Son to every believer, and in this gift is included all that the Christian can need for life, work, and testimony. For the gifts of the Spirit are great and manifold. They are—

1. **Very diversified.** In 1 Corinthians 12. 8-10 there are nine different gifts specified, and these are represented as given to as many different individuals. All these various gifts were in operation in the days of the infant Church, and were all the outcome of the working of " *One Spirit.*" Mark, these are not natural gifts, but spiritual; not the development of a something good from within, but the implantation of a new spiritual faculty from without, and that by the hand of the omnipotent Spirit of God.

2. **Sovereignly bestowed.** " The Spirit divideth to every man severally as *He will*" (1 Cor. 12. 11). The building up of the holy temple—the Church—is the work of the Spirit (Eph. 2. 22). And surely He knows best upon what part to bestow any particular gift or grace. Therefore, as spiritual stones, we must be entirely submissive to His holy will, allowing Him to have the fashioning and fitting; believing that He is both. able and willing to make the greatest possible use of every one committed to His will.

3. **For the profit of all.** " The manifestation of the Spirit is given to every man to profit withal" (1 Cor. 12. 7). All (*i.e.*, the whole body or Church) is to be profited by the Spirit's gifts and revelations to *every man*. Every believer ought to be a *profitable* member of the body of Christ. For this end the common manifestation of the Spirit is given to every man. And being convinced that we have the Spirit within us, we may be assured that

Almighty sufficiency (Mark 9. 23) is within our reach, so that we need not always be groaning out " unprofitable servants" as if that were an attainment in grace.

4. To be earnestly desired. " Covet earnestly the best gifts" (1 Cor. 12. 31). " Desire spiritual gifts, but rather that ye may prophesy " (1 Cor. 14. 1). " Covet to prophesy" (v. 39). Paul mentions prophecy as the gift to be most earnestly sought. The reason for this is very explicitly stated in verses 22-25. That the unlearned and unbelieving may be *convinced* and *converted* and bear *testimony* to the truth, so that God may be glorified. The apostle's whole soul was set on this. It is no vain thing to covet even " *the best gift* " if we seek only the glory of God, for no good thing will He withhold from them that LOVE HIM.

5. Suited to each possessor. " Every man hath his *proper gift* of God: one after this manner, and another after that" (1 Cor. 7. 7). Not only is it true that every man hath his gift, but the gift every man hath is his own proper gift, exactly suited to himself, and becoming in him. I have no gift, say some; but what saith the Scripture? "Every man hath." Perhaps you have not the gift of your eminent friend, but you have *your own gift*. Yes, and your own *proper gift* too. But what is it? Search and see

6. To be carefully used. " Neglect not the gift that is in thee" (1 Tim. 4. 14). How many hide their precious talents in the earth as useless, because they are not the same as others? (Matt. 25. 18). What if your ear would refuse to hear because it is not an eye? Many complain of their leanness and fruitlessness, and no wonder, when they are *imitating* the gifts of others, and *neglecting* their own. And so the whole body suffers loss by their *one part* lacking (Eph. 4. 16). Be content to be nothing but what

God means you to be, then you shall be all that God wishes you to be.

7. To be constantly improved. " Stir up the gift of God which is in thee" (2 Tim. 1. 6). The gift may be in thee as a smouldering fire, but must be stirred up and kept brightly burning. All the resources of our being must be directed to, and concentrated on, the development of this heavenly gift. " Striving according to His working, which worketh in me mightily" (Col. 1. 29). What can you do *best* for God? Then stir up that gift, and you will have power both with God and men.

---

10. THE TEACHING OF THE SPIRIT.

MAN needs not only a Divine Saviour, but also a Divine Teacher. The Holy Spirit has come to teach us, just as really as the Lord Jesus came to save us. We must trust Him to do His work *in* us, as we trust the Lord to do His work *for* us. Notice—

1. The characteristics of this Teacher. He is—

1. INDISPENSABLE. " The things of God knoweth no man" (1 Cor. 2. 11); " Neither can he know them" (v. 14); "His ways are past finding out" (Rom. 11. 33). Seeing, then, that man in his natural state is totally incapable of himself to know God, or the things of God, he must have a teacher; for no man can know God except he is taught of God, and this the Holy Ghost alone can do.

2. INFALLIBLE. " The Spirit searcheth *all things*, yea, the deep things of God" (1 Cor. 2. 10); " Who hath directed the Spirit, or hath taught Him?" (Isa. 40. 13). If we despise this Teacher in vain we seek for spiritual wisdom. We never repent of nor even forget what we have learned of Him. " My Spirit is upon thee, and *My words shall not depart* out of thy mouth" (Isa. 59. 21).

3. ALL-SUFFICIENT. " The anointing abideth in you,

and ye need not that any man teach you" (1 John 2. 27)
The Lord hath ordained pastors and teachers for the
perfecting of the saints, and we must esteem them
highly for their work's sake. Although such teachers are
abundantly needed in these days, still "ye need not
that any man teach you." "He shall teach you *all
things*" (John 14. 26); "He will guide you into all
truth" (John 16. 13). Who is better able to explain a
book than the one who wrote it?

4. UNASSUMING. "He shall not speak of Himself"
(John 16. 13). He hides Himself that He might all the
more glorify Christ. In this He is an example to all
teachers. If the Great Teacher Himself is so unassuming,
how should the scholar appear?

2. The methods of His teaching. He teaches by—

1. ENLIGHTENING THE MIND "That God may give
you the Spirit of wisdom; the *eyes* of your understanding being enlightened" (Eph. 1. 17, 18); "Satan
hath blinded the mind" (2 Cor 4. 4); "Darkness hath
blinded his eyes" (1 John 2. 11). Unless the eyes of the
understanding are enlightened by the Holy Ghost, man's
best effort is but teaching the blind.

2. POINTING TO THE SUFFERINGS OF CHRIST. "He will
convince the world of sin" (John 16. 18). How does
He do this? "I will pour the *Spirit of grace*, . . . and they
shall *look upon Me*" (Zech. 12. 10). And while looking
on Him whom they have pierced, they shall mourn and
be in bitterness. The kind and thoughtful mother convinces the child of its guilt by quietly pointing to the
mischief done.

3. QUICKENING THE UNDERSTANDING. "The Spirit of
the Lord shall rest upon and make him of quick understanding" (Isa. 11. 2, 3). Quick to discern the mind
and will of God, and to take pleasure in doing it. His will

should be to our mind and heart what the sweet smell is to our sense, a positive, sensible delight.

4. COMPARING THINGS THAT ARE SPIRITUAL. "The Holy Ghost teacheth, comparing spiritual things with spiritual" (1 Cor. 2. 13). He compares the spiritual things of the Old Testament with those of the New. He expounds spiritual things to those only who are spiritual, because they are spiritually discerned. There will always be ample proof for those things taught by the Spirit, as He compares one spiritual thing with another. But believe not every spirit, as some are always comparing spiritual things with the reasonable, the temporal, and the natural, instead of spiritual.

5. REVEALING HIDDEN THINGS. "It was revealed unto Simeon by the Holy Ghost" (Luke 2. 26); "He shall receive of Mine, and show it unto you" (John 16. 14); "Eye hath not seen; . . . but He hath revealed them unto us by His Spirit" (1 Cor. 2. 9, 10). The deep things of God are being constantly unveiled before the enraptured vision of those who humbly sit at the feet of this Great Teacher come from God.

6. RECALLING FORGOTTEN THINGS. "He shall bring all things to your remembrance, whatsoever *I have said* unto you" (John 14. 26); "The words of Christ which have been *hidden* in the heart" (Psa. 119. 11). Although presently forgotten they are not lost. They are as weapons laid past for the Holy Spirit, and in due time *He will bring them*. If the message you wish to deliver is only an address framed in the head, and a burden on the memory, you cannot expect the Spirit's help; but if it is a burden on the heart, fear not.

7. HINDERING SELFISH THINGS. "Paul and Silas were *forbidden* of the Holy Ghost to preach in Asia. They assayed to go into Bithynia, but the Spirit *suffered* them *not*" (Acts 16. 6, 7); "It is not in man to direct his steps;

commit thy ways unto the Lord, and He shall bring it to pass'' (Isa 37. 5). It is one thing to form plans, and *then* ask His guidance; it is quite another thing to trust Him to form the plans. The hindrances of the Holy Spirit are but part of His helps.

3. The attitudes of the taught. He teaches—

1. WHILE WE OBEY. '' The Lord said unto Philip, Arise and go, and he arose and went. *Then* the Spirit said, Go near'' (Acts 26. 28). He was in the way of the Lord when the Spirit taught him. The disobedient need not expect the special ministry of the Holy Ghost. Soul-winners are always Spirit-taught workers.

2. WHILE WE MEDITATE. '' While Peter *thought* the Spirit said'' (Acts 10. 19); it is in the calm waters that the image is clearly reflected. How many hear of those things which are true, honest, and of good report, but don't '' *think* on these things?'' (Phil. 4. 8). Reflection is a positive necessity for growth in grace and usefulness. '' Meditate upon these things that thy profiting may appear unto all'' (1 Tim. 4. 15). Read Psalm 119. 99.

3. WHILE WE SERVE. '' As they ministered to the Lord, the Holy Ghost said'' (Acts 13. 2). He who serves with his eye on his Master will be guided by the Master's eye. The Spirit rejoices to guide and instruct the willing heart. And in our most *active moments*, if we are still submissive to Him, we will be wisely taught.

4. WHILE WE WAIT. '' Simeon was *waiting* for the consolation of Israel when the Holy Ghost revealed to him'' (Luke 2. 26). '' *If* the blessing tarry, wait for it.'' If the promise has been believed the answer will surely come. But it will prove vain waiting unless there is a well-grounded expectation (Ruth 3. 18).

5. WHILE WE LISTEN. '' He that hath ears to hear, let him *hear what the Spirit saith*'' (Rev. 2. 7). The Lord

saves every believing soul, the Spirit speaks to every open ear. The *Spirit* of prayer is better than *times* of prayer. So the Spirit of understanding is better than all commentaries (good as they are). Every Christian might be as Bezaleel, filled with wisdom and understanding (Exod. 31. 2). Daniel was taught of the Spirit, and so could read and interpret the Divine handwriting. "Covet earnestly the best gift."

11. THE WORK OF THE SPIRIT.

IN these studies much has been already indicated regarding the Spirit's work. But we might look at the various aspects in a more connected way.

The work of the Spirit in connection with the life of Christ was clearly manifest, and should be recognised with equal distinctness in the life of every Christian. With regard to His incarnation, it is said, "The *power* of the Highest shall overshadow thee" (Luke 1. 35), and "that which is conceived in her is of the Holy Ghost"(Matt. 1. 20). At His baptism the Holy Ghost descended *upon Him*. Here we have both *conception* and *anointing*, which are very distinct. Then He was *led* by the Spirit into the *wilderness*, and *returned* in the power of the Spirit (Luke 4. 1-14). The secret temptation always precedes the coming forth in power. Then He preached in the Spirit, and they wondered at His gracious words (Luke 4. 18-32). He cast out devils by the Spirit (Matt. 12. 28), and at last offered Himself through the eternal Spirit (Heb. 9. 14). From different Scriptures we learn some of the active aspects of His work. The Holy Spirit—

1. Strives. "My Spirit shall not always strive with man" (Gen. 6. 3). This striving evidently implies that man by nature is *opposed* to the Spirit of God. "My ways are not your ways, nor My thoughts your thoughts." The Spirit strives because He is resisted, as Jacob resisted the angel at the brook, and may be finally resisted as in the days of Noah.

2. Convinces. "He will convince the world of sin" (John 14. 8). *Conviction* is the first object of His striving. He labours to make the sinner sensible of his guilt. This is exactly what the sinner does not seek to know, but rather to hide. He seeks to press home to the heart and conscience the truth regarding our state in the sight of God.

3. Quickens. "It is the Spirit that quickeneth" (John 6. 63). "Except a man be born of the Spirit" (John 3. 5, 6). Although a man is made deeply conscious of his guilty state he is still as helpless as the child unborn, or as the dead in the grave. But the Spirit is promised to them that ask Him (Luke 11. 13). The life-giving touch is His. He quickens into life man's dormant spirit, so that it awakens up, asserts its power, and rules the man. He becomes "a new creature" (2 Cor. 5. 17).

4. Seals. "*After ye believed* ye were sealed with the Holy Spirit" (Eph. 1. 13). "Grieve not the Spirit whereby ye are sealed" (chap. 4. 30). The bargain is struck the moment we trust in Christ, and then the seal of *ownership* is set upon us as His property. Ye are not your own, ye are bought, therefore glorify God.

5. Reveals. (1) The love of God by shedding it abroad in our hearts (Rom. 5. 5). (2) The things of Christ (John 16. 14). (3) The things God hath prepared (1 Cor. 2. 10). (4) The way into truth (John 16. 13). (5) The valley of need (Ezek. 37. 1). He only can make us see the spiritual death that exists. (6) The suffering Saviour (Zech. 12. 10). (7) The path of service (Acts 8. 29).

6. Witnesses. "The Spirit beareth witness with our spirit" (Rom. 8. 16). Our *quickened* spirit testifies that we are the children of God, and God's Spirit corroborates this testimony. We are witnesses of these things. So is also the Holy Ghost (Acts 5. 32). This is the witness that cannot lie: "A faithful witness delivereth souls" (Prov. 14. 25).

7. Intercedes. "God hath sent forth the Spirit of His Son into your hearts, *crying Abba*, Father" (Gal. 4. 6). The Spirit also helpeth our infirmities and maketh intercession for us (Rom. 8. 26, 27). The sphere of His advocacy is *within* the soul of man. The Spirit of prayer is little understood. Contrast the Holy Spirit's "unutterable groanings" with the frivolous prayers of many. No wonder that our petitions are so seldom answered when the Spirit's groanings are so little heeded. Holy Ghost prayers are as "God going up with a shout."

8. Calls. "The Holy Ghost said, Separate *Me* Barnabas and Saul for the work whereunto *I have called them*" (Acts 13. 2). "Called of God," as was Aaron, is true of every real servant of God. Separate Me, said the Holy Spirit, as if to teach us that only those who have been wholly set apart and consecrated to Him can be used by Him. Christian worker, think of this important truth.

9. Ordains. "Take heed unto *yourselves*, and to the *flock* over the which the Holy Ghost hath made you overseers" (Acts 20. 28). Every man is ordained an overseer over himself by the Holy Ghost, but those who attempt to *feed* the flock without being ordained by the Spirit will be but clouds without water. This is the ordination that will glorify God in fruit-bearing (John 15. 16).

10. Commissions. "The Lord God and His Spirit hath sent me" (Isa. 48. 16). "And they being *sent forth* by the Holy Ghost, departed" (Acts 13. 4). The Holy Ghost is the Lord of the harvest. Pray ye Him to thrust forth labourers (Matt. 9. 38). For when *He* sends them out a harvest is sure to be gathered, for such are "able ministers" (2 Cor. 3. 6; see 1 Cor. 12. 11).

11. Invites. "The Spirit says, Come" (Rev. 22. 17). In this the Spirit and the " Bride" are co-workers together. They unite in inviting the " bright and Morning Star." *This is* the night. But the night is far spent, *the day* is at hand. And so the Spirit works, and waits, and longs with us in this world of darkness till Jesus comes, and the shadows flee away.

12. Leads. " If ye be led of the Spirit ye are not under the law" (Gal. 5. 18). " For as many as are led by the Spirit of God are the sons of God" (Rom. 8. 14). Jesus was led by the Spirit into the wilderness (Luke 4. 1). This was in itself a proof of Christ's *Sonship*. Those who are under the law, however earnest and active in religious work, are not led by the Spirit. All God's sons are to be divinely guided. " He will guide you."

13. Comforts. " He shall give you another Comforter, even the Spirit of truth" (John 14. 16). " They had rest in the comfort of the Holy Ghost" (Acts 9. 31). He who dwells with us *for ever* (John 14. 16) knows as none other can the nature of our troubles, the real depth of our need, the very comfort that is wanted, and the best time and way to administer the succour and apply the things of Christ. Eliezer comforted Rebekah with the things of Isaac, "And the servant brought forth jewels of silver, and jewels of gold, and gave them to Rebekah" (Gen. 24. 53).

14. Overcomes. " When the enemy shall come in like a flood the Spirit of the Lord shall put him to flight" (Isa. 59. 19, margin). " Not by might, nor by power, but by My Spirit, saith the Lord" (Zech. 4. 6). " We have no power nor might, but our eyes are upon THEE" (2 Chron. 20. 12). It is when opposition comes in like a deluge that we are apt to summon our own forces, or else to give up in despair. Then is the time to *trust*, to fix the eye on the overcoming *One*.

12. THE FRUIT OF THE SPIRIT.

THERE is evidently a difference between the *work* of the Spirit and the *fruit* of the Spirit. The work of the Spirit may be regarded as the direct result of the Spirit's *active* energy, the fruit as the outcome of His indwelling presence. In Galatians 5. 19-22 we see the *works* of the flesh contrasted with the *fruit* of the Spirit. The works of the flesh are the natural outcome of an active evil principle within. The *fruit* of the Spirit does not spring from anything naturally in us, but is the result of the new life begotten in us by the Holy Ghost and maintained by His continued abiding. "In me, that is in my *flesh*, dwelleth no good thing." The fruit of the Spirit is not spoken of in the plural as the *works* of the flesh are. This signifies the *oneness* of the fruit. Every grace mentioned is but part of a whole, so that no Christian is complete unless he is characterised by all these nine graces (Gal. 5. 22). The fruit of the Spirit is *in all* goodness, righteousness, truth (Eph. 5. 9). What is fruit? Fruit is—

1. An evidence of death. "Except a corn of wheat die it abideth alone, but if it die it bringeth forth much fruit" (John 12. 24). I am crucified, nevertheless I live, yet not I, *but Christ*. This new life alone can bring forth fruit to the glory of God. We conclude, then, that one reason why so many Christians are fruitless is that self has not died, and so they abide *alone*.

2. The necessity of grace. "Every branch *in* Me that beareth not fruit He taketh away" (John 15. 2). I shall dig about it, "and if it bear fruit well, and if not, *then after* that thou shalt cut it down" (Luke 13. 9). The branch was in the vine, the fig-tree was in the vineyard, both in the place of grace and privilege. To maintain this high privilege fruit must be found. The fruitless cannot long enjoy the privileges of the fruitful; sooner or later they will sink into the place of the withered branch.

Fruitlessness and favour cannot live together, there must be a divorce.

3. The manifestation of character. "The *tree* is known by its fruit" (Matt. 12. 33). "*Ye* bear much fruit, so shall ye be My disciples" (John 15. 8). They showed them the fruit of the *land* (Num. 13. 26) just to prove the character of the land. Fruit then manifests: (1) The character of the tree. (2) Of the men. (3) Of the land. By their *fruits* ye shall know them, not by their appearance. If the Holy Spirit dwell in us, the fruit of the Spirit must be witnessed through us. There are no figs on thistles, nor grapes on thorns (Matt. 7. 16).

4. The result of abundance of life. "From ME is thy fruit found" (Hosea 14. 8). I am come that ye might have life more abundantly (John 10. 10). Fruit can only come where there is life to spare, where there is more than what is needed for self-support. The fruit of the Spirit in us is the result of *floods* upon the dry ground. The soul itself must first be abundantly satisfied before fruit will be found. The well must be full before it can run over.

5. The outcome of steadfast abiding. "As the branch cannot bear fruit except it *abide* in the vine, no more can ye except ye abide in *Me*" (John 15. 4). "Bring forth *with patience*" (Luke 8. 15). The tree that is not *rooted* will as a consequence be fruitless. "That Christ may dwell in your hearts by faith, that ye being *rooted* and grounded *in love* may be able" (Eph. 3. 17, 18). In Colossians 2 the order is—Rooted and *abounding with thanksgiving* (Col. 2. 7). Be not driven about, like a rootless, fruitless branch. Abide in ME.

6. Something for the good of others. "He sent His servants that *they* might receive the fruits" (Matt. 21. 34). Fruit is not for the good of the tree. Although it is *the good of the tree*. The fruit of the Spirit is in all "goodness." That they may see your good works, and glorify your Father (Matt. 5. 16). If we seek fruit merely for our own name we dishonour the Father. Remember Jesus said, "My Father is the Husbandman." Many pine away for want of this fruit (Lam. 4. 9).

7. The object of the Master's search. "Behold I come seeking fruit" (Luke 13. 7). Behold, the Husbandman waiteth for the fruit of the earth, and hath long patience (James 5. 7). Bring forth fruit *unto God* (Rom. 7. 4). The fruit of the Spirit in us is what the blessed Lord seeks from us. He is a patient Husbandman. How long has He waited? Until the early and *latter* rain. The early rain of conversion and the latter of consecration.

8. The natural method of propagation. "God said, Let the earth bring forth, the fruit tree, yielding fruit after his kind, whose *seed is in itself*" (Gen. 1. 11). The seed is in the fruit. If there is no fruit there is no seed. If then the fruit of the Spirit is not manifest in our lives, we are a positive hindrance to the extension of the kingdom of God. May "God Almighty make thee fruitful" (Gen. 28. 3). "Fruitful in every good work" (Col. 1. 10). Beware of thorns which choke (Mark 4. 7).

FAITH: AS EXHIBITED IN HEBREWS 11.
FAITH.—STUDY 1.

1. Nature of faith (vs. 1, 2). It is the *substance or* ground of things hoped for; it is neither a shadow nor a feeling; it is the *evidence* of things not seen. Jacob exercised it when he prized the birthright and sold the pottage. He laid hold on the promise, and made no provision for the *flesh*, so by faith he obtained a good report. Faith gives a good report of God, and gains a good report for the believer. I believe, and therefore have I spoken.

2. Knowledge of faith (v. 3). "Through faith we

understand." Seeing is believing, says the world. Believe, and thou shalt *see*, says the Word. By faith we understand that Christ has died, that sin has been put away, that we have eternal life, and are accepted in the Beloved. Unbelief cannot understand this; no unbeliever ever knew it. Do you know these things? "These things have I written unto you that believe that *you* may know" (1 John 5. 13).

3. Worship of faith (v. 4). "By faith Abel offered unto God." He that cometh to God *must* believe. God is a Spirit. Faith enters within the veil and adores. Of the outside worshippers it may be said they worship they know not what. Remember the three *musts*. The first lies at the door of the kingdom: "Ye must be born again" (John 3. 7); the next at the door of prayer: "must believe" (v. 6); the third at the door of worship: "must worship in the Spirit" (John 4. 24).

4. Translation of faith (v. 5). "By faith Enoch was translated." We often speak of justification by faith, but seldom of translation by faith; every believer has been translated by faith into the kingdom of His dear Son (Col. 1. 13), and seated with Christ in heavenly places, *far above* all principality, and power, and might, and dominion, and *every name* that is named, *not only in this world*. This is the victory that overcometh the world. You often think about the higher Christian life, and long to be delivered from the stifling atmosphere and deadening influences of the present world. Did you ever try Enoch's way? Have faith in God.

5. Preciousness of faith (v. 6). "Without faith it is impossible to please God." Faith is precious because it pleases God. There are two great things that please God: (1) The precious Blood of Christ. Are you pleased with that? (2) Faith in that Blood. *God* is pleased with that. Here are two truths, grasp them by faith, then all things are possible: 1st, believe that *He is*; 2nd, that He is what He says He is—*a Rewarder*. Many believe in His existence who practically deny His gracious character. Have you received like precious faith?

6. Testimony of faith (v. 7). "Noah prepared an ark, by the which He condemned the world." The works of every believer should condemn the world. The building of the ark was Noah's *everyday* work for 120 years. Every stroke of the hammer said, salvation to his house, but the echo whispered, condemnation to the world. Every conversation and every transaction of the Christian should have this testimony.

7. Obedience of faith (v. 8). "Abraham when he was called went, not knowing whither he went." Faith does not question, but follows. To the Israelites God said, "Go forward." They obeyed, and step by step the waters fled from before them. He always makes a way of escape for the faithful. The Lord called Peter on to the troubled waters with Himself, and he obeyed, although he had not gone that way heretofore. The obedient follow Jesus anywhere. The Master hath come and calleth for *thee*. To the questioning ones He says, "What is that to thee? Follow thou Me."

8. Walk of faith (v. 9). "By faith he sojourned in the land of promise." Every believer has been called out from the world to be a sojourner *with God* in the land that is His (Lev. 25. 23). With such a companion you need take no thought for your life. "My God shall supply all your need; be not afraid, only believe."

FAITH.—STUDY 2.

1. Aspiration of faith (v. 10). "Looks for a city whose Builder and Maker is God." Faith will not be satisfied with temples made with hands. It looks higher up for God's building, and sees the Holy City, the New Jerusalem, coming down from God. Faith seeks eternal realities; only the things unseen are eternal. Lord, increase our faith.

2. Fruit of faith (vs. 11, 12). "Through faith Sara conceived seed." Many as well as Sara have at first laughed at God's exceeding great and precious promises, but afterwards have judged Him faithful, and, like Isaac, have sown the seed and received in the same year an hundredfold (Gen. 26. 12). Unbelief is barren. Have you not been glorifying the Father in bearing much fruit, O ye of little faith?

3. Vision of faith (v. 13). "Having seen them afar off." It is only the anointed eyes that can see at all. Faith climbs to Pisgah's top and views the land that is afar off. It is the privilege of faith not only to dream of a ladder that reaches to Heaven, but to gaze on it continually. Unbelief is blind. " The pure in heart shall see God."

4. Confession of faith (vs. 13, 14). " Confessed and declared plainly." The faithful are not ashamed to confess that they are strangers and pilgrims on the earth. There was no ambiguity about the declarations of Ruth (chap. 1. 16). The plain, practical confession of the young widow is much wanted among present-day saints with regard to Christ.

5. Devotedness of faith (vs. 15, 16). " If they had been *mindful* they might have returned, but *now* they desire a better country." Faith has but one hand, and it reaches forth to those things which are *before*, *forgetting* the things that are behind, The language of faith is, " *One* thing I do" (Phil. 3. 13).

6. Trial of faith (vs. 17-19). " By faith Abraham offered up Isaac." The trial of faith is more precious than gold. Your faith will be tried · if it is real it will stand the fire, like the Hebrew youths. The young ruler's faith was tried and found wanting; but Abraham was ready to sell all that he had. *Are you?* Our Lord and Master sold all that He had and bought the field—the field is the world.

7. Blessings of faith (vs. 20, 21). " By faith Isaac and Jacob blessed." The promise is to you and to your children. The believing parent receives it by faith, and lays it on the head of his offspring. Faith is able to claim blessing for others (Matt. 8. 13). Are others blessed through our faith? The prayers of the righteous availeth much. How much?

8. Remembrance of faith (v. 22, margin). " By faith Joseph remembered the departing of Israel." We often talk about *realising* the promise, but all faith needs is to remember it. The butler said, " I do remember my faults this day." So did Peter when the Lord looked on him. Remember the words of the Lord Jesus.

9. Secrets of faith (v. 23). " By faith Moses was hid three months." Some read this as if by *fear* Moses was hid; but they were " not afraid of the king's command." Like the parents of Moses, every believer has his hidden hopes and secret expectations that no stranger can inter-meddle with; every child of faith is a " goodly child."

FAITH.—STUDY 3.

1. Choice of faith (vs. 24, 25). " By faith Moses refused, . . . choosing rather to suffer." Lot chose the well-watered plains, which were just pleasures for a season. Esau preferred the pottage; this also was pleasure for a season. Sense chooses in the light of the present; faith in the light of Eternity. Faith refuses the honours of the world at the cost of Christ, and such faith never blunders.

2. Estimate of faith (v. 26). Faith esteems the " reproach of Christ greater riches than all the treasures of Egypt." If you are reproached for the Name of Christ, happy are ye, your position is to be coveted. Why? Because the Spirit of glory and of God resteth upon you (1 Peter 4. 14). If we believe this, would we not more willingly go forth without the camp bearing His reproach?

3. Flight of faith (v. 27). " By faith he forsook Egypt." This may look like cowardice, but faith never fears. " *Not* fearing the *wrath of the king*." We are constantly surrounded with those temptations and snares, and hurtful lusts which drown men, but Paul sounds the note of warning, "O man of God, flee these things." Are you living with any lust acquired in your youth? " Flee also youthful lusts." Are you often tempted to sin? Have the courage, like Joseph, to flee (Gen. 39. 12).

` **4. Means of faith** (v. 28). " Through faith he kept . . . the sprinkling of blood." Human means can only accomplish a human purpose. Faith uses, with all confidence, the divinely appointed means, no matter how feeble or ridiculous they appear to the world. God has no faith in rods, small stones, ram's horns, jawbones, or broken pitchers; but God has faith in His own *Word*, and faith lays hold on that as the means omnipotent.

5. Boldness of faith (v. 29). " By faith they passed through the Red Sea." Faith has boldness to enter anywhere if invited, even into the Holiest. Faith is Divine authority, and is more mighty than any of David's three mighty men. It marches courageously through the foe, the furnace, and the flood, and speaks as one having authority. The word of faith is with power.

6. Victory of faith (v. 30). " By faith the walls of Jericho fell." Jacob heard of Esau's 400 men, and was greatly afraid, but at Penuel he got the victory through faith. Those who would win *open* victories for God must first conquer in the *closet* (Matt. 6. 6). We have this treasure (the *light* of the knowledge of the glory of God) in the earthen vessel; that our light may shine the pitcher must be broken. Broken pitchers precede victory. '' I tell you even weeping.'' This is light from a broken pitcher.

7. Salvation of faith (v. 31). '' By faith Rahab perished not.'' '' Whosoever believeth in Him should not perish.'' Israel would have been unjust if they had forgotten Rahab. The butler forgot Joseph. We have a just God and a Saviour who is faithful that hath promised. Rahab was willing and obedient because she believed. If ye be willing and obedient ye shall eat the good of the land. '' By grace are ye saved through faith, and that not of yourselves, it is the gift of God'' (Eph. 2. 8), but ''faith without works is dead'' (James 2. 17).

8. All-sufficiency of faith (vs. 32-35). '' What shall I say more, time would fail me to tell of . . . who through faith.'' Faith is one of the three that never faileth. If thou canst believe, *all things* are possible to him that believeth. What wilt thou that I should do unto thee? According to your faith be it unto you.

9. Sufferings of faith (vs. 36-38). Mocked, scourged, imprisoned, stoned, sawn, destitute, afflicted, tormented. We have left *all* and followed Thee. What shall we have? An hundredfold *now* in this life, with persecutions, and in the world to come eternal life; but the '' with persecutions'' is accompanied with the blessedness of Matthew 5. 10: '' He for the joy that was set *before* Him endured the Cross, despising the shame.'' If we suffer with Him we shall also reign with Him. '' In the world ye shall have tribulation, but be of good cheer, I have overcome the world'' (John 16. 33).

YOUR ADVERSARY THE DEVIL.
1 Peter 5. 8.

"Your adversary the Devil." These are ominous words, and suggest at once our privilege and our warfare. We fight, not against flesh and blood, not with human beings, but against principalities, and powers, and wicked spirits ruling and reigning in the hearts of ungodly men.

1. His personality. He is called "that old serpent, the Devil," and "Satan, your adversary." The personality of the Devil is about as little realised by the world as the personality of the Holy Spirit is by the Church. How real he was to the Lord Jesus Christ (Matt. 4. 3).

2. His character. He is described by the unerring Word as—

1. MOST SUBTLE (Gen. 3. 1-7). *As cunning as a serpent.* It is part of his cunning to appear as an angel of light.

2. A TEMPTER (Matt. 4. 1). He tempts by presenting desirable objects before the eye. He seeks to pamper our pride that we might forget or deny God. He succeeded with Eve; he failed with Christ.

3. AN ADVERSARY. He is opposed to every holy resolution, every good work, every heaven-born desire.

4. A DECEIVER (1 John 5. 19, R.V.). Deceit is the poison of the serpent. He deceives men with the pleasures of sin, nations with the rule of unrighteousness. We are not ignorant of his devices.

5. A MURDERER (John 8. 44). He murdered from the beginning, and will do so until the end, all who come under his destroying sway, every power, and faculty.

3. His purpose. The Devil has a purpose, and is in desperation to carry it out. In the following texts we observe its working in a sevenfold manner. He—

1. STEALS (Luke 8. 14). He snatches away the

Word from off the heart; the Word that is hidden *in* the heart is beyond his reach.

2. POLLUTES (Matt. 13. 38). The tares are the children after his own heart. His object is to spoil the good by overcrowding it with evil.

3. SUGGESTS (John 13. 2). In these two texts we have him dealing both with God and man. In Christ he found nothing; in Judas' heart the fiery darts found wood, hay, stubble.

4. PROVOKES (1 Chron. 21. 1-14). A man is easily provoked when he thinks it will promote his own honour. His provocations are all to the dishonour of God.

5. SIFTS (Luke 22. 31). The Devil's sieve rejects the good and preserves the bad.

6. DEVOURS (1 Peter 5. 8). What an awful thought— to be swallowed by the Devil, food for a fiend.

7. RESISTS (Zech. 3. 1). The Devil is quick to point out man's filthiness and God's holiness, and to forget the precious Blood.

4. His power. That the Devil has great power there can be no doubt (see Job 1). He is described as—

1. A LION (1 Peter 5. 8). A stranger to mercy, and one whose *nature* is to destroy.

2. THE GOD OF THIS WORLD (2 Cor. 4. 4). The object of the worldlings' worship, because the world lieth in his lap (Matt. 4. 8, 9).

3. HAVING THE POWER OF DEATH (Heb. 2. 14). As the author of sin he wields the power of death.

4. ABLE TO FILL THE HEART (Acts 5. 3). It must be a sorry house when the Devil keeps the key.

5. His defeat. To the believer the Devil is a defeated foe. Christ, as our David, has destroyed this giant's authority by the power of His own sword (Heb. 2. 14).

And the God of peace, who hath given us peace, will shortly bruise him under our feet. It is our privilege NOW to be more than conquerors. We overcome him by—

1. THE ARMOUR OF GOD (Eph. 6. 11). Put on Christ.

2. THE WORD OF TRUTH (Matt. 4. 4). "It is written." It is by this power demons are to be driven out of the hearts of men.

3. THE RESISTANCE OF FAITH (James 4. 7). Have the courage to *stand* in these backsliding days (Eph. 6. 13).

4. THE INDWELLING SPIRIT (1 John 4. 4). In the face of this there is no excuse for defeat.

6. His doom. The way of sin is ever downward. Satan fell from Heaven to the air, from the air to the earth, and soon from the earth to the bottomless pit, and again into the lake of fire (Rev. 20. 1-10). Then our enemies will be seen no more for ever. The way of the transgressor is hard.

———

JOSHUA ;
Or, THE HIGHER CHRISTIAN LIFE.

THE character and life of Joshua gives us a striking illustration of how the promises of God are to be received and enjoyed. Canaan represents the better land, or what God Himself designates "My rest" (Heb. 3. 11). This rest did not mean a folding of the arms and a lying down at ease. It meant hardship, warfare, and victory. It simply meant an entering into the plans and purposes of God, and a quiet resting on Him alone, to accomplish all that He had promised.

The Christian life is a life of—

1. Faith in the promises of God. "Every place that the sole of your feet shall *tread upon, that have I given you*" (chap. 1. 3). There can be no real progress without a planting of the foot of faith upon the "sure word of

promise.'' **All** other ground is sinking sand. There will
not be a close following of the Lord unless there is a constant trusting in Him. The believer must be prepared
to venture, like Peter, on the deep waters at His bidding.
Faith will be tried, it is too precious not to be tested.
There will be Jordans in our path and Jericho walls in our
way, difficulties which *faith alone* can surmount. '' But
nothing shall be impossible to them that believe,'' and
continue believing. It was when the feet of the priests
were *dipped in the brim of the water* that the waters stood
(chap. 3. 15, 16).

2. Consecration to the will of God. At Ai we see
failure for want of being consecrated wholly (as a body)
to the revealed purpose of God (chap. 6. 18, 19).

To live the consecrated life there must be—

1. An understanding of the *Word of God*. '' The book
of the law shall not depart out of thy mouth, thou shalt
meditate therein day and night'' (chap. 1. 8).

2. An unquestioning obedience to the mind and will
of God. '' Turn not from it to the right hand or the
left'' (chap. 1. 7). To turn from the Word is to turn
from God, and many are the temptations to turn aside,
arising from our own feelings and the likings of
carnal-minded men.

3. A sanctifying of ourselves (chap. 3. 5). If we
would see the *wonders* of the LORD this is needful. A
setting apart of ourselves unto God (chap. 23. 11, 12).

3. Fellowship in the presence of God. The promise
given was clear and comforting: '' I will be with thee:
I will not fail thee nor forsake thee'' (chap. 1. 5). How
full of grace. Then the promise was confirmed: '' As I
was with Moses, *so* will I be with thee'' (chap. 3. 7). The
promises of God are just as good to the believer as they
were to His own Son, and His presence should be to us
as real and as abiding. Joshua believed the Word, and

so he said, "The living God is among you" (chap. 3. 10).
How striking is verse 15 of chapter 5. We see Joshua in
fellowship with the Captain, Prince of the Lord's hosts.
He said: "Loose thy shoe from off thy foot, for the
place whereon thou standest is holy. And Joshua did
so." Then the scene abruptly closes, leaving Joshua
standing with unshod feet in the holy presence of his
mighty Lord, typical of the Christian's constant attitude
toward his Lord and Master. Then in chapter 6. 27 we
read: "*Lo*, the Lord *was* with Joshua." And Joshua's
dying testimony was, "The Lord your God, He it is that
fighteth for you, *as He hath promised*" (chap. 23. 10).
He is faithful that hath promised.

4. Testimony to the honour of God. The whole life
of Joshua was a testimony for God. But the twelve stones
which he pitched at Gilgal were to stand as a special
testimony to the mighty saving power of God in opening
a new way for His trusting people. These stones were the
works of faith, and others seeing them would glorify God.
The fruit of all testimony is that men "might fear the
Lord your God for ever" (chap. 4. 21, 24), and this testimony is to be to " all the people of the earth" (v. 24).

5. Warfare against the enemies of God. As soon
as Jordan is passed, and the witness pitched, they find
that Jericho is straitly shut up (chap. 6. 1). So that
aggressive warfare is at once needed if the promises of God
are to be realised. The enemies are great and many.
"*All the kings* gathered themselves together to fight with
Joshua *with one accord*" (chap. 9. 1, 2). There are many
kings to fight. There is King Pride, King Lust, King
Love-ease, King Fearful, and King Please-all. There is
also King Fashion, King Hate-the-truth, King Love-the-
dark, King Worldly-mind, King Unbelief. Everything
not pleasing to God is our enemy.

6. Victory in the Name of God. "No man shall

be able to stand before thee *all the days of thy life*"
(chap. 1. 5). It is a life of constant victory. If there
is defeat, as at Ai, " it is because of sin." Every wall
must come down before the shout of faith (chap. 6. 5).
Every opposer may be smitten and the land possessed
for God (see chap. 12). When men are faithful to God,
then the terror of God is sure to fall upon the enemies
(chap. 2. 9). If your life is not victorious, then it is
time you were searching your heart.

7. **Rest in the faithfulness of God.** They divided
the land (chap. 14. 5), and they rested from wars
(chap. 15), so they rested in the good gift of God. A
land which they did not purchase, cities and vineyards
which they made not (chap. 24. 13). Not one thing
had failed (chap. 23. 14). But while we rest in the
possessions given us of God, still we must not rest from
war as long as there is yet much land (blessing) to be
possessed (chap. 13. 1; 18. 3). If we rest short of the
fulness, then the likelihood is we will not enjoy what
we have. The enemies spared became thorns in their
side. Rest in the Lord.

SIN AND SALVATION.

THE inhabitants of the tropical zone, where the severity
of winter is never felt, cannot have the same appreciation
of the freshness of spring. They have never seen the nakedness of winter, and so are unable to experience the delight
of approaching summer. Those who have never felt the
coldness of their own spiritual death, or seen their own
nakedness as sinners before God, will not rejoice at the
springtime of God's redeeming love. To appreciate the
grace that is offered in Christ's atoning death, the darkness
and emptiness of sin must be felt. It was the man who was
wretched that thanked God for His great deliverance
(Rom. 7. 24, 25).

GOSPEL OUTLINES.

THE SACRIFICE OF CHRIST.
Ephesians 5. 1, 2.

FROM Eden down to the Cross of Christ the red line of sacrifice was unbroken. But all the sacrifices found their culmination in the Lamb of God. All *man*-provided offerings came far short of the righteousness of God. In mercy to a sin-smitten world God provided for Himself a Lamb (John 1. 29).

1. What this sacrifice was. "He gave *Himself* for us." Not only His love, His time, His power, His wisdom, His blood, but HIMSELF, in all the fulness of His life and moral worth.

2. To whom it was made. "He gave Himself *to God*." To God as the universal Ruler and righteous Judge of all. Forgiveness was needed, and only God could give it. If God will save, He will do it *justly*. He is a just God and a Saviour. Just *first*.

3. For whom it was made. "He gave Himself *for us*." In this *us* Paul includes himself, who was a blasphemer and injurious. Us, poor and needy, morally deformed and alienated from God. As the sinner's *Substitute* He died.

4. How it was made. It was entirely voluntary. "He *gave* Himself." He who had *life in Himself* could alone give Himself for others. It was His own choice, and He was able to do it. "I have power to lay it down."

5. The nature of it. "An offering and a sacrifice." Two aspects of the one offering. The meat-offering and the sin-offering in one person. The *offering* shows the

"Beloved Son," well-pleasing unto God; the *sacrifice* shows the Substitute *made a curse* for us. The first is the blameless *life* of Jesus Christ, the second is the atoning *death*.

6. The preciousness of it. " To God a sweet-smelling savour." There was that in Christ's death which was infinitely *sweet* to Him. This is how the *Blood* of Christ is called precious. We rejoice in His death, because it is a savour of delight to God.

7. The constraining motive for it. " Christ hath *loved* us." It was because He loved us He gave Himself for us. So He exhorts us to " love one another, as I have loved you" (John 13. 34).

8. The purpose of it. " That we should *imitate* God by walking in love" (v. 1). Imitate His self-sacrificing life. He pleased not Himself. " If any man would follow Me, let him deny himself, and take up his cross" (Matt. 5. 44). The child may be but a poor imitation of the father, but through obedience it may grow up into the perfect likeness. "Walk worthy of the Lord in all well pleasing" (Col. 1. 10).

THE CHRISTIAN LIFE.
Hebrews 12. 1, 2.

THE great outstanding feature of the Christian is that he has *life*. Not the common natural life of the flesh, but the new Spirit-begotten life of God, which makes him a new creation. Notice its characteristics. It is—

1. An energetic life. " Let us run *the race*." A man in a race is always wide awake. "This one thing I do" seems written on his countenance. This is after the fashion of Christ, who " set His face like a flint."

2. An ordered life. " The race *set before us*." It is not a rush at random. The *course* of the Christian is well defined. The Word of God and the example of Christ make his way plain. This is the way, run ye in it. "Not My will, but Thine be done" (Luke 22. 42).

3. A persevering life. "Run with patience." There must be patient continuance in well doing in those who seek for glory and honour (Rom. 2. 7). It is the patient endurance of *faith* as seen in the previous chapter.

4. An upward life. "Looking unto Jesus." We look unto Him because we press on for the prize of His eternal glory and reward. In steadily beholding Him we are lifted up above the things of earth and sense, and conformed into His likeness (Phil. 3. 13, 14). The apostle said, "I press on."

5. A believing life. "Looking unto the Author and Finisher of our faith." It is simply a life of faith on the Son of God. Faith that He who hath begun the good work of faith in our hearts will finish it (2 Tim. 4. 7, 8). A *finished faith*. What will that be? It will just be according to your faith. Faith, when it is finished, bringeth forth satisfaction. Great faith is great capacity.

6. A self-denying life. "Lay aside every weight." I keep my body under, lest I myself should be a castaway— a disqualified runner. When a man is going to run a race he has little regard for the prevailing fashions of the day. If any man will come after Me let him deny himself. Our own will and thoughts are but weights to be laid aside.

7. A hopeful life. "Who for the joy that was *set before* Him." Christ lived, and suffered, and died in the hope of seeing of the travail of His soul. The faithful servant will be rewarded. Enter thou into the joy of thy Lord. Salvation is all of grace, but the *works* of the saved will all be rewarded.

8. A public life. "We also are compassed about with a great cloud of witnesses." *We*, like those mentioned in the eleventh chapter, are also surrounded with a cloud of witnesses. Every individual Christian has a cloud of witnesses. May we so run our heavenward course that they, too, will be led to glorify our Father in Heaven. Are you booked for this race?

A BLESSED FEAR.

"THEN they that feared the Lord spake often one to another, and the Lord hearkened and heard" (Mal. 3. 16, 17).

1. Three things about the Lord's people. Their—

1. REVERENCE. "They fear the Lord." This is not the fear of a cringing slave, but of a dutiful child. The fear of holy worshippers.

2. THOUGHTFULNESS. "They thought upon His Name." His Name means His character, therefore it is precious, something well worth thinking about. "Where two or three are gathered together in My Name, there am I." Those who *think* upon His Name will now be found speaking lovingly of Him (Luke 24. 15).

3. TESTIMONY. "They spake often one to another." Those who love the Lord, love one another, and feel their kinship in Him. "Come all ye that fear the Lord, and I will declare what He hath done for my soul" (Psa. 66. 16).

2. Three things about the Lord. His—

1. INTERESTEDNESS. "The Lord hearkened and heard." He that formed the ear, shall He not hear? He *hearkens* as if bending down His ear to catch every whisper spoken of Him. He is interested for our sakes. "If the Lord should not be with me," said a preacher, "I will speak well of Him behind His back."

2. CAREFULNESS. "A book of remembrance was written before Him." The names of all fellow-labourers are written in the Book of Life (Phil. 4. 3). Every word is noted, because by our *words* shall we be justified or condemned

(Matt. 12. 36, 37). Let the *word* of Christ dwell in you richly, then you shall speak and sing with grace in your hearts to the Lord (Col. 3. 16).

3. FAITHFULNESS. '' They shall be Mine when I make up My jewels.'' '' All which the Father hath given Me, I shall lose nothing'' (John 6. 39). This assurance is again given in His great prayer in John 17. '' Father, I will that they also whom Thou hast given Me be with Me where I am.'' The Lord knoweth them that are His. They shall be Mine; Mine to save, and keep, and feed, and teach, and lead, and glorify. ———

THE GIFT OF GOD.

'' WHEN thou hast eaten and art full . . . thou shalt bless the Lord thy God for the good land which He hath given you'' (Deut. 8. 10).

1. **What this gift was.** '' The good land.'' They could not purchase it, neither could they *work for it*. It was the gift of His grace, as is the Lord Jesus Christ His Son. ''The gift of God is eternal life'' (Rom. 6. 23).

2. **To whom it was given.** '' Which the Lord thy God giveth *thee*.'' It was given to those who had been redeemed by the blood of the paschal lamb, and who had by *faith* gone into it. The good land of promise for us is in Christ Jesus in whom are all the promises of God. Through His redeeming Blood we may by faith enter into possession of these unsearchable riches which are in Him (Prov. 10. 22).

3. **The enjoyment of the gift.** '' When thou hast *eaten* and art *full*.'' There was sufficiency in the good land to satisfy every soul *in it*. There is exceeding abundant grace for all who are *in* Christ Jesus (1 Tim. 1. 14). Eat, O beloved. This is a land without scarceness. They did all eat. and were *filled* when our Lord fed the hungry multitude. If our eyes are on Him He will ''satisfy the hungry with good'' (Psa. 107. 9).

4. The blessed result. '' Thou shalt bless the Lord.'' Godless fulness only makes men, in the pride of their hearts, to kick (Deut. 32. 15). Fulness of *grace* makes thankful. It is His desire to so satisfy us that we will be constrained to bless the Lord. Bless the Lord, O my soul, and forget not all His benefits (Psa. 103. 1-4).

BUY OF ME.
Revelation 3. 18.

In addressing the Church of Laodicea our Lord uses terms that must have been very familiar to them. The city was noted for wealth, wool, and ointment, while the Church was charged with lukewarmness and self-satisfaction. The message of the Saviour was tender, timely, and merciful. In this great world's '' vanity fair'' there are many voices clamouring for patronage, so that the still small voice of the heavenly merchantman is but seldom heard. These simple words, '' Buy of Me,'' constrain us to think of—

1. Our need. Why does He ask us to buy? Just because He sees our nakedness and need, and knows that we are ignorant of our own condition. Can you afford to do without Him and His gifts?

2. The wares He offers. What are they?

1. GOLD TRIED IN THE FIRE. His precious Word (Psa. 19. 8-10) that has passed through the fiery trials of many a persecution. The word of the Gospel of Salvation that brings life and comfort to the believing heart.

2. WHITE RAIMENT. Robes washed in the Blood of the Lamb (Rev. 7. 14). The righteousness of God which is unto all and upon all that believe. Not the withering fig leaves of man's making (Rev. 19. 8).

3. EYE SALVE. This wonderful '' eye salve'' is the Holy Spirit, who is offered to all who have believed His *Word* and been adorned with the ''white raiment'' of

justification before God. This holy eye salve enables us to discern the things freely given us of God (1 John 2. 20-27; Eph. 1. 18).

3. The Merchantman Himself. "Buy of ME." He is the alone agent for these precious things. No servant of His can bestow them, although they may speak much about them. There must be *personal dealing* with the Lord Himself. The goods He wishes to sell are the purchase of His own Blood.

4. The price quoted. "Come, buy, without money and without price" (Isa. 55. 1). *Buying* implies *claiming* after the conditions have been fulfilled. The condition is come *without money*, without any price, for such priceless gifts cannot be bartered for anything of man's, and claim on this condition His offered gifts. A king does not sell, he gives (Rom. 6. 23).

5. Our present opportunity. "Buy of Me." "Now is the day of salvation." "Behold, I stand at the door and knock." This is the world's *market day*, when God's gifts of grace are being sold without money. Happy is the man that findeth this merchandise (Prov. 3. 13-17).

6. The possibility of losing such a bargain. It is said that a man on a wager failed to sell real sovereigns at one penny each. The people would not believe him, and the opportunity was soon gone. How shall ye escape the suffering of eternal loss if ye neglect so great Salvation? Yet a little while is the light with you. Walk while ye have the light (John 12. 35; Luke 19. 42).

ARE WE SERVANTS OR FRIENDS?

"HENCEFORTH I call you not servants: for the servant knoweth not what his Lord doeth, but I have called you friends" (John 15. 15).

There are two classes spoken of here, *servants and friends*.

These may represent two classes of Christians, or two different experiences in the Christian life. Those living in the outer and those in the inner court of communion. From these deeply significant words we may learn—

1. That it is a privilege to be a servant, but a greater privilege to be a friend. A man's servants may not always be his friends. We may serve the Lord in a way without being happy in His friendship.

2. That servants are hired, but friends are made by voluntary choice. It is easy to get servants if the hire is very liberal. Friends are not purchased for money. Are we only serving the Lord for the material or social advantage it brings, or are we connected with Him by our own hearty voluntary choice? Servants or friends?

3. The servant knoweth not his master's secret purposes, but his friends do. It is enough for the mere servant to *obey*, but the friend has the hidden things revealed to him (1 Cor. 2. 10). The hireling cannot receive the gift of the Holy Ghost, just because he is an hireling, and so the hidden wisdom cannot be imparted. The *friends* are wise in Christ, they have an unction from the Holy One, and know all things (Psa. 25. 14).

4. The servant works for wages, the friend serves for love. The love of Christ constrains those who live in the inner circle of His friendship. Those who serve for wages long for the lengthening of the shadow that they may cease their work. They are always glad when the given task is over. It is not so with the friends. They are found constantly saying, "What may I do for thee now?" They *live* for His Name's honour and His cause's good. To me to live is Christ.

5. The servant suggests obedience, but the friend fellowship. The Lord said, "Shall I hide from Abraham that thing which I do?" (Gen. 18. 17). Abraham was

more than a servant, he was the *"friend of God."* Friends
will show themselves friendly. If a man love Me he will
keep My words. "Ye are My friends if ye do whatsoever
I command you." What are ye? Hired servants or
loving friends? ———

IS GOD YOUR FATHER?

" IF God were your Father you would *love Me*, for I
came from God" (John 8. 42).

Much is taught in these days about the Fatherhood of
God. It is a most precious truth, but according to the
declaration of the Son of God only those who *love Him*
have any evidence at all that God is their Father. God
the Father was in Christ, and is revealed to us *in* Him.
To deny the Son is to deny the Father. We are made
the children of God *by faith*. "Whosoever *believeth* that
Jesus is the Christ is *born of God*" (1 John 5. 1). The
doctrine of the *universal* Fatherhood of God is a contradiction of the teaching of Jesus Christ. If God were
your Father, says Christ, *you would love Me*. Love to
the Son of God is the evidence that we are under the
Fatherhood of God. How does this love show itself?

1. By trusting Him. We cannot say that we *love*
Him if we have not in our hearts believed in Him as the
One who came from God to lay down His life for us.

2. By receiving His words. The truth has been told
us, in and by Him (v. 45). Where there is love there
will be a joyful reception of His words into the heart.
If God is our Father we will never have a shadow of doubt
concerning the sayings of His Son (John 8. 47).

3. By delighting in His company. We cannot help
drawing near to and keeping in company with those we
sincerely love. Having the spirit of *prayer* is another
proof that we are the children of God. If we love not
to *draw nigh* to God we have no evidence that God is our

Father. He is the God of all, but only the Father of them that believe (Rom. 8. 15, 16).

4. By speaking about Him. Love will find some way of manifesting its tender regard. Those who love the Lord take pleasure in speaking to others of Him. We cannot but speak the things which we have seen and heard.

5. By suffering willingly for Him. Suffering gladly for Christ's sake is another token that God is our Father, because it reveals our love to the Son. If ye be without chastisement, whereof all are partakers, then are ye bastards and not sons.

6. By longing to be like Him. Every true child desires to be like his noble, godly father. It is an assurance of sonship that our souls pant and yearn to be conformed into our Heavenly Father's likeness.

7. By desiring to please Him. " One is your Master, even Christ." " I delight to do Thy will, O God," was the language of the Son. It will also be the language of every one who *loves* the Son. "He that honoureth Me honoureth the Father also. I and My Father are one."

TRUE HEARTED SEEKERS.

"THEY shall ask the way to Zion with their faces thitherward, saying, Come, let us join ourselves unto the Lord in a perpetual covenant that shall not be forgotten" (Jer. 50. 5). They ask—

1. The way to Zion. They are honest enough to confess that they do not know the way. They are not ashamed to take the place of *anxious inquirers*, acknowledging that they have been in the wrong way. They declare plainly that they seek a city (Heb. 11. 14).

2. With their faces thitherward. This is another evidence of an *honest* inquirer. They don't inquire with their faces toward Sodom, like Lot's wife. They ask, not theoretically, not for curiosity, not hypocritically, but honestly and with a downright practical object in view. "Ye receive not because ye ask amiss" (Jas. 4. 3).

3. That they might join themselves unto the Lord. They are anxious not merely to join the Church, but to join themselves to the Lord. It is Himself they seek. They know that there is Salvation in none other Name. Like the Greeks, they say, "Sir, we would see Jesus." When a man has deserted from the service of Satan he will surely be desirous to enter the Zion of Salvation.

4. That they might make a perpetual covenant. They are willing and prepared now to bind themselves to the Lord and His service all the days of their life (Luke 1. 74, 75). To be saved by the Lord means to be *married* to Him. "Ye are not your own, ye are bought with a price, therefore glorify Him in your body and your spirit which *are His*" (1 Cor. 6. 20; 7. 23).

THE MAN THAT SAVES.

"A MAN shall be as an hiding place from the wind, and a covert from the tempest, as rivers of water in a dry place, as the shadow of a great rock in a weary land" (Isa. 32. 2).

There are many false refuges to which men resort when in danger (chap. 31. 1). Refuges of lies. The arm of flesh will fail you. Notice—

1. Who this Man is. "A *man* shall be as an hiding place." This is *the Man* who is God's fellow (Zech. 13. 7). The one Mediator between God and men, *the Man* Christ Jesus (1 Tim. 2. 5).

2. What this Man does. "Thou shalt call His Name Jesus, for He shall *save* His people from their sins." He—

1. SAVES. "He is an *hiding place* from the wind and the tempest." This rock was strong to bear the tempest of suffering and judgment that came upon Him for us. "There is therefore now no condemnation" (Rom. 8. 1).

2. SHELTERS. "He is a *covert.*" He is the Ark of refuge from the coming storm. He is the Mercy-seat (propitiation) that covers a broken law, and through which we may stand accepted before God. He Himself is the tabernacle of covering for the soul (Isa. 4. 6; Psa. 32. 7).

3. SATISFIES. "He is as *rivers of water in a dry place.*" He not only shelters but supplies the need of all who hide in Him. "If any man thirst let him come unto Me and drink."

4. SUCCOURS. "He is the *shadow* of *a great Rock* in a weary land." In the weary land of our earthly pilgrimage His succouring shadow will be cast over us while bearing the burden and heat of the day. The day of active service for Him. "They drank of that Rock which *followed them*, and that Rock was Christ" (1 Cor. 10. 4).

THE NEED OF TESTIMONY.

" Go home to thy friends, and tell them how great things the Lord hath done for thee, and hath had compassion on thee" (Mark 5. 19). Note concerning this Testimony—

1. Where is it to begin? " Go home to thy friends." The first disciples were commanded to begin at Jerusalem (John 1. 40-42).

2. Who are to give it? " Those for whom the Lord has done great things." Personal experience must come before witness-bearing. This was David's order (Psa. 51. 12, 13; 66. 16).

3. What is the nature of it? The *great things* which the Lord had done for him implied many things. There was a deliverance from—

1. SELF. "No *man* could tame him" (v. 4). But Jesus did. He is able to subdue the most stubborn will.

2. THE DEVIL (v. 15). "And such were some of you; but ye are washed, sanctified, and justified in Name of the Lord Jesus" (1 Cor. 6. 11).

3 INSANITY. " He was clothed and in his *right mind*" (v. 15) The prodigal was first brought to himself before he came to his father (Luke 15 17) A Christless life is a life of madness. "They know not what they do."

4. DEATH " He dwelt among the tombs" (v. 3). The spiritually dead prefer the company of the dead, they walk according to the course of this world.

5. SUFFERING. " He was in the tombs *cutting himself* with stones." The life of unbelief is a life of self-destruction. O Israel, thou hast destroyed thyself. Every sin committed is a cut inflicted on the soul.

6. FEAR. When the Lord came near, he said, " What have I to do with Thee, Jesus, Thou Son of God ?" (v. 7), but after his salvation he " prayed that he might be with Him" (v. 18) The result of his testimony was that " All men did marvel" (v. 20). Great and marvellous are Thy works, O Lord. " Let the redeemed of the Lord *say so*" (Psa. 107. 2). ⸻

A THREEFOLD SALVATION.
Hebrews 9. 24-28.

1. He hath appeared to put away sin.
2. He now appears in the presence of God for us.
3. He shall appear the second time.

These three appearings represent three aspects of the great Salvation (past, present, and future), and correspond with the three deliverances mentioned in 2 Corinthians 1. 10.

1. From the guilt of sin. " He hath appeared to put away sin by the sacrifice of Himself." This is a *past* deliverance. Christ once suffered for sins, the Just for the unjust, that He might bring us to God (1 Peter 3. 18). This He did once for all. There is therefore now no condemnation to those who are in Christ Jesus.

2. From the power of sin. " Christ is entered into

Heaven, now to appear in the presence of God for us"
(v. 24). This is a *present* Salvation. In this sense we are
being saved day by day. With regard to our guilt we *are*
saved by the Blood of atonement; but with regard to sin
in us we need to be constantly saved. The appearing
of Christ on the Cross puts away the guilt of sin; the
appearing of Christ in the presence of God gives power
to overcome sin within us. "If any man sin we have
an *Advocate* with the Father, Jesus Christ the *righteous*"
(1 John 2. 1; Rom. 8. 34).

3. **From the presence of sin.** "He shall appear
the second time without sin (sin-offering) unto Salvation"
(v. 28). This is a *future* Salvation. So we, in this sense,
hope to be saved. We shall never be saved from the
presence of sin till we are saved from this " vile body."
We shall be saved from this vile body when He shall
appear and change it, and fashion it like unto His own
glorious body. Then this corruptible shall put on incor-
ruption (Phil. 3. 20, 21).

Salvation from the guilt of sin by the Sacrifice of Christ.

Salvation from the power of sin by the Intercession
of Christ.

Salvation from the presence of sin by the Coming of
Christ.

A SPIRITUAL CRISIS.

" I WILL not let thee go except thou bless me" (Gen.
32. 26). The angelic man who wrestled with Jacob said,
" Let me go." Heaven-sent privileges may be very
short. The feet of God's messengers are never tardy.

1. **A precious privilege.** There wrestled a man with
him. He was—

1. MET BY ONE WHO COULD BLESS HIM. "Except
Thou bless me." God has sent His Son to bless you
(Acts 3. 26). In the reading or preaching of the Word
you may meet Him. Behold, I stand at the door and

knock." "Come unto Me," said the second Man, the Lord from Heaven.

2. BROUGHT INTO PERSONAL CONTACT WITH HIM. "There *wrestled* a man with him." It is a solemn thing to get into grips with the striving Spirit of God. My Spirit shall not always strive with man. He comes to convince of sin, He wrestles with us because we struggle against Him.

3. AWARE THAT THE TIME WAS UNCERTAIN. The day was breaking and He may soon depart. The *day* will either bring deliverance or disappointment. "Behold, *now* is the day of salvation. To-day, if you will hear His voice, harden not your heart" (2 Cor. 6. 2, 3).

2. A definite purpose. "I will not let thee go except thou bless me." He was—

1. CONVICTED OF HIS NEED. "His resisting power was broken down" (v. 25). It is not easy to wrestle with a thigh out of joint. When the Spirit convinces of *sin* there will soon follow the cry for mercy. When the fountain of earthly pleasure has been dried up there will be a crying after Him who is the Fountain of living water. Bless me, O my Father, also.

2. CONSCIOUS OF HIS PRESENT OPPORTUNITY. He realised that the victory must be now or never. What a crisis! Is he to be blessed or unblessed by this special time? What is this day of grace, this day of Divine pleading, going to bring forth for you? Remember the time is short, and remember Lot's wife.

3. THOROUGHLY DECIDED IN HIS HEART. "I *will not* let thee go *except*." Such a holy determination will never go unblessed. Thou shalt find Me when thou shalt seek for Me with all thy heart. "Great is thy faith, be it unto thee even as thou wilt" (Matt. 15. 28). What wilt thou that I should do unto thee? By faith the walls of Jericho fell down. And He blessed him there (v. 29).

TO HIM BE THE GLORY.

" Now unto Him who is able . . be glory" (Jude 24, 25). Worthy is the Lamb, for He was slain for us. To Him be the glory, because He is—

1. The " Only wise God." The wisdom of man is but foolishness with God. "Unto you, O men, I call" (Prov. 8. 4).

2. " God our Saviour." All the wisdom and omnipotence of Jehovah in exercise for our redemption. What a Gospel! What a refuge! What a Saviour!

3. "Able to keep you from falling." " His is the power to *establish* you" (Rom. 16. 25). He is able to keep you from falling out by the way, from falling in love with other gods, from falling into error, and from falling out of fellowship with Himself. Kept by the power of God through faith.

4. Able to " present you faultless." Praise be to His Name. This will be to the honour of His own saving grace and *cleansing* Blood. As faultless ones we shall sing, " Unto Him who loved us and washed us from our sins, in His own Blood" (Eph. 5. 25-27).

5. Able to present us " with exceeding joy." He for this joy that was set before Him endured the Cross. He shall see of the travail of His soul and be satisfied. His joy will be our joy. Enter into the joy of thy Lord.

THE PURIFYING HOPE.
1 John 3. 2, 3.

1. What is this hope? It is the hope of—

1. HIS APPEARING. " We know that when He shall appear." He will come again according to His promise (John 14. 3). " Christ, who is our life, *shall appear*" (Col. 3. 4).

2. BEING LIKE HIM. " We shall be like Him." This

mortal shall put on immortality. "Our vile body shall be fashioned like unto His glorious body" (Phil. 3. 21).

3. SEEING HIM. "We shall see Him as He is." "I will behold Thy face in righteousness, I shall be satisfied when I awake in Thy likeness" (Psa. 17. 15). "Now we see through a glass darkly, but then face to face" (1 Cor. 13. 12). What a bright and glorious prospect!

2. What is the effect of this hope? "He that hath this hope in Him *purifieth* himself even as He is pure." There is—

1. PERSONAL PURITY. "Purifieth *himself*." This sure and blessed hope constrains to voluntary purity. It is intensely practical (1 John 3. 5), as all real faith is.

2. PURITY AFTER HIS EXAMPLE. "As He is pure." He willingly separated Himself unto God for the joy that was set before Him. Be ye holy, for I am holy. I live, yet *not I*, but Christ liveth in me. Those who look for His coming will long to *live* like Him, that there be no shame before Him at His appearing (1 John 2. 28).

3. PURITY AS AN EVIDENCE OF FAITH. Every man that *hath this hope* purifieth himself. If a man is not seeking to purify himself, it is clear that *this hope* is not in him, there is no *faith* in the coming Saviour. "Dearly beloved, let us cleanse ourselves" (2 Cor. 7. 1).

FRUITFUL CHRISTIANS
Genesis 49. 22-24.

THE name *Joseph* means "increase," health and prosperity. Health is essential to fruitfulness. Is thy soul in health? If so, then may you expect to be fruitful in the work of the Lord. Let us think of his—

1. Character. "Joseph is a fruitful bough." Not a barren, withered branch in the vine. He is full of sap as by the Spirit of the Lord. "Herein is My Father glorified that ye bear much fruit" (John 15. 8).

2. Position " A fruitful bough *by a well*." The roots have found out a place of fulness, and they abide there. A tree planted by rivers of water (Psa. 1. 3). All fulness is in Christ, abide in Him. Let the roots of your heart's affections be planted in Him, and you shall not know when drought cometh.

3. Usefulness. " His branches run over the wall." Over the wall of selfishness and sectarianism. Something offered to outsiders and passers-by. Freely ye have received, freely give. Let your light so shine.

4. Sufferings. " The archers sorely grieved him, and shot at him, and hated him." " Blessed are ye when men shall revile you" (Matt. 5. 11). On your part He is glorified (1 Peter 4. 13, 14).

5. Strength. " His bow abode in strength, and his hands were made strong by the hands of the mighty God of Jacob." My grace is sufficient for thee. Strengthened with all might according to His glorious power (Col. 1. 11; Psa. 27. 14).

_____

ALL GRACE ALWAYS ALL-SUFFICIENT.

" GOD is able to make all grace abound toward you; that ye, always having all-sufficiency in all things, may abound to every good work" (2 Cor. 9. 8).

1. The nature of it. It is—

1. ALL GRACE. It is all of grace from beginning to end.

2. All grace ABOUNDING. Deep and overflowing like the waves of the sea.

3. All grace abounding TOWARD YOU. To meet your individual need, to fill up that which is lacking in your own soul and life. They drank of that Spiritual Rock that *followed* them.

2. The measure of it. The measure is deep and

capacious, it is "according to His riches in glory" (Phil. 4. 19). It is—

1. ALL-SUFFICIENCY. The source is unfailing and abundant. HE is the Fountain of living waters.

2. All-sufficiency ALWAYS. In every time of need, at every stage of life, and every hour of the day.

3. All-sufficiency always IN ALL THINGS. In all the details that go to make up both the inward and outward experiences of life.

3. The assurance of it. " God is able."

1. BELIEVE IT. Have faith in God. Prove Me and try Me, He says. Fear not, only believe. God is able.

2. EXPECT IT. If ye ask anything in My Name I will do it. Reckon on it. God is able.

3. THANK HIM FOR IT. There is nothing too hard for the Lord. Praise Him and prove Him.

4. The outcome of it. The results of such fulness of blessing should be abundance of service. That ye may—

1. WORK. The grace of God not only saves, but makes bone and muscle, that we may be strong to serve. Occupy till I come. " Son, go work."

2. Be found in EVERY GOOD WORK. Whatsoever ye do, do it heartily as unto the Lord. In all well-pleasing.

3. ABOUND to every good work. Abounding grace should produce abounding work. Why stand ye here all the day idle? God is able to make all grace abound toward you.

SAFETY AND QUIETNESS.
Proverbs 1. 33.

1. A Great Blessing,	..	..	"Dwell safely."
2. A Simple Condition,	..	..	"Hearken unto Me."
3. A Happy Result,	..	..	"Quiet from fear."
4. A Wide Offer,	..	..	"Whoso."

WHO IS ON THE LORD'S SIDE?
Exodus 32. 25-27.

1. There are but two sides.

1. THE LORD'S SIDE. The side of infinite wisdom and power.

2. THE ENEMIES' SIDE. The side of human pride and devilish hate. A company of blind weaklings, glorying in their strength, and making gods for themselves out of their own perverted imaginations.

2. These two sides may be indiscriminately mixed up. It was so here in the camp of Israel. The idolaters and the worshippers of Jehovah mingled freely together. So is it now. The tares and the wheat are growing up together.

3. The need of separation. The—

1. CALL FOR IT. "Who is on the Lord's side? Let him come unto Me." Let him come out and take his stand by him who lives and witnesses for God. "Come out from among them, and be ye separate" (2 Cor. 6. 17).

2. REASON FOR IT. "The sword of vengeance was about to go through the camp" (v. 27). The judgments of God are sure to overtake the presumptuous sinner.

3. RESPONSE TO IT. "The sons of Levi gathered unto him." Faithful preaching will always bring some right out for the Lord.

4. What this separation implies.

1. A PUBLIC STAND AGAINST EVERYTHING OPPOSED TO GOD. Public sins call for the public testimony of the servants of Christ.

2. A CONSECRATION OF THEMSELVES TO THE LORD. "Consecrate yourselves to-day to the Lord" (v. 29). Dead to sin and *alive* unto God. To me to live is Christ. Who is on the Lord's side?

GOD OUR SAVIOUR.

"GOD our Saviour, who will have all men to be saved, and to come unto the knowledge of the truth" (1 Tim. 2. 3, 4).

1. The need of man. The need, as brought before us here, is twofold—

1. SALVATION. "Who will have men to be *saved*." What must I do to be *saved?* is the first cry of a spirit-convicted soul. Salvation is man's first necessity in the sight of God (John 3. 17).

2. A KNOWLEDGE OF THE TRUTH. Man in his soul must be adjusted with God before he can know and appreciate the truth as it is in Jesus. "If any man will *do* His will, he shall *know* of the doctrine" (John 7. 17).

2. The character of Christ. "God our Saviour."

1. HE IS A SAVIOUR. "Thou shalt call His Name Jesus, for He *shall save*" His death atones, His resurrection justifies. There is none other Name.

2. HE IS GOD. "God in Christ reconciling the world unto Himself" (2 Cor 5. 19). As God He is mighty to save.

3. The will of God. "I know the thoughts that I think toward you, thoughts of peace" (Jer. 29. 11). His will is—

1. THAT MEN SHOULD BE SAVED. "Have I any pleasure at all, that the wicked should die? saith the Lord God" (Ezek. 18. 33). "God so loved the world, that He gave His only begotten Son, that whosoever believeth in Him should not perish, but have Everlasting Life" (John 3. 16).

2. THAT ALL MEN SHOULD BE SAVED. Go into all the world and preach the Gospel to every creature. "If *any man* thirst let him come unto Me." "The grace of God hath appeared, bringing salvation to all men" (Titus 2. 11, R.V.).

FEAR AND TRUST.

"WHAT time I am afraid, I will trust in Thee" (Psa. 56. 3). It is a blessed fear that frightens us to God. Fear and trust are two very common feelings of the soul.

1. The object of trust. "I in Thee." This implies—

1. KNOWLEDGE. "Trust in *Thee*." Thee, the living God, who hath delivered mightily in times past. Thee, the eternal God revealed to us in Christ Jesus.

2. CONFIDENCE. "I will *trust*" or commit my case to Thee. This is the confidence that we have in Him.

3. DETERMINATION. "I *will*." There is no doubt or uncertainty here. I know whom I have believed.

2. The time of trust. "What time I am afraid." Blessed are all they who know God as a refuge for the fearful. Adam hid from God, David would hide in Him. Trust in Him when afraid of—

1. GUILT AND WRATH. There is no condemnation to them who are *in* Christ Jesus. He hath made peace by the blood of His Cross.

2. INDWELLING SIN. There is no hope of deliverance in our own strength or wisdom.

3. WEAKNESS AND FAILURE. We are nothing but weakness, and of ourselves can do nothing but fail. When conscious of these, *then* is the time to trust. When I am weak, then am I strong.

4. TRIALS AND TEMPTATIONS. These often look upon us with frightful countenance, and we instinctively dread the contact. A MAN shall be a hiding place from the storm and the tempest. Only believe.

5. SICKNESS AND DEATH. Death has shadows that are dark and dismal, but *faith* gains the victory. They overcame by the Blood of the Lamb. "He shall not be afraid; his heart is fixed, trusting in the Lord."

YE SHALL SEE THEM NO MORE.
Exodus 14. 13.

THE Israelites had their last look at their Egyptian enemies at the Red Sea. There is a time coming when all the people of God will see their enemies no more for ever. Learn that—

1. Great changes may come suddenly. To-day the foe is pressing them, to-morrow he will be overwhelmed in the deep. He that hardeneth his neck shall suddenly be destroyed.

2. Opportunities may quickly vanish. These Egyptians had seen much of the power and greatness of God, but they remained in wilful rebellion. Harden not your heart.

3. Self-confidence leads to ruin. "The Egyptians went *after them*," but in their own strength. They dug their own grave, they rushed into the place of doom. The wages of sin is death. The heart is deceitful above all things.

4. The Salvation of the believer is certain. "Ye shall see them again no more for ever." The besetting sins, the snares of the Devil, the lusts of the flesh, the pride of life, ye shall see them no more. Full and eternal deliverance is sure.

5. The separation between the believer and the unbeliever will be complete. "See them no more." The chaff will be driven away. The wheat and the tares will not always grow together. Judas went to *his own* place.

6. Salvation is of the Lord. The almighty supernatural power of Jehovah was needed to deliver the children of Israel. This saving power of God is now manifested in His Son. Christ is the power of God, He came to seek and save. "He is able also to *save* to the uttermost, those who come unto God, by Him" (Heb. 7. 25).

7. They had to stand still to see the Salvation of the Lord. Man can never make a way of deliverance through the Red Sea of his fathomless guilt. The Lord alone can roll these dark and deadly billows back. Stand still, cease from your works. "Behold the Lamb of God which taketh away the sin of the world."

Unsaved ones, give earnest heed now to your Bibles, your Christian friends, and your privileges, or the time will come when you will see them again "no more for ever."

THE INFALLIBLE SAFEGUARD.

"Abide thou with me, fear not; for he that seeketh my life seeketh thy life, but with me thou shalt be in safeguard" (1 Sam. 22. 23). Observe that—

1. David is a type of Christ. *Chosen* of God and *anointed* for his work, but just now *rejected* and despised as a king.

2. With him implies suffering. "He that seeketh my life seeketh thy life." Identifying ourselves with the rejected Christ means suffering with Him; we have the same enemies to oppose. If any man live godly he must suffer.

3. With him implies safety. "With me thou shalt be in safeguard." I flee to Thee to hide me. God in Christ is our refuge. With Him we are in safeguard from the—

1. WRATH TO COME (1 Tim. 1. 10). He is the shadow of a great rock. He bore our sins.

2. CURSE OF THE LAW. "He was made a curse for us." Now no condemnation.

3. POWER OF SIN. With Him, abiding in Him, sin shall not have dominion over you; by His indwelling Spirit He breaks the power of it.

4. FEAR OF MAN. With Him, in His *love*, all fear is cast out. If God be for us, who can be against us?

5. WORRIES OF LIFE. Abiding with Him, His peace will rule (garrison) the heart. "My God shall supply all your need." "Take no thought for your life," "with ME thou shalt be in safeguard."

6. DREAD OF DEATH. With Him we can shout "O death, where is thy sting? Though I walk through the valley of the shadow of death I will fear *no evil*, for *Thou art with me.*" Are you *with Him*? He invites you, "Come unto Me, and I will give you rest" (Matt. 11. 28).

ABUNDANT GRACE.

" THE grace of our Lord was exceeding abundant with faith and love which is in Christ Jesus" (1 Tim. 1. 14).

The apostle has just been speaking of his guilty past as a blaspheming persecutor, and in using the above words he proves conclusively that he was saved only by the GRACE of God. Not of works, lest any man should boast. In this short but most suggestive account of Saul's salvation we note the—

1. Means. "GRACE." "Where sin abounded grace did *much more* abound" (Rom. 5. 20). It is the nature of Divine grace to flood all the depths and to overflow all the heights of a sinner's need. " By grace are ye saved " (Eph. 2. 8).

2. Source. "The grace of OUR LORD." "Ye know the grace of our Lord Jesus Christ, that, though He was rich, yet for your sakes He became poor, that ye through His poverty might be rich" (2 Cor. 8. 9). He loved us, and gave Himself for us.

3. Fulness. "It was EXCEEDING ABUNDANT." Far above what we ask or think. In this ocean fulness of infinite mercy there is room enough for the chief of sinners. "Exceeding abundant." Who can fathom it? " My grace is sufficient for thee" (2 Cor. 12. 9).

4. Channel. " IN CHRIST JESUS." It is *through* Him

that the renewing of the Holy Ghost is shed on us abundantly (Titus 3. 5, 6). There is but one Mediator between God and men, the Man Christ Jesus. By Him also He made the worlds.

5. **Accompaniments.** "WITH FAITH AND LOVE." The grace of God which bringeth salvation, bringeth with it faith and love, without which salvation could not be received and enjoyed. The begetting of faith and love in the heart is part of that grace which is exceeding abundant (Eph. 2. 7-9). Faith lays hold on, and love constrains to serve and adore.

THE PRECIOUS NAME.

"THY Name is as ointment poured forth, therefore do the virgins love thee" (Song of S. 1. 3).

1. **Its character.** "It is as ointment." This teaches us that it is—

1. PRECIOUS. His *Name*, like precious ointment, is a compound of great value. There are five marvellous ingredients in it. His Name shall be called: (1) Wonderful; (2) Counsellor; (3) The Mighty God; (4) The Everlasting Father; (5) The Prince of Peace (Isa. 9. 6). What a Name!

2. FRAGRANT. All who come into gracious contact with Jesus Christ will be so perfumed with His Spirit that others will take knowledge of them that they have been with Jesus (Acts 4. 13).

2. **Its mission.** "As ointment *poured forth*." This is most expressive. His *Name*, which is His character and life, poured forth. Then it is—

1. REVEALED. There has been no keeping back, the precious treasure of His life's Blood has been poured out as a sacrifice for us (Eph. 5. 2). He poured out His soul unto death. In this was *manifested* the love of God.

2. OFFERED. The *pouring out* is the offering of all that that Name and life means to every one who feels their need of the Divine odour instead of their own. Those who receive Jesus as the Son of God may have the whole house of their heart and life filled with the odour of this ointment.

3. Its influence. "Therefore do the virgins love Thee." It—

1. SAVES. "They shall call His Name Jesus, because He shall save" (Matt. 1. 21). This is an eye-opening salve (Rev. 3. 18) and a sin-cleansing ointment. "If ye ask anything in My Name I will do it." There is none other Name under Heaven, none other ointment for the sore of sin (Acts 4. 12).

2. CONSTRAINS. "Therefore do they *love Thee*." Those made virgins by the pouring forth of His Name cannot but love Him. The love of Christ constrains them. They love so much that they give themselves to Him and delight to follow Him (Rom. 12. 1, 2). Lovest thou Me?

A UNIVERSAL CHALLENGE.

"WHO can say, I have made my heart clean?" (Prov. 20. 9). This clearly implies that—

1. The heart needs cleansing. "If we say that we have no sin we deceive ourselves" (1 John 1. 8). The heart is deceitful above all things. There is none that doeth good, no, not *one*. "They that are *in the flesh* cannot please God" (Rom. 8. 8). The carnal mind is enmity against God.

2. No man can make his own heart clean. "Who can bring a clean thing out of an unclean? Not one" (Job 14. 4). Outward reformation is but the whitening of the sepulchre, ornamenting a charnel-house, painting the dead. "Marvel not that I said unto thee, Ye must be born again." That which is born of the flesh is flesh.

3. The Lord alone can cleanse the heart. "There is nothing too hard for the Lord." "*Create* in me a clean heart, O Lord, and renew a right spirit within me" (Psa. 51. 10). "If we *confess our sins*, He is faithful and just to *cleanse us* from all unrighteousness" (1 John 1. 8, 9). The heart may be cleansed as a fountain, like the stream at Jericho, by the putting in of the new cruse of the Spirit, with the salt of the Word of God (2 Kings 2. 20, 21).

THE FUTURE JOY OF JESUS.

"HE shall see of the travail of His soul and be satisfied" (Isa. 53. 11).

1. The way into it. Through "the travail of His soul" It was—

1. SOUL TRAVAIL. My soul is exceeding sorrowful, even unto death. The sorrow of His soul was the soul of His sorrow. Being in agony He sweat great drops of blood.

2. SOUL TRAVAIL FOR OTHERS. "He was made sin *for us*, who knew no sin" (2 Cor. 5. 21). "By the obedience of One shall many be made righteous" (Rom. 5. 19). He suffered for us, the Just for the unjust.

2. The promise of it. "He shall see." He for the joy that was set before Him endured the Cross. The purchase of His pain shall be a people saved for His Name. He shall see them—

1. CONVICTED AND CONVERTED. Awakened by the Spirit, and turned about by that word which converteth the soul (Psa. 19. 7). He shall see His seed.

2. PRESERVED AND GATHERED. Kept by the power of God, and brought into the home of God. After that ye believed ye were *sealed* with the Holy Spirit of promise (Eph. 1. 13, 14). "They shall be Mine when I make up My jewels" (Mal. 3. 17).

3. The fulness of it " He shall be satisfied." Satisfied with their—

1. NUMBER. "A great multitude which no man can number. All that the Father hath given Me shall come unto Me. *Every knee* shall bow and *every tongue* shall yet confess that He is Lord." The kingdoms of this world shall become the kingdom of our Lord and of His Christ.

2. CHARACTER. "A *royal priesthood* that shall show forth His praises" (1 Peter 2. 9). He is able to present you *faultless* before the presence of His glory (Jude 24). It should be satisfying now to the suffering servants of the Saviour to know assuredly that in that day HE SHALL BE SATISFIED, although through the wide gate "many have gone in thereat."

_____

LIFE AND ABUNDANCE.

" I AM come that they might have life, and that they might have abundance" (John 10. 10, R.V., margin).

1. A great need. " That they might have life." It is—

1. UNIVERSAL. " As in Adam all die " (Gen. 2. 17). " By one man's offence death reigned " (Rom. 5. 17).

2. VITAL. It is a death and life question (Rom. 6. 23). "You hath He quickened who were dead" (Eph. 2. 1).

2. A marvellous condescension. " I am come."

1. THE PERSON. " I." He by whom the worlds were made (John 1. 3). The eternal and beloved Son, the image of the invisible God. The Word made flesh.

2. THE PURPOSE. "That they might have life." "He hath brought life and immortality to light" (2 Tim. 1. 10). He came not to be ministered unto, but to give His life a ransom for many. " He that hath the Son hath life" (1 John 5. 11, 12).

3. An ample provision. " That they might have abundance." That is—

1. ABUNDANCE OF LIFE. Life, in all its fulness, as a branch in the living vine, drawing its life from a living source, as a member of His body. The woman who touched the hem of His garment got life abundantly.

2. ABUNDANCE TO MEET THE NEEDS OF THAT LIFE. In Him there is all-sufficiency to satisfy the daily wants, and to sustain amid all the trials and temptations of that new life. "My God shall supply all your need" (Phil. 4. 19).

INVITED TO SERVE.
Exodus 3. 10-12.

LET us take heed that we don't treat lightly any whisperings of the indwelling Spirit. We shall lose much precious teaching if we refuse to turn aside and inquire when some fresh light has been given. Some of the greatest spiritual treasures have been found by at once following what was but a faint indication. Moses turned aside and he found the salvation of Israel. In the above verses we note—

1. The invitation. "Come now therefore." All who would hear His voice may hear this gracious entreaty. "Come now, let us reason together. Come, for now is the accepted time."

2. The commission. "I will send thee." We must *come* to Him before we can *go* for Him. We have to be receivers before we can be witnesses. Let all who *come* be prepared to *go*.

3. The purpose. "That thou mayest bring forth My people." He was now to be used of God in delivering others from the bondage of slavery. Should not every one who has come to Christ be helpful in the bringing forth of others into the liberty of sons?

4. The excuse. "Moses said unto God, Who am I, that I should go?" Jeremiah said in like circumstances,

"Ah, Lord God! behold, I cannot speak" (chap. 1. 4-7).
When we are able to realise the greatness of the work
given us to do we will apprehend at once our utter in-
ability *in ourselves* to do it. This self-emptying is a
needful process.

5. The promise. "Certainly I will be with thee."
God now takes the place of our weakness, and so our
strength is exchanged. If God be for us, who can be
against us? "Most gladly *therefore* will I rather glory in
my infirmities, that the power of Christ may *rest upon
me*" (2 Cor. 12. 9). When I am weak then am I strong.

6. The assurance. "This shall be a token unto thee
that I have sent thee." His *presence with us* is the token
to us that we have been *sent by Him*. He is with every
sent one (Matt. 28. 19, 20). If we have this token with
us we may rest satisfied about results. The results are
with Him who worketh in us (Phil. 2. 13).

7. The prospect. "Ye shall serve God upon *this
mount*." This was a guarantee that his mission would
finally be a great success. His brethren, now bondslaves
in Egypt, would yet worship God upon this mount where
he now stood. We must stand on the mount with God
if we are to be the means of lifting our fellowmen up to
this same privilege. This experience is always the beginning of a mighty work for God. "Be strong in the
Lord, and in the power of His might" (Eph. 6. 10).

THE GREAT PASSAGE.

He that heareth My word, and believeth on Him
that sent Me, hath everlasting life, and shall not come
into condemnation, but is *passed from death unto life*"
(John 5. 24).

Conversion is the emigration of a soul from death into
life. Many fear the *passage*, or, as a negro puts it, " I
would like to be saved, but I dreads de process." There

are two states mentioned here, death and life, and the passage between them.

1. The state of death. '' Passed from death.'' *Death* is the name given to our own native country. A city of destruction. It is a place of—

1. MISERY. All guilty before God. Condemned already. Death's dark and dismal shadow is stretched over all.

2. HELPLESSNESS. No power at all to resist or escape. Without strength. Being without Christ we can do nothing.

3. SEPARATION. Death is always separation. We can have no fellowship with the dead, neither can God. God is not the God of the dead, but of the living. Sin is death, and alienates from the life of God. ''The soul that sinneth it shall die'' (Ezek. 18. 4).

2. The state of life. '' Passed from death unto life.'' This implies—

1. DELIVERANCE. The power of sin and death has been overcome, and the soul emancipated from its bondage and misery. Christ's atoning death is the price paid. Life means liberty.

2. FULNESS. The life here contrasted with death is much more than mere existence. A man may be living while he is half dead. In this life in Christ there is all the fulness of God to meet every pure and holy longing of the soul. Fulness of blessing. Life and abundance (John 10. 10).

3. HAPPINESS. When the prodigal came home to his father's house he passed from death into life. ''This my son was dead, but is alive again; and they began to be merry.'' When did they cease?

3. The passage between. '' He that believeth on Him is passed.'' It is—

1. A SHORT PASSAGE. It is the trust of the heart, being

transferred from self to Christ. This may be done in a moment, although one may *think* about it for months and years. *Thinking* about emigrating will never take you across the sea. " I will," and it is done.

2. A SAFE PASSAGE. None perish that trust in Him. If there is failure it is for want of actually stepping on board the ship of His promise. "Him that cometh UNTO ME I will in no wise cast out." " He that believeth *on Him hath* everlasting life, and shall not come into condemnation."

3. A FREE PASSAGE. " *Whosoever* will may come." "He that believeth." "I am the Door, by Me if *any man* enter in he shall be saved." Wilt thou go? (Gen. 24. 58).

4. The simple condition. " He that *heareth* My word and *believeth* on Him that sent Me." Hearing the *word* of Christ leads to believing in God the Father. Observe the vital relationship that here exists between the words of the Son and the honour of the Father, that no man can really believe in God who will not *hear* the Son. " I and My Father are one." ———

THE SINGLE EYE AND FULNESS OF LIGHT.

" THE light of the body is the eye: therefore when thine eye is single, thy whole body also is full of light" (Luke 11. 34).

1. The light is needed. There was no light in creation till God said "Let there be light." "I am the Light of the World." Without Him all are the children of darkness. All who are wise in their own eyes put darkness for light (Isa. 5. 20, 21).

2. The light has come. " He that followeth Me shall not walk in darkness, but shall have the light of life" (John 8. 12). "In Him was life, and the *life* was the *light* of men" (John 1. 4). This light shineth in darkness, but the darkness comprehended it not.

3. The eye needs opening. '' The natural man cannot receive the things of God, because they are *spiritually discerned*'' (1 Cor. 2. 14). ''Open Thou mine eyes that I may behold'' (Psa. 119. 18). ''Who hath opened thine eyes? A Man called Jesus'' (John 9. 25).

4. The whole body is illuminated through the eye. It may be a very narrow channel, but it is not the eye, but the light that fills with brightness. The *faith* may be weak and narrow, but it is not the faith that saves, but the great Christ that it rests on. The root fibres of a plant may be weak and small, but the fulness of the earth gets through sufficient for the life of the plant.

5. The single eye brings fulness of light. The pure healthy eye will always take in as much of the light as the body needs. A simple honest faith will expect from the Lord grace sufficient for every time of need. God who commandeth the light to shine out of darkness will always cause it to shine in the hearts that are single and pure, and they shall have the light of the knowledge of the glory of God in the face of Jesus Christ.

6. The light must come into contact with the eye. The light is for the eye. Christ is for the heart. It is a pleasant thing for the eye to behold the Sun of righteousness. There are diseased eyes that cannot bear the light of revealed truth. They love the darkness rather than the light, because their deeds are evil. Lift up thine eyes and behold. '' Behold the Lamb of God.''

7. The evil eye fills with darkness. '' When thine eye is evil, thy body also is full of darkness'' (v. 34). A faith that does not receive the light is unbelief. The light that is in such is darkness. The heart that seeks only its own selfish ends cannot enter into the light; it is an evil heart, shutting out the light, and filling itself with darkness (Matt. 6. 23).

SEED THOUGHTS.

SALVATION.
Titus 2. 11, 12.

1. What all men need—" Salvation."
2. What all men should know—" That salvation hath appeared."
3. How this salvation has come—" Through the grace of God."
4. What this grace teaches—" To deny ungodliness."

A HAPPY DELIVERANCE.
Psalm 40. 1-3.

1. The condition of the sinner—" In a horrible pit."
2. The power of the Saviour—" He brought me up out."
3. The security of the saved—" Feet upon the Rock."
4. The walk of the saved—" Established my goings."
5. The song of the saved—" A new song in my mouth."
6. The testimony of the saved—" Many shall see it."
7. The influence of the saved—" Many shall see, fear, and trust in the Lord."

THE ONLY NAME.
Acts 4. 11, 12.

1. An urgent need,   .. " We must be saved."
2. An only hope,   .. " None other Name."
3. A universal offer, .. " Name given among men."
4. A foolish work,   .. " Set at naught of you builders."

A THREEFOLD PRIVILEGE.
Jude.

1. Called (v. 1). 2. Preserved (v. 1). 3. Sanctified (v. 1).

THE MYSTERY OF GODLINESS.
1 Timothy 3. 16.

This mystery was seen in the burning bush, in the Holy of Holies, in the Person of Christ. Notice here the relationship of God the Son—

1. To the Flesh, ... " Manifested."
2. To the Spirit, ... " Justified."
3. To the Angels, ... " Seen by them."
4. To the Gentiles, ... " Preached."
5. To the World, ... " Believed in."
6. To the Glory, ... " Received up."

" As He is, so are we."

THOUGHTS FOR WORKERS.
Jude 20-23.

1. A needful work—" Building up yourselves."
2. A holy work—" Praying in the Holy Ghost."
3. A happy work—" Keep yourselves in the love of God."
4. A watchful work—" Looking for the mercy of our Lord Jesus Christ."
5. A compassionate work—"Of some have compassion."
6. An urgent work—" Others save with fear, pulling them out of the fire."
7. An unselfish work—" Hating even the garment spotted by the flesh."

THE BEGINNING AND THE ENDING.
Revelation 1. 8.

These are two of our Lord's many titles. He is the Beginning and the Ending.

1. Of Creation,   ..   Prov. 8. 22, 23; John 1. 1-3
2. Of Redemption, ... Rev. 1. 18
3. Of Experimental Salvation, ... Phil. 1. 6
4. Of Christian Service,   ..   Eph. 3. 20; Phil. 2. 13; Col. 1. 29

A WEEPING SAVIOUR.

" And when He came near He beheld the city, and
wept over it" (Luke 19. 41).

1. The approach of GRACE. " He came near." Grace
and truth came by Jesus Christ.

2. The look of LOVE. " He beheld the city."

3. The tears of SYMPATHY. " He wept over it."

SALVATION OF THE LORD.

" The word of the Lord came unto Abram in a vision,
saying, Fear not, I am thy shield, and thy exceeding
great reward" (Gen. 15. 1). This Salvation contains—

1. A REVELATION OF GRACE. " The word of the Lord
came." The " Word was made flesh and dwelt among
us" (John 1. 14).

2. A PROMISE OF SHELTER. " I am thy shield." A
man shall be an hiding place.

3. AN ASSURANCE OF SUFFICIENCY. " I am thy
exceeding great reward." " Whoso findeth *Me* findeth
life" (Prov. 8. 35).

4. A WORD OF COMFORT. " Fear not." " Perfect love
casteth out fear" (1 John 4. 18). " Lo, I am with
you alway" (Matt. 28. 20).

A RANSOM FOR ALL.
1 Timothy 2. 4-6.

1. The need implied. " Who will have all men *to
be saved.*"

2. The desire of God. " *Who will have all* men."

3. The provision made. " Who gave Himself a ransom for all."

4. The way appointed. " One Mediator between God
and men, the Man Christ Jesus "

GRACE EXCEEDING ABUNDANT.
1 Timothy 1. 12-14.

1. WHAT I WAS. "A blasphemer."
2. WHAT I AM. A servant "put into the ministry."
3. HOW IT CAME ABOUT. (1) I obtained mercy;
(2) Through the grace of Christ; (3) By faith and love.
4. WHAT I NOW DO. "I thank Christ Jesus our Lord."

THE SERVANT'S PRAYER.

"Give Thy strength unto Thy servant" (Psa. 86. 16).
Give—

1. For I am Thy *servant*.
2. For Thy servant is *very weak*.
3. For Thy servant is *very poor*.
4. For *Thy strength* is needed.
5. For Thy strength is *sufficient*.
6. That Thy servant may be *worthy of such a Master*.

SERVING THE LORD.
Acts 20. 19.

1. WHOM HE SERVED. "The Lord."
    1. As his Saviour.
    2. As his Master.
    3. As his God.

2. HOW HE SERVED.
    1. With humility (Matt. 20. 28).
    2. With tears (2 Cor. 2. 4).
    3. With temptations (1 Peter 1. 6; 2 Cor. 11. 24-27).

HOW TO USE HIS WORDS.
Deuteronomy 11. 18-20.

1. Lay them up.   2. Bind them.   3. Teach them.
4. Speak of them.   5. Write them.

"Whatsoever He saith unto you, do it" (John 2. 5).

POWER FOR SERVICE.
Haggai 2. 4.

1. The assuring promise. "I am with you" (Phil. 4. 13; John 15. 5).

2. The inspiring command. "Be strong" (Eph. 6. 10).

3. The noble purpose. "Be strong *and work*" (Judges 6. 14).

NEARNESS IN CHRIST.
Ephesians 2. 13.

1. What we were, ... "Afar off."
2. Where we are, ... "In Christ Jesus."
3. What we enjoy, ... "Made nigh."
4. When this is enjoyed, .. "Now."
5. How this is attained, .. "By the blood of Christ"
--- (Heb. 2. 14; 9. 12).

JESUS SENT TO BLESS YOU.
Acts 3. 36.

1. THE SAVIOUR.

   1. The Son of God, ... Titus 2. 13, 14
   2. Sent by God, ... Eph. 1. 3
   3. Raised from the dead, .. 1 Peter 1. 15, 16

2. THE SALVATION. "To bless you." This saving blessing—

   1. Was needful. "From *iniquity*."
   2. Was powerful. "Turning away from" (1 Peter 1. 15, 16).
   3. Was general. "Every one of you" (Rom. 8. 32).

"As many as *believed* were ordained to eternal life" (Acts 13. 48).

RECEIVING HIM.
John 6. 21.

1. Who? "They."
2. When? "Then."
3. What? "Received."
4. Whom? "Him."
5. How? "Willingly."
6. Where? "Into the ship.'
   7. Result. "Immediately at the land "

LIGHT IS COME.
John 12. 36.

1. A Present Privilege, .. "Ye have the light."
2. A Present Obligation, " Believe in the light."
3. A Passing Opportunity, "While."
4. A Glorious Possibility, " May become the children of light."

CONFESSION.
Hosea 6. 1.

1. A Confession of Need, .. "The Lord."
2. A Confession of Sin, ... "Return."
3. A Confession of Suffering, .. "Torn."
4. A Confession of Faith, .. "He will heal."

THREE MIGHTIES.
1 Corinthians 1. 30.

1. The desperate condition of the Christless implied.
2. The blessed inheritance of the Christian stated.
3. The marvellous grace of God revealed.

CHOSEN AND HOLY.
Deuteronomy 14. 2.

Here the Lord's people are said to be—

1. A *chosen* people.
2. A people chosen *by the Lord*.
3. A people chosen *to be holy*.
4. A people chosen *to be peculiar*.
5. A people chosen *unto Himself*.
6. A people chosen *above all other*.

THE LORD'S HOWS.

1. The How of Rebuke, ... Mark 4. 40
2. The How of Entreaty, ... Matt. 23. 37
3. The How of Warning, ... Heb. 2. 3
4. The How of Promise,

　　For temporal things, ... Luke 12. 28
　　For spiritual things, ... Luke 11. 13

COMFORTING PROMISES IN HOSEA.

1. I will be thy King, ...   Hosea 13. 10
2. I will Ransom, ...   Hosea 13. 14
3. I will Redeem, ...   Hosea 13. 14
4. I will Heal, ...   Hosea 14. 4
5. I will Love, ...   Hosea 14. 4
6. I will be as the Dew, ...   Hosea 14. 5

NOW HE IS COMFORTED.
Luke 16. 25.

This is the *now* of—

1. DELIVERANCE. " He has come out of great tribulation" (Rev. 7. 14).

2. TRANSFORMATION. " He has washed his robes and made them white in the Blood of the Lamb" (Rev. 7. 14).

3. ETERNITY " Therefore is he before the Throne of God" (Rev. 7. 15).

A BLESSED ASSURANCE.

" Thou art my hope in the day of evil" (Jer. 17. 17).

1. WHO? " Thou art,"   ..   ..   ..   Psa. 4. 6
2. WHAT? " My hope," ..   .. Psa. 30. 5; Rom. 5. 5
3. WHEN? " In the day of evil,"   ..   Psa. 59. 16

     In the day of evil thoughts.
     In the day of evil temptations.
     In the day of evil companions.

SANCTIFICATION.

1. THE NATURE OF IT.

1. It is a cleansing from sin, ...   Eph. 5. 26
2. It is a separation unto God,   Lev. 20. 24-26, Psa. 4. 3

2. THE MANNER OF IT.

1. By God the Father, ...   Jude 1
2. By God the Son, ...   Heb. 13. 12
3. By God the Spirit, ...   1 Peter 1. 2
4. By the Word of Truth, ... John 17. 17-19
5. By the will of the believer, ...   Lev. 20. 7

THE BLOOD THAT SPEAKETH.
Hebrews 12. 24.

The blood of Abel speaks of sin and guilt; the blood of Christ speaks of better things.

1. It speaks of Love, ...   John 3. 16
2. It speaks of an Eternal Purpose,   ..   Rev. 13. 8
3. It speaks of Suffering, ...   Rev. 5. 9
4. It speaks of Substitution, ...   John 1. 29
5. It speaks of Redemption, ...   Col. 1. 14
6. It speaks of Cleansing, ...   1 John 1. 7
7. It speaks of Liberty, ...   Heb. 10. 19
8. It speaks of Peace, ...   Col. 1. 20
9. It speaks of Heaven, ...   Rev. 7. 14, 15

THE UNIVERSAL GOSPEL.
John 3. 16.

1. The Object, ...   '' The World.''
2. The Gift, ...   '' His only Son.''
3. The Cause, ...   '' God so *loved*.''
4. The Offer, ...   '' Whosoever.''
5. The Condition, ...   '' Believeth in Him.''
6. The Promise, ...   '' Shall not perish, but have everlasting life.''

DELIVERING LOVE.
Isaiah 38. 17.

1. A Helpless Condition. '' In the pit of corruption.''

2. A Miserable Experience. '' For hope I had great bitterness.''

3. A Great Deliverance. '' Thou hast delivered from the pit.''

4. A Merciful Motive. '' In love to my soul.''

5. A Comforting Assurance. '' Thou hast cast all my sins behind Thy back.''

ILLUSTRATIONS.

SPIRITUAL BLINDNESS

In Kentucky there is a great deep cave which stretches away for several miles under ground, and is inhabited by blind fishes. In loving the darkness rather than the light these poor fishes have lost the power of sight. Eyes they have, but they see not. Man's love for the darkness of sin deprives him of all spiritual vision. He is in darkness until now. In *loving* the darkness the power of sight is lost. It would not be enough that light should shine into that cavern of darkness; those benighted fishes must have their power of vision born again if the light is to be enjoyed. The light of the Gospel has come, but without the eye-opening power of the Holy Spirit that is not sufficient to save from the darkness of death. "It is the Spirit that quickeneth" (John 6. 63).

OUTWARD APPEARANCE AND INWARD CHARACTER.

The outward life of Christ was true to His inward character, but, alas, how many of us claim the Name of Christ while we are destitute of His Spirit. Like the peacock, which is famed for its beauty and gluttony, there be many that have an attractive appearance, but at the same time an insatiable desire for self-gratification. Self-complacent boasting is just about as equally unpleasant as the horrid scream of the peacock. "As a man *thinketh in his heart* so is he" (Prov. 23. 7).

COURAGE.

It has been said that what has been attributed as ferocity to the tiger is due to its "incredible audacity and courage." It simply sees no danger, knows no fear, brooks no delay, uses no artifice, abandons no object of attack. Are these the elements of Christian courage? If we were filled with a deep sense of God's presence and power, and of our own privileges and responsibilities, would this not blind us to many of the things that disturb and terrify, and inspire to many an act and work which we now dread? "Be strong and of a good courage" (Deut. 31. 6).

WORLDLY WISDOM.

IT is a well known scientific fact that the illuminating power of phosphorus is due to the process of decomposition, the outcome of putrefaction, although no appearance of it may be visible. The wisdom of this world may be very attractive in certain circumstances, but with regard to spiritual things it is only phosphorescence as compared with the wisdom of God in Christ Jesus. It may be beautiful, but it is ephemeral and delusive, being only the product of corrupt man. In the Scriptures we have "the sure word of prophecy, wherein we do well to take heed" (2 Peter 1. 19).

CHRIST-LIKENESS.

THE caterpillar of a moth, we are told, becomes like the colour of the leaf upon which it feeds. Its colour in this way indicates the character of the food it eats. If we would be like Christ we must feed on Him. Our moral character will always manifest the colour of our mental food. Christ lived upon the Word of God His Father, and so maintained a life that was like God. If we would be His disciples we must come after Him in this matter. Man shall not live by bread alone, but by every word that proceedeth out of the mouth of God. "Eat, O friends" (S. of S. 5. 1).

THE SWORD OF THE WORD.

WE are told that the grey heron has a very singular mode of defence. When attacked by the eagle or falcon it simply stands quiet and firm, using its bill as a sword, allowing the enemy to pierce himself through by his own force. The Christian's method of defence is very similar. We have the sword of the Spirit which is the Word of God. When attacked by the enemy, without or within, stand firm and display the Word, hold it forth. The more fiercely the foe attacks the more surely shall they pierce themselves with it. His Word is a fire, all that cross it shall be burned. " Stand therefore, having your loins girt about with truth" (Eph. 6. 14).

BEHOLD NOW.

IN the Polar regions the summer season causes much joy and brightness. Every hour is utilised, as they well know that in a *few weeks* the opportunity will be gone, and the severity of a long winter will again set in. They act as those who believe that the time is short. Such is " the accepted time, the day of salvation." A brief but precious season. Yet many heed not this, their only chance of a harvest of eternal bliss before the long winter of death and eternal gloom sets in. " Arise, shine, for thy light is come" (Isa. 60. 1).

SPIRITUAL WARFARE.

THE greatest athlete in Britain is weakness itself in the grasp of the fierce gorilla that can twist a gun barrel like a rotten stick. Just as helpless are we to wrestle with spiritual wickedness in high places without the armour of God and the sword of the Spirit which that great gorilla, the Devil, can neither bend nor break. The weapons of our (gorilla) warfare are not carnal, but spiritual. " Put on the whole armour of God that ye may be able to stand" (Eph. 6. 11).

TRANSFORMING GRACE.

CHEMISTRY has performed many wonderful feats of transformation. What is more black and dirty and unpromising
than coal-tar, yet it has been changed into the most beautiful and useful colours ? But the grace of God has wrought
still more marvellous wonders. What could be more
filthy and unpromising than a God-hating, blaspheming
sinner, steeped as in a cesspool of iniquity, and possessed
by the spirit of the Devil? Yet the grace of God, as by
a spiritual chemistry, has transformed such depraved and
hopeless characters into the most beautiful and useful
lives. '' By grace are ye saved'' (Eph. 2. 5).

ONE IS YOUR MASTER.

Two queen bees will not live together in the same hive.
'' Ye cannot serve God and mammon.'' It would be well
with us if, when we yield ourselves to Christ, we would do as
some barbarous princes, who when they are honoured with
a crown immediately cast into prison or put to death all
those likely to usurp or hinder them from using their
authority. Everything that hinders Christians from
exercising their rightful privileges and authority as sons
and servants of God should at once be subdued or cast
out. With regard to sin and worldliness, the Christian
spirit is severely autocratic.

AFFLICTION.

THE tortoiseshell is a valuable article of commerce. To get
the turtle to freely yield its beautiful plates the natives
kindle a fire upon the animal's back. This is a cruel
process, but the fires of affliction may need to be kindled
around us and on us to make us yield the precious fruits
of the Spirit. We don't like the process of burning,
'' no affliction for the present seemeth to be joyous, but
rather grievous; nevertheless, *afterwards* it yieldeth the
peaceable fruit of righteousness'' (Heb. 12. 11).

SOMETHING IN NOTHING.

THE cipher 0 standing by itself means *nothing*, and is frequently used only to fill up an *empty* space. But it is a capital thing for filling up, without attracting any attention, or lessening the value of others. When we sing, " O to be nothing," do we mean 0 to fill some empty space, without having any value at all in the eyes of men? This is indeed a low service. Two such 0's with Christ as the 1 in front will make 100. " I can do all things through Christ which strengtheneth me" (Phil. 4. 13).

LIVING WATER WITHIN.

ON the sands at Saltcoats there is a spring of fresh water, but as it is within the tide-mark, it is frequently buried beneath the briny waves. But every time the tide recedes the spring appears as fresh and full as ever. If there is within us what our Lord offers to give us, " a well of living water springing up within," it will manifest itself. The billows of temptation or the flood-tide of sorrow and affliction may overflow for a season, but as sure as every living thing must move, so sure will it spring up again untainted by the contact. Its source is not in its surroundings, but deep in the heart of God, the Fountain of eternal life and love (John 4. 14).

CHOKE-DAMP.

CARBONIC acid gas, commonly known as *choke-damp*, is usually found in pits or the bottom of old wells. It is so called because it has often suffocated those who came into contact with it. In the pit of iniquity and in the old wells of worldliness this soul-choking damp still abounds. If you wish your spiritual life choked just *go down* into the darkness of prayerlessness, into the empty well of the world's pleasures. There is always as much poisonous gas there as will take your heavenly breath away

GIVING.

It has been said that "many littles make a muckle." A single bee does not collect more than one teaspoonful of honey in a season. Yet in a single hive there is often found as much as eighty pounds. We should not refuse to give for the cause of Christ because we cannot give large sums. The teaching of the bee is that every one should give. The united littles of God's poor ones will be enough to please Him. But don't forget that the bee gives its very life to do that little. " The Lord loveth a cheerful giver" (2 Cor. 9. 7).

LIFE IN DEATH.

It is a most remarkable fact that the most beautiful bird in the world has been known to build its nest in the most deadly tree in creation. The humming bird or birds of Paradise build their nest and live on the poision of the deadly manchineel. What a connection! The most deadly tree to the Son of Man was the Cross, yet it is the life of all the sons of Paradise. It is life in death. Sin is an awful poison. Christ on the tree of death drank the terrible fruit of the curse. Now every son of Paradise builds his hopes upon it, and finds the strength of his life in it. We live by faith upon the Son of God (Gal. 2. 20).

CANNIBAL TONGUES.

Cannibals are called "man-eaters" because they kill and devour one another. There may be different ways of killing and devouring one another. You may do it with the *tongue* as successfully as with the teeth. Does not the apostle speak of those who *bite and devour* one another? (Gal. 5. 15). It is quite possible to kill and devour a man's influence by backbiting and evil speaking. Such an unchristian spirit is but a remnant of the cannibal age. Pray for them that despitefully use you.

SEEING THINGS INVISIBLE.

WHEN any one is in a state of clairvoyance they are supposed to be, according to the meaning of the word, in a state of *clear-sightedness*, so that they can see things that are invisible to others. There is certainly a state of spiritual clairvoyancy in which one can see things in a way that others whose eyes have never yet been opened cannot understand. Moses " endured as seeing Him who is invisible" (Heb. 11. 27). We look not at the things which are seen, but at the things which are unseen and eternal.

TRANSFORMED.

EVERY plant and flower that has come into the hands of cultivation has been improved, beautified, and made more useful. Every soul that has come into the hands and under the skill of Jesus Christ has also been immensely improved, in that it has been beautified with the righteousness of God, transformed into His likeness, and made useful in His service and kingdom. As the plant does improve by being perfectly passive in the hands of the skilful gardener, so will the soul be wonderfully *enlarged* by being entirely submissive to the wise and tender treatment of Him who doeth all things well, and who is willing and able to make the most out of little things.

RUINOUS REFUGES.

THE flying fish, when terrified and pressed by their enemy, will fly out of the water and sometimes take refuge on a passing ship, where the sailors find great delight in catching them, and where the poor breathless things find their doom. At the sight of sin as an enemy, and through fear of coming judgment, terrified souls will often fly out of their old surroundings, but instead of fleeing to Christ, the only saving One, they take refuge on the ship of mere outward reformation, and fall an easy prey to pride and self-sufficiency, which work death as surely as any other sin " GOD is our Refuge" (Psa. 46. 1).

VAIN HOPE.

MANY are familiar with that very pathetic picture called " The lang awa' ship." The young maiden is seen sitting on a rock, with her left hand above her eyes, looking most pitifully across a shipless ocean.

> "Wearisome long the maiden must wait,
> Months and years ere her watching be o'er,
> For a lover that never will come to land,
> For a ship that never will touch the shore."

Such is not the hope of the Christian, for hath Christ not said, "I will come again, and *receive you unto Myself?*" (John 14. 3). But, like this maiden, may we *watch* for the coming of Him whom we love, and who at His coming will bless us with the glory of His eternal presence.

HEAVENLY-MINDEDNESS.

IF, as Emerson says, " The eye of Lyncaus could see *through* the earth," then what else but the *Heavens* could be seen in the distance? It is not always the best bargain that you can see through. What would it profit a man though he should gain the whole world when he became able to see through it? All those whose eyes have been opened by the Spirit of God can see through the earth unto the things which are spiritual and eternal. They are but short-sighted creatures who cannot see through the earth into the Heavens beyond. It is sad when the earth is allowed to come between and blind the eyes to the abiding inheritance in the everlasting kingdom.

SUBTLE SELF.

THE glass snake, it is said, is the most difficult creature to catch. You lay hold on its tail, but it leaves its tail in your hand and quickly disappears. It will even divide its body into pieces to elude being entrapped. What a resemblance there is here to the glassy, sinful, slippery snake of *self* You lay hold on it, you mortify (make dead) its members, you crucify it, and reckon it dead, yet it lives, and if allowed will soon restore itself to its original form and vitality. Like the head of that old serpent the Devil it takes the power of the Almighty Christ to bruise it.

THE BREAD OF LIFE.

THE body has a remarkable power of assimilation. No matter how *varied* the articles of food, all are received and so assimilated that the eater is made strong thereby. The soul as well as the body needs a variety of food if it is to grow up thoroughly developed in every part. This wholesome variety is found in the Word of God. Every truth revealed by God that is believed and accepted becomes assimilated by the new man, who is strengthened and built up thereby. Hence, if we would be healthy men of full stature, the whole "bread tree" of Divine revelation must be our food. The work of assimilation may go on unconsciously, but the building process is none the less sure It takes a whole Bible to reveal a whole Christ as the Bread of Life for the whole man. Eat, O friends, that ye may be perfect and entire, wanting nothing.

PRAYER.

PHYSIOLOGISTS declare that " whatever hinders the blood discs in the process of exhalation causes death." It is possible for the blood not to alter its appearance and yet be dead. Whatever hinders the spirit of prayer works spiritual death. The form of prayer and the appearance of holy vitality may remain the same while the power and virtue of it are clean gone. Whatever hinders our desires from rising up to God, and our delight in His presence, is working death in the soul. Everything that arrests the process of life causes death. "Men ought always to pray, and not to faint " (Luke 18. 1)

DELIGHTING IN DARKNESS.

A TRAVELLER in the Isthmus of Darien tells us of a tribe of Indians who have such weak eyes that they cannot endure sunshine. They sleep in the day time, and are all alive in the night. They do what a great many in our own country do: they love the darkness rather than the light. They do not like the bright shining of the Word of God; it is not pleasant to their weak half-blinded eyes. They are sleepy and sluggish to all spiritual things, but ever wide awake about the things of the world. Their weak eyes are the result of *loving the darkness* rather than the light.

CHANGING THE APPEARANCE.

IN South America some curious birds are seen with yellow feathers. The Indians have learned the art of making these birds change the colour of their feathers. They pluck them out, then inoculate the fresh wound with a secretion from the skin of a toad. The feathers which afterwards grow are of very different colour. But the changed appearance of the feathers does not in any way alter the *character* of the bird. A man may have the colour of his outward life completely changed and yet remain the same unregenerate soul before God. There may be reformation without regeneration. A better appearance does not always mean a better character. Temperance and other societies have inoculated many with better views of life, but they cannot transform the carnal mind, which is enmity against God.

THE GOSPEL.

WHEN John Knox landed in Scotland from Geneva the news flew like lightning over the country. The inhabitants of Edinburgh rushed into the streets. All business was instantly given up. Mounted messengers sped everywhere shouting the joyful tidings, '' John Knox is come.'' The whole land was moved and stirred by the inspiration of " Knox is come.'' It meant to Scotland Salvation from the tyranny of Popedom. But here is better news, would that it had the same effect: '' The Son of Man has come to seek and save the lost '' (Matt. 18. 11). Messengers of God shout it out, ''Christ has come.'' It means a present Salvation from the thraldom of sin and self. Groaning Scotland still needs this.

PLANTED IN CHRIST.

IT is a singular and beautiful providence of God that nearly all the plants in hot climates, where the rain is scarce and the rivers few, have '' tubrous roots buried far beneath the ground,'' so that they know not when drought cometh, and are almost independent of their outward circumstances. Such is the special privilege of the children of God who are planted in Christ. The roots of their life are down into the depths of the fulness of God. This life is entirely independent of outward surroundings of the pleasures or fashions of the world. They shall not see when drought cometh. They are like trees planted by rivers of water, whose roots lie buried beneath in the ever flowing stream of God's eternal love and unchanging grace. So their leaf shall not wither (Psa. 1. 3).

THE TIME IS SHORT.

The time is short!
If thou wouldst work for God it must be now;
If thou wouldst win the garland for thy brow,
Redeem the time.

With His reward
He comes; He tarries not; His day is near;
When men least look for Him will He be here;
Prepare for Him!   H. BONAR.